Government as Entrepreneur

GOVERNMENT AS ENTREPRENEUR

Albert N. Link and Jamie R. Link

OXFORD
UNIVERSITY PRESS

2009

OXFORD
UNIVERSITY PRESS

Oxford University Press, Inc., publishes works that further
Oxford University's objective of excellence
in research, scholarship, and education.

Oxford   New York
Auckland   Cape Town   Dar es Salaam   Hong Kong   Karachi
Kuala Lumpur   Madrid   Melbourne   Mexico City   Nairobi
New Delhi   Shanghai   Taipei   Toronto

With offices in
Argentina   Austria   Brazil   Chile   Czech Republic   France   Greece
Guatemala   Hungary   Italy   Japan   Poland   Portugal   Singapore
South Korea   Switzerland   Thailand   Turkey   Ukraine   Vietnam

Published by Oxford University Press, Inc.
198 Madison Avenue, New York, New York 10016

www.oup.com

Oxford is a registered trademark of Oxford University Press

Library of Congress Cataloging-in-Publication Data
Link, Albert N.
Government as entrepreneur / Albert N. Link and Jamie R. Link.
    p. cm.
Includes bibliographical references and index.
ISBN 978-0-19-536945-8
1. Technological innovations—Government policy—United States.
2. Entrepreneurship—Government policy—United States. I. Link, Jamie R.
II. Title.
HC110.T4L56 2009
338'.040973—dc22   2008050774

9 8 7 6 5 4 3 2 1
Printed in the United States of America
on acid-free paper

For Carol and Kevin

Acknowledgments

Our sincere thanks to the many individuals who were directly and indirectly involved in the writing and publication of this book. We are very appreciative for the confidence of Terry Vaughn, Executive Editor at Oxford University Press, in our ability to address such a provocative subject as government as entrepreneur and to deliver a treatise that identifies the intersection of two important fields, entrepreneurship and public policy.

We imposed on many individuals—some of whom are professional friends, some of whom are co-authors, and some of whom are among the leading scholars in the fields of entrepreneurship and public policy (and these three groups are not mutually exclusive)—to read and offer comments and suggestions on earlier versions of the material that formed the basis for this book. Those "imposed upon" include (alphabetically): Cristiano Antonelli of the University of Turin, David Audretsch of the University of Indiana and the Max Planck Institute of Economics, Barry Bozeman of the University of Georgia, Wes Cohen of Duke University, Denis Gray of North Carolina State University, Bronwyn Hall of the University of California at Berkeley, Chris Hayter of the National Governors Association, John Jankowski of the National Science Foundation, Dennis Leyden of the University of North Carolina at Greensboro, Stan Metcalfe at the University of Manchester, Fiona Murray of the Massachusetts Institute of Technology, Phil Phan of Rensselaer Polytechnic Institute; Sean Safford of the University of Chicago; Rosalie Ruegg of the former Advanced Technology Program, John Scott of Dartmouth College,

Don Siegel of the University at Albany, Paul Stoneman of the University of Warwick, Greg Tassey of the National Institute of Standards and Technology, Marie Thursby of the Georgia Institute of Technology, Nick Vonortas of The George Washington University, and Chuck Wessner of the National Academy of Sciences.

As well, we received many useful comments and suggestions from participants at various National Science Foundation, National Academy of Sciences, and Technology Transfer Society workshops where we presented some of the material herein. Our focus on government as entrepreneur as a global phenomenon came especially from comments and suggestions that we received from participants at a United Nations Economic Commission for Europe conference where we were privileged to present earlier versions of the concepts herein.

Of course, our family's support throughout this project has been invaluable.

Contents

About the Authors

Albert N. Link is Professor of economics at the University of North Carolina at Greensboro. He received the B.S. degree in mathematics from the University of Richmond and the Ph.D. degree in economics from Tulane University. His research focuses on innovation policy, university entrepreneurship, and the economics of R&D. He is the Editor-in-Chief of the *Journal of Technology Transfer*. Professor Link's most recent books include: *Cyber Security: Economic Strategies and Public Policy Alternatives* (Edward Elgar, 2008) and *Entrepreneurship, Innovation, and Technological Change* (Oxford University Press, 2007). Much of Professor Link's research has been supported by the National Science Foundation, the OECD, the World Bank, and various science and technology ministries in developed nations. Currently, Professor Link is serving as the vice-chairperson of the Innovation and Competitiveness Policies Committee of the United Nation's Economic Commission for Europe (UNECE).

Jamie R. Link is a research staff member at the Science and Technology Policy Institute in Washington, D.C. She received the A.B. degree from Princeton University and the Ph.D. degree in chemistry from the University of California, San Diego. Link's current research is related to science and technology policy, with an emphasis on sustainable energy solutions. Her research has appeared in various academic journals various as *Science, Nature Materials*, and the *Proceedings of the National Academy of Sciences*. She was named as one of *Technology Review*'s "World's 100 Top Young Innovators under 35" in 2004. She has served as a AAAS Congressional Science Fellow and as a Fulbright Scholar at The Energy and Resources Institute (TERI) in New Delhi.

Government as Entrepreneur

1

Government as Entrepreneur

An Introduction

1.1. Introduction

Throughout intellectual history as we know it, the entrepreneur has worn many faces and played many roles. The entrepreneur is the person who assumes the risk associated with uncertainty, the entrepreneur is the person who supplies financial capital, the entrepreneur is an innovator, the entrepreneur is a decision maker, the entrepreneur is an industrial leader, the entrepreneur is a manager or superintendent, the entrepreneur is an organizer and coordinator of economic resources, the entrepreneur is the owner of an enterprise, the entrepreneur is an employer of factors of production, the entrepreneur is a contractor, the entrepreneur is an arbitrageur, and the entrepreneur is an allocator of resources among alternative uses.

These themes are not mutually exclusive descriptions of his or her roles or actions, but they all are themes that have been offered by scholars as identifiable entrepreneurial activities that occur within a market setting. But government actions, which are a theme of this book, are not necessarily market based.[1] Markets operate through the laws of supply and demand, and economic actors within markets respond to explicit and implicit prices.[2] A similar analogy does not always hold for public-sector actors or activities.[3]

What do we mean by the phrase *government as entrepreneur*?[4] Based on the economic principle of market failure, government involvement in market activity—the provision of technology infrastructure, in particular, to remove the innovation barriers that bring about the market failure, technology market

3

failure, in particular—is warranted. The marginal social benefit of involvement is greater than the marginal social costs, assuming of course that government involvement is efficient.[5]

Not all such government involvement is entrepreneurial. We argue, based on the historical perspective of who the entrepreneur is and what he does, from a technology-based perspective, that *government acts as entrepreneur in the provision of technology infrastructure when its involvement is both innovative and characterized by entrepreneurial risk.* The programmatic mechanism or organizational structure for this involvement, at least based on the experiences in the United States that we discuss in this book, is the public/private partnership.[6]

Thinking of government as entrepreneur is a unique lens through which we characterize in this book a specific subset of government policy actions.[7] As such, our viewpoint underscores the purposeful intent of government, its ability to act in new and innovative ways, and its willingness to undertake policy actions that have uncertain outcomes.

Of course, we do not believe that all government policy actions are entrepreneurial. Certainly, aspects of monetary and fiscal policy are theoretically based and have predictable outcomes. Such policy actions are not necessarily innovative, and aside from timing issues are generally not, in our view, characterized by entrepreneurial risk.[8]

We do not take the position, much less advocate, that government should be more or less entrepreneurial. Rather, we argue that a new aspect of a taxonomy of government policy actions should be considered, and we are sanguine about its usefulness. Viewing particular policy actions through an entrepreneurial lens could be useful in at least two broad dimensions. One, viewing particular government policy actions as entrepreneurial underscores the forward-looking nature of policymakers as well as the need to evaluate the social outputs and outcomes of their behavior in terms of broad spillover impacts. Two, government acting as entrepreneur parallels in concept similar activities that occur in the private sector. Baumol, Litan, and Schramm (2007, p. 2) recently suggested that: "if the United States wishes to continue enjoying rapid growth, it must find a way both to launch and promote the growth of innovation entrepreneurial enterprises. . . . " And relatedly, viewing government as entrepreneur, albeit in selected areas and for selected policies, places a realistic (and positive, we believe) spin on such activities because it equates entrepreneurial government policy actions with the spirit of the private sector that has led to economic growth and prosperity in all industrial nations.

Viewing particular innovative policy actions through an entrepreneurial lens does not necessarily imply that all such policy actions are productive. Baumol (1990, p. 3) argued, within the context of a market, that " . . . at times the entrepreneur may even lead a parasitical existence that is actually damaging to the economy." He went on to say that, within the market context, the impact of entrepreneurship on the economy is determined by a set of rules that affects the allocation of entrepreneurial resources, a point that we revisit below.

In subsequent chapters, we discuss six such selected public/private partnerships associated with government's provision of technology infrastructure. The word *technology* is important, but not delimiting for generalizations, in our concept of infrastructure and hence our focused definition of government as entrepreneur. The partnerships discussed throughout this book are related to the creation or support of new technologies. Our selection process of these partnerships is not random, and the partnerships discussed are not representative of all entrepreneurial activity by the government. Rather, the partnerships we discuss are those to which we have devoted years of study and which illustrate clearly programmatic mechanisms that support our view of government as entrepreneur. This lack of representativeness in the partnerships discussed in this book is not problematic; our purpose is to foster a new way of thinking about selected government policy actions. If the lens of government as entrepreneur is not used, certain policy actions could mistakenly be judged narrowly in terms of some ad hoc predictability of outputs and outcomes. When policy actions per se are viewed through the lens of government as entrepreneur, they will logically be judged more broadly in terms of their innovative nature and their entrepreneurial risk.

1.2. An Historical Perspective of the Entrepreneur

While there is a rich intellectual history on each of the following themes of entrepreneurship, only the writings and ideas of selected individuals are summarized briefly in this section.[9] Generally, our trace focuses on the earliest writers associated with a specific theme so as to place the entrepreneur in a truly historical perspective, but in this trace we emphasize the perspicuity of authors' intent. Our purpose in this summary is to demonstrate that entrepreneurship is not a topical area of study but certainly one based on a rich tradition of idea development. We emphasize, through example, that scholars have traditionally ideated about the entrepreneur as one who operates within a market setting; this emphasis sets the stage for our views about government as entrepreneur. It is important to point out that there is significant overlap among writers on the twelve themes below.

Not all of the themes of the entrepreneur that we discuss are relevant to our notion of government as entrepreneur, but all are important to intellectual thought. With the advantage of hindsight and knowledge about classical writers, we borrow from this historical trace to ground our notion of entrepreneurial activity in the public sector. In particular, we borrow the themes of assuming the risk associated with uncertainty and being an innovator.

1.2.1. The Person Who Assumes the Risk
Associated with Uncertainty

Richard Cantillon (1680?–1734) is associated with the view that the entrepreneur is one who assumes the risk associated with uncertainty. In his historic *Essai sur la nature du commerce en general* (Cantillon 1931) he depicted the entrepreneur as someone who engages in exchanges for profit; specifically, the entrepreneur is someone who exercises business judgment in the face of uncertainty. This uncertainty (of future sales prices for goods on their way to final consumption) is rather carefully circumscribed. As Cantillon described it, entrepreneurs buy at a certain price to sell again at an uncertain price, with the difference being their profit or loss.

Cantillon took uncertainty for granted as something inherent in the economic activity of the marketplace. He did not provide a detailed analysis of the nature of risk and uncertainty; he merely related the function of the entrepreneur to uncertainty. Since the writings of Frank Knight (1921), it has been customary in economics to distinguish between risk and uncertainty. Knight pointed out that some forms of risk can be mitigated by insurance. To be insurable, there must be a known probability distribution associated with risk, either because of a large number of individuals exposed to risk or repeated exposures to the same risk by the same individual.[10]

Although we cannot credit Cantillon with this distinction, it is reasonably clear that the concept of uncertainty central to his analysis is not of the insurable kind. In Cantillon's world, not only is the information about the future unknown, it is also, for the most part, unknowable. Yet Cantillon's entrepreneurs are constantly called upon to exercise their business judgment, and if they guess wrong, they must pay the price.

Cantillon argued that the origin of the entrepreneur lies in the lack of perfect foresight individuals have about the future. Rather than considering this lack of foresight as a defect of the market system, Cantillon accepted it as part of the human condition. Uncertainty is a pervasive fact of everyday life, and those who must deal with it continually in their economic decisions are entrepreneurs. Consequently, it is the function of the entrepreneur, not his personality, which counts for economic analysis. Cantillon was quite emphatic that this function lies at the very heart of a market system, and that without it, the market as we know it does not operate.

Some other aspects of Cantillon's conception are noteworthy. His portrayal of the entrepreneur's role in a market economy has a distinct supply-side emphasis. His entrepreneur does not create demand through new production or merchandising techniques; he merely follows the dictates of a class of fashion leaders (the landlords of his time). The entrepreneur thus provides appropriate goods or services at the right time and place in order to satisfy preordained consumer wants. To be effective, he must be forward-looking. He must be alert, for when particular supplies and demand do not match, the theory calls for the entrepreneur to spring into action. But Cantillon's entrepreneur is not required to be innovative in the strict sense of the term.

Cantillon's view of the entrepreneur was later widened by J. H. von Thünen (1785–1850), John Stuart Mill (1806–73), H. K. von Mangoldt (1824–58), Frederick B. Hawley (1834–1929), Ludwig von Mises (1881–1972), Frank Knight (1885–1972), Arthur H. Cole (1889–1974), and G. L. S. Schackle (1903–92).

1.2.2. The Person Who Supplies Financial Capital

The locus classicus of economic analysis in the eighteenth century was Adam Smith's (1723–90) *An Inquiry into the Nature and Causes of the Wealth of Nations* ([1776] 1976a). But Smith discussed entrepreneur types earlier in *The Theory of Moral Sentiments* ([1759] 1976b). In *Wealth*, the entrepreneur is encountered in three different forms: the adventurer, the projector, and the undertaker. Smith spoke disparagingly of the first two and with unqualified approbation only of the undertaker, whom he identified with the prudent man—a concept developed at length in *Moral Sentiments*.

Of the prudent man Smith ([1759] 1976b, p. 215) said that: " ... if he enters into any projects or enterprise, they are likely to be well concerted and well prepared. He can never be hurried or drove into them by any necessity, but has always time and leisure to deliberate soberly and coolly concerning what are likely to be their consequences." The prudent man is frugal (i.e., he accumulates capital) and is an agent of slow but steady progress.

This kind of treatment in which the entrepreneur is either a menace or a boon leaves the concept of entrepreneurship muddled. As a result, erudite scholars have derided Smith. Spengler (1959, pp. 8–9) characterized Smith's entrepreneur as essentially passive: "a prudent, cautious, not overly imaginative fellow, who adjusts to circumstances rather than brings about their modification."

Joseph Schumpeter, who established his own distinctly dynamic notion of entrepreneurship, was unsympathetic to Smith in many ways, not least of which was his view of the role of the entrepreneur. According to Schumpeter (1954, p. 555), if pressed, Smith would not have denied that no business runs by itself, yet " ... this is exactly the overall impression that his readers get. The merchant or master accumulates 'capital'—this is really his essential function—and with this 'capital' he hires 'industrious people,' that is, workmen, who do the rest. In doing so, he exposes these means of production to risk of loss; but beyond this, all he does is to supervise his concern in order to make sure that the profits find their way to his pocket."[11]

Other writers who emphasized that the entrepreneur is the person who supplies financial capital include A. R. J. Turgot (1727–81), Francis Y. Edgeworth (1845–1926), Eugen von Böhm-Bawerk (1851–1914), A. C. Pigou (1877–1959), and Ludwig von Mises.

1.2.3. An Innovator

Among those who emphasized the innovative nature of the entrepreneur are Abbé Nicholas Baudeau (1730–92) and Joseph Schumpeter (1883–1950).

Baudeau treated the agricultural entrepreneur as a risk bearer, in the manner of Cantillon (i.e., uncertainty), but he added a distinctly modern twist. He made the entrepreneur an innovator as well, one who invents and applies new techniques or ideas in order to reduce his costs and thereby raise his profit.[12] This new aspect of entrepreneurship, innovation, represents an important advance over Cantillon's theory because it anticipated the twentieth-century reformulation of entrepreneurship by Schumpeter, whose theory of creative destruction dominates many contemporary discussions of the subject.

For Schumpeter, the main instrument of change in a theory of economic development is the entrepreneur. Development is a dynamic process, a disturbing of the economic status quo. He viewed economic development not as a mere adjunct to the central body of orthodox economic theory, but as the basis for reinterpreting a vital process that had been crowded out of mainstream economic analysis by the static, general equilibrium approach of his predecessors. The entrepreneur is the key figure for Schumpeter because, quite simply, he is the persona causa of economic development.

Schumpeter combined ideas from many earlier writers but mostly from the Germanic tradition. His entrepreneur is a disequilibrating force. For Schumpeter, the concept of equilibrium that dominated twentieth-century economics served as a mere point of departure. The phrase he coined to describe this equilibrium state was the circular flow of economic life. Its chief characteristic is that economic life proceeds routinely on the basis of past experience; there are no forces evident for any change of the status quo—cumulative drift in a sense. Within this system, the production process is invariant, although factor substitution is possible within the limits of known technological horizons. The only real function that must be performed in this state is "that of combining the two original factors of production, and this function is performed in every period mechanically as it were, of its own accord, without requiring a personal element distinguishable from superintendence and similar things" (Schumpeter 1934, p. 45). In this situation, the entrepreneur is a nonentity. "If we choose to call the manger or owner of a business 'entrepreneur'," wrote Schumpeter (1934, pp. 45–46), then he would be an entrepreneur "without special function and without income of a special kind."

For Schumpeter, the circular flow is a mere foil. The relevant problem, he wrote in *Capitalism, Socialism and Democracy* (1950, p. 84), is not how capitalism administers existing structures, but how it creates and destroys them. This process—what Schumpeter called "creative destruction"—is the essence of economic development. In other words, development is a disturbance of the circular flow. It is a process defined by carrying out of new combinations in production. It is accomplished by the entrepreneur.

Schumpeter admitted that the essential function of the entrepreneur is almost always mingled with other functions, such as management. But management, he asserted, does not elicit the truly distinctive role of the entrepreneur. "The function of superintendence in itself, constitutes no essential economic distinction," he declared (1934, p. 20). The function of making decisions is another matter, however. In Schumpeter's theory, the dynamic entrepreneur is the person who innovates, who makes new combinations in production.

Schumpeter described innovation in several ways. Initially he spelled out the kinds of new combinations that underlie economic development. They encompass the following: (1) creation of a new good or new quality of good; (2) creation of a new method of production; (3) the opening of a new market; (4) the capture of a new source of supply; (5) a new organization of industry. Over time, the force of these new combinations dissipates, as the new becomes part of the old circular flow. But this does not change the essence of the entrepreneurial function. According to Schumpeter (1934, p. 78), "everyone is an entrepreneur only when he actually 'carries out new combinations,' and loses that character as soon as he has built up his business, when he settles down to running it as other people run their businesses." In Schumpeter's theory, successful innovation requires an act of will not of intellect. It depends, therefore, on leadership, not intelligence, and it should not be confused with invention.

The leadership that constitutes innovation in the Schumpeterian sense is not homogeneous. An aptitude for leadership stems in part from the use of knowledge, and knowledge has aspects of a public good. People of action who perceive and react to knowledge do so in various ways; each internalizes the public good in potentially a different way. The leader distances himself from the manager by virtue of his aptitude. According to Schumpeter (1928, p. 380), different aptitudes for the routine work of "static" management results merely in differential success at what all managers do, where different leadership aptitudes mean that "some are able to undertake uncertainties incident to what has not been done before; [indeed]...to overcome these difficulties incident to change of practice is the function of the entrepreneur."

Other writers, besides Baudeau and Schumpeter, who emphasized the theme of the entrepreneur as an innovator and leader *comme aucun autre*, include Jeremy Bentham (1748–1832), J. H. von Thünen, Gustav Schmoller (1838–1917), Werner Sombart (1863–1941), and Max Weber (1864–1920).

1.2.4. A Decision Maker

With the publication of his *Principles of Economics* in 1871, Carl Menger (1840–1921) established himself as the founder and early leader of the Austrian School. The central concern of Menger was to establish the subjectivist act of human valuation as the starting point of economic theory. In the subjectivist view, economic change arises not from circumstances themselves but from an individual's awareness and understanding of them. His analysis, in particular, relied heavily on the role of knowledge in individual decisions.

Although his theory of production is secondary to his theory of value, it is in the theory of production where one finds his views on the entrepreneur. According to his general theory of production, the entrepreneur is the person who handles the intertemporal coordination of the factors of production. Menger recognized that industry is vertically disintegrated and that somebody has to align productive resources over time. That someone—a decision maker—is the entrepreneur.

Menger ([1871] 1950) established that entrepreneurial activity includes (1) obtaining information about the economic situation; (2) economic calculation—all the various computations that must be made if a production process is to be efficient; (3) the act of will by which goods of higher order are assigned to a particular production process; and (4) supervising the execution of the production plan so that it can be carried through as economically as possible.

The decision-making theme of the entrepreneur is also present in the writings of Cantillon, Amasa Walker (1799–1875), Francis Walker (1840–97), Alfred Marshall (1842–1924), Friedrich von Wieser (1851–1926), John Maynard Keynes (1883–1946), Ludwig von Mises, Arthur H. Cole, G. L. S. Shackle, and T. W. Schultz (1902–98).

1.2.5. An Industrial Leader

J. B. Say (1767–1832) followed in the French tradition inaugurated by Cantillon. Say's theory of the entrepreneur was influenced by his practical experience as an industrial entrepreneur—he managed a textile mill—rather than his academic acquaintance with other French economists. His theory of the entrepreneur is part of a threefold division of human industry into distinct operations. The first step is the scientific one. Before any product can be made, such as a bicycle, certain knowledge about the nature and purpose of it must be understood. It must be known, for example, that a wheel is capable of continuous, circular motion and that a force exerted on a chain and sprockets can propel the wheel forward. The second step, the entrepreneurial one, is the application of this knowledge to a useful purpose (i.e., to the development of a mechanism—the bicycle) with one or more wheels capable of transporting someone from one place to another. The final step, the productive one, is the manufacture of the item by manual labor.

Say's entrepreneur performs a social function, even though Say does not make him a member of a distinct social class. He is a principal agent of production, whose role is vital to the production of utility. His applications of knowledge must not be mere random events. They must meet a market test, that is, in order to be entrepreneurial each application must lead to the creation of value or utility. This requires sound judgment, one of the key characteristics of Say's entrepreneur. According to Say, an entrepreneur must be able to estimate customers' needs and the means to satisfy them; he might lack the personal knowledge of science, and he can avoid dirtying his own hands by employing others, but he must not lack judgment, for without it he might "produce at great expense something which has no value" (Say 1840, vol. 1, p. 100).

Say's entrepreneur is an economic catalyst, a pivotal figure. But Say did not follow Cantillon's lead in making uncertainty the mainstay of entrepreneurship. Risk is incidental to Say's notion of entrepreneurship because he saw no necessary dependency of entrepreneurial action upon capital accumulation. For the first time in economic literature, entrepreneurial activity became virtually synonymous with industrial management or leadership in the contemporary sense of that term.

This theme of industrial leadership is also present in the writing of Henri de Saint-Simon (1760–1825), Amasa Walker, Francis Walker, Alfred Marshall, Friedrich von Wieser, Werner Sombart, Max Weber, and Joseph Schumpeter.

1.2.6. A Manager or Superintendent

John Stuart Mill (1806–73), along with Say, Marshall, and Menger, characterized the entrepreneur as a manager, gerent, or superintendent. Mill's *Principles of Political Economy* ([1848] 1965) is a watershed in British classical economics, yet he contributed little that was new to the theory of entrepreneurship. He lamented the fact that *undertaker*, the English equivalent to the French term *entrepreneur*, referred to someone who set out to do a job or complete a project and this was an inadequate characterization of what an entrepreneur was. But, throughout his *Principles*, Mill spoke ambiguously of the entrepreneur and of his economic reward. Mill identified the entrepreneur's functions as direction, control, superintendence, and not much more.

1.2.7. An Organizer and Coordinator of Economic Resources

Léon Walras (1834–1910), a French economist, is recognized today as the founder of the general equilibrium theory. The hallmark of the general equilibrium theory is the all-pervasive interdependence of economic affairs and markets. As developed by Walras, the theory was static rather than dynamic, but it offered nevertheless a limited view of economic change. His analysis showed a state of ultimate and timeless adjustment maintained by the competitive self-interest of the individual suppliers of productive services. In this world, each productive service contributes technically and essentially to the production, transport, and sale of goods, thereby earning each day that amount by which the withdrawal of one such productive unit would reduce the daily output of the system as a whole. Furthermore, in this analytic system the total of all the payments to the suppliers of productive services exactly exhausted their total product.

Walras's lasting contribution to economic theory was architectonic, that is, it was more a contribution of form than of substance. He constructed an elegant system of mathematical equations to represent the totality of the economic system and to emphasize the interdependence of constituent parts. Outwardly, Walras considered the entrepreneur an important figure separate and apart from the capitalist. In *Elements of Pure Economics* ([1874] 1954), he characterized the entrepreneur as an intermediary, or coordinator of resources, between production and consumption, an equilibration agent egged on by profit opportunities in the marketplace. It would thus appear, from his writings, that he envisioned the entrepreneur operating in an arena of disequilibrium.

Similar ideas about the entrepreneur appear in the writings of J. B. Say, Friedrich von Wieser, Gustav von Schmoller, Werner Sombart, Max Weber, John Bates Clark (1847–1938), Herbert J. Davenport (1861–1931), Joseph Schumpeter, and Ronald Coase (1910–).

1.2.8. The Owner of an Enterprise

François Quesnay (1694–1774) analyzed the nature and operation of agrarian capitalism. His analytic system featured three economic classes, which can be distinguished from each other by their respective functions. A proprietary class owns property rights in the land that it leases to the productive class (i.e., farmers), who in turn produce the raw materials demanded by a third class, the artisans. The chief merit of Quesnay's analysis is that it underscores the vital importance of capital to economic growth. In the physiocratic system (the term *physiocracy* means rule of nature), capital comes from the landlords, who are best positioned to accumulate wealth. Entrepreneurs are present in the economy as farmers, large farmers specifically (*grande culture*). He described the rich farmer as an entrepreneur who "manages and makes his business profitable by his intelligence and wealth" (Quesnay 1888, pp. 218–19). He had in mind a capitalist farmer who owns and manages his business on land owned by another. Thus, his entrepreneur is the independent owner of a business, as was the entrepreneur in the subsequent writings of Frederick Hawley (1843–1929), Friedrich von Wieser, and A. C. Pigou.

1.2.9. An Employer of Factors of Production

Amasa Walker recognized the important role of the entrepreneur in creating economic wealth, but his discussion of this special resource did not range beyond the act of production. He defined the entrepreneur simply as one who brings about "an advantageous union between labor and capital," and he identified this special agent, variously, as employer, manager, entrepreneur, projector, contractor, businessman, merchant, farmer, or "whatever else he may be called, whose services are indispensable" (Walker 1866, p. 279). His son Francis Walker shared this thematic view, as did Friedrich von Wieser and John Maynard Keynes.

1.2.10. A Contractor

Jeremy Bentham, a follower of Smith, disagreed with him about entrepreneurship. Bentham's entrepreneur is an exceptional individual, one above the common herd; a minority in society. Smith's entrepreneur is a common type, widespread in society, one who exercises self-control in the exercise of economic activity in order to receive the approval of his fellow man.

For Bentham, economic development is activated by discontinuous changes involving improvements (in the broadest sense), and resulting in a nonlinear path of progress. Smith's notion of economic progress is slow, gradual, uniform, and not subject to sudden variations. Bentham was virtually alone among British classical economists in his emphasis on the entrepreneur as an agent of economic progress. He illustrated the role of the entrepreneur as a contract manager of a new administrative arrangement using an example of a prison system. An entrepreneur in this setting would be an independent contractor who through competitive bidding would purchase a prison and run it more profitably than the state.

1.2.11. An Arbitrageur

Israel Kirzner (1930–), following the seeds of thought sown by Cantillon and Walras, argues that the essence of entrepreneurship is alertness to profit opportunities. Kirzner accepts the Austrian idea that the role of the entrepreneur is to achieve the kind of adjustment necessary to move economic markets toward an equilibrium state, but he emphasizes that the crucial role of the entrepreneur is on the process of moving toward equilibrium rather than the equilibrium itself.

An entrepreneur is an alert person who acts quickly to an opportunity. By stressing pure alertness, Kirzner emphasizes the quality of perception, recognizing an opportunity that is a sure thing, whereas in reality every profit opportunity is uncertain. Like an arbitrageur, the entrepreneur, because of differences in intertemporal and interspacial demands, discovers the opportunity to buy at a low price and sell the same item at a high price.

1.2.12. An Allocator of Resources among Alternative Uses

Cantillon, Kirzner, and Schultz all discussed the entrepreneurial theme of resource allocation among alternative uses. Schultz argues that within contemporary economic literature there is a persistent failure to see the rewards that accrue to those who bring about economic equilibrium, especially as it occurs in certain nonmarket activities. He advanced thought on the entre- preneur in two ways. First, he redefined the concept of entrepreneurship as the ability to deal with disequilibria, and he extended the notion to market activities and nonmarket activities (e.g., household decisions, allocation of time, etc.). Second, he provided evidence on the effects of education on people's ability to perceive and react to disequilibria. More specifically (Schultz 1980, p. 443), he wrote the following passage:

> The substance of my argument is that disequilibria are inevitable in [a] dynamic economy. These disequilibria cannot be eliminated by law, by public policy, and surely not by rhetoric. A modern dynamic economy would fall apart were it not for the entrepreneurial actions of a wide array of human agents who reallocate their resources and thereby bring their part of the economy back into equilibrium. Every entrepreneurial decision to reallocate resources entails risk. What entrepreneurs do has an economic value. This value accrues to them as a rent, i.e., a rent which is a reward for their entrepreneurial performance. This reward is *earned*. Although this reward for the entrepreneurship of most human agents is small, in the aggregate in a dynamic economy it accounts for a substantial part of the increases in national income. The concealment of this part in the growth of national income implies that entrepreneurs have not received their due in economics.

In summary, the above trace of intellectual history shows that there is no surfeit of themes about who the entrepreneur is and what he does. See table 1.1. In our development of the concept of government as entrepreneur we borrow from Cantillon, Baudeau, and Schumpeter and we assert that the public sector both acts as an innovator and assumes entrepreneurial risk.

1.3. Market Failure and Government Intervention

Frequently cited as the author of the pioneering research on market failure, Bator (1958) defined this concept to mean "the failure of a more or less idealized system of price-market institutions to sustain 'desirable' activities or to stop 'undesirable' activities," where market activities are "broadly defined to cover consumption as well as production" (Bator 1958, p. 351). Generally speaking, there are three broad categories of reasons or explana- tions for market failure: one, economic agents possess some degree of market power so that the market does not operate in a perfectly competitive manner; two, externalities are associated with the activities of economic agents; and three, there are ill-defined property rights associated with the provision or use of goods and services.[13,14]

The examples of government as entrepreneur in this book focus on innovative policy actions (i.e., the provision of technology infrastructure) to

Table 1.1.   Summary Of Who the Entrepreneur Is and What He Does

The entrepreneur is...	Classical or Key Writer(s)
the person who assumes the risk associated with uncertainty	Richard Cantillon
the person who supplies financial capital	Adam Smith
an innovator	Abbé Nicholas Baudeau and Joseph Schumpeter
a decision maker	Carl Menger
an industrial leader	J. B. Say
a manager or superintendent	John Stuart Mill
an organizer and coordinator of economic resources	Léon Walras
the owner of an enterprise	François Quesnay
an employer of factors of production	Amasa Walker
a contractor	Jeremy Bentham
an arbitrageur	Israel Kirzner
an allocator of resources among alternative uses	T. W. Schultz

lessen barriers to innovation that cause dimensions of market failure. Of course, government can and does act in an entrepreneurial manner in many policy areas, and certainly technology policy is only one. Technology policy is, however, our own research and practitioner area of interest, and hence it is the focus of this book. That said, the arguments that we make about government as entrepreneur are, in concept, applicable across much if not all of the policy landscape.

Technological market failure refers to a condition under which the market, including both the research and development (R&D)–investing producers of a technology and the users of the technology, underinvests, from society's standpoint, in a particular technology.[15] Such underinvestment occurs because conditions exist that prevent organizations from fully realizing or appropriating the benefits created by their investments.

Arrow (1962, p. 609) identified three sources of market failure related to knowledge-based innovative activity—"indivisibilities, inappropriability, and uncertainty." Consider a marketable technology to be produced through an R&D process where conditions prevent full appropriation of the benefits from technological advancement by the R&D-investing firm. Other firms in the market or in related markets will realize some of the profits from the innovation, and of course consumers will typically place a higher value on a product than the price paid for it. The R&D-investing firm will then calculate, because of such conditions, that the marginal benefits that it can receive from a unit investment in such R&D will be less than could be earned in the absence of the conditions reducing the appropriated benefits of R&D below their potential, namely the full social benefits. Thus, the R&D-investing firm will underinvest in R&D, relative to what it would have chosen as its investment in the absence of the conditions. Stated alternatively, the R&D-investing firm will determine that its private rate of return is less than its private hurdle rate—its minimal accepted rate of return—and therefore it will not undertake socially valuable R&D. Thus, the principle market failure in this example relates to appropriability of returns to investment.[16]

Following Link and Scott (2005a), there are a number of nonmutually exclusive factors than can explain why a firm will perceive that its expected rate of return will fall below its hurdle rate. First, high technical risk (i.e., the outcomes of its R&D might not be technically sufficient to meet needs) might cause market failure given that when the firm is successful, the private returns fall short of the social returns.[17] The risk of the activity being undertaken is greater than the firm can accept, although if successful there would be very large benefits to society, hence it would like the investment to be made.

Second, high technical risk can relate to high commercial or market risk as well as to technical risk when the requisite R&D is highly capital intensive.[18] The investment could require too much capital for a firm—any firm—to feel comfortable with the outlay, and thus the firm will not make the investment although it would be better off if it had, and so would society.

Third, many R&D projects are characterized by a lengthy time interval until a commercial product reaches the market. The time expected to complete the R&D and the time to the commercialization of the R&D are long, and thus any realization of a cash flow from the investment is in the distant future. If the firm faces greater risk than society, and thus requires a greater return than society, the firm will apply a higher discount rate than society and will value future returns less than society, and it will underinvest.

Fourth, it is not uncommon for the scope of potential markets to be broader than the scope of the individual firm's market strategies so the firm will not perceive economic benefits from all potential market applications of the technology. As such, the firm will consider in its investment decisions only those returns that it can appropriate within the boundaries of its market strategies.

Fifth, the evolving nature of markets requires investment in combinations of technologies that, if they existed, would reside in different industries that are not integrated. Because such conditions often transcend the R&D strategy of firms, such investments are not likely to be pursued.

Sixth, a situation can exist when the nature of the technology is such that it is difficult to assign intellectual property rights. Knowledge and ideas developed by a firm that invests in technology can spill over to other firms during the R&D phase or after the new technology is introduced into the market. If the information creates value for the other firms that benefit from the spillovers, then other things being equal, the innovating firm might underinvest in the technology.

Table 1.2.   Factors Creating Barriers to Innovation that Lead to Technological Market Failure

---

High technical risk associated with the underlying R&D
High capital costs to undertake the underlying R&D
Long time to complete the R&D and commercialize the resulting technology
Underlying R&D spills over to multiple markets and is not appropriable
Market success of the technology depends on technologies in different industries
Property rights cannot be assigned to the underlying R&D
Resulting technology must be compatible and interoperable with other technologies
High risk of opportunistic behavior when sharing information about the technology

---

Sources: Link and Scott (1998, 2005a).

Seventh, industry structure can raise the cost of market entry for applications of the technology. The broader market environment in which a new technology will be sold can significantly reduce incentives to invest in its development and commercialization because of what some scholars have called technological lock-in or path dependency.[19]

Eight, situations can exist where the complexity of a technology makes agreement with respect to product performance between buyers and sellers costly. Sharing of the information needed for the exchange and development of technology can render the needed transactions between independent firms in the market prohibitively costly. And, sellers of the technology and buyers of the technology can be exposed to hazards of opportunism.

These eight factors, summarized in table 1.2, that individually or in combination create barriers to innovation thus lead, because of the technological market failure, to a private underinvestment in R&D.[20, 21, 22]

1.4. Government as Entrepreneur

1.4.1. Defining the Concept

As we have stated, government acts as entrepreneur in the provision of technology infrastructure when its involvement is both innovative and characterized by entrepreneurial risk (i.e., uncertainty). Our conceptualization of government as entrepreneur draws directly from the intellectual thought of Cantillon, those scholars who built upon his idea that the entrepreneur is one who assumes the risk associated with uncertainty—entrepreneurial risk[23]—and Baudeau and Schumpeter, who fostered the idea that the entrepreneur is one who innovates and applies new techniques. As our brief historical perspective on the entrepreneur above points out, Cantillon's entrepreneur was not an innovator, but the entrepreneur of Baudeau and Schumpeter was as he assumed entrepreneurial risk and undertook uncertainties.

We draw specifically on Schumpeter's (1928, p. 380) characterization of entrepreneurial leadership: "some are able to undertake uncertainties incident to what has not been done before; [indeed] ... to overcome these difficulties incident to change of practice is the function of the entrepreneur."

Many of the earlier writers about the entrepreneur envisioned his actions within a market setting, and his actions led to or maintained market equilibrium. Schumpeter, writing about the entrepreneur in the context of a theory of economic development, envisioned economic growth occurring through the innovative actions of the entrepreneur who, through creative destruction, moved an economy away from its current static equilibrium toward a new one in which there is greater efficiency. With respect to government policy actions, following Schumpeter, the public sector embraces new combinations of policy tools to move an effected segment of the market from inefficiency (e.g., market failure) toward efficiency.

Consider the schematic in figure 1.1. Government as entrepreneur is shown as a continuum, without regard to the exact slope of the arrowed line in the figure and without regard to alternative levels of efficiency (i.e., a band around the arrowed line).[24] Government can be more or less entrepreneurial as it assumes greater or lesser entrepreneurial risk, and as it is more or less innovative in its development and application of relevant policy actions.[25] Entrepreneurial action by the government, as we define it, involves the acceptance of entrepreneurial risk that is involved in the development and application of innovative policy actions.

Alternatively, consider the schematic in figure 1.2. There, government as entrepreneur is represented statically. Government either assumes, or not, entrepreneurial risk, and it is either innovative, or not, in its development and application of relevant policy actions. When government does both, it is within our framework entrepreneurial (the labeled cell in figure 1.2). Cell A

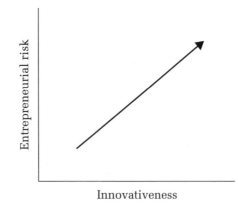

Figure 1.1. Government as Entrepreneur: A Continuous Representation

	No entrepreneurial risk	Assumes entrepreneurial risk
Not Innovative	A	B
Innovative	C	Government as entrepreneur

Figure 1.2. Government as Entrepreneur: A Static Representation

in the figure represents a government that is in what we call cumulative drift, that is, the government is neither innovative in the development and application of relevant policy actions nor willing to assume entrepreneurial risk. Cell B represents a government that is willing to assume entrepreneurial risk in implementing status quo policies, and cell C represents a government that is unwilling to assume entrepreneurial risk in developing and applying innovative policy actions.

Cell B and cell C might be unrealistic situations. Can there be uncertainty in the implementation of status quo policies? One could envision the application of a status quo policy to a situation in which it had never previously been applied, and such direct action could be labeled as innovative, and thus entrepreneurial risk could be present. Can there be an absence of uncertainty in the implementation of an innovative policy? By the fact that the policy is innovative, there must be some degree of uncertainty, along perhaps with measurable risk, in terms of its outcomes, timing issues aside.

1.4.2. Technology Infrastructure and Government as Entrepreneur

The government, by providing technology infrastructure, acts in a Schumpeterian manner as entrepreneur. In a dynamic fashion, government exhibits leadership by perceiving opportunity and acting on that perception.[26] The opportunity at hand with respect to technology policy is the provision of a public or quasi-public good—the technology infrastructure itself—that leverages the ability of firms and other actors in a national innovation system to participate efficiently in the innovation process (a concept developed in chapter 2) and thereby to contribute to technology-based economic growth.

Technology infrastructure, or a technology-based institution, has many dimensions. It supports the design, deployment, and use of individual technology-based components that comprise a knowledge-based economy. Technology infrastructure can be classified legitimately by the set of physical and virtual tools, methods, and data that enable all stages of technology-based economic activity: the conduct of R&D, the control of production processes to achieve target quality and yield, and the consummation of market transactions at minimum time and cost. The government, primarily at the national level, provides technology infrastructure through public and quasi-public institutions, as well as through public and quasi-public goods and services that leverage the innovation process. Government supports, through public/ private partnerships (a concept also developed in chapter 2), mechanisms, institutions and platforms that lessen innovation barriers that bring about market failure as related to investments in all stages of technology-based economic activity; government supports the design, deployment, and use of both individual technology-based component goods and the systems of such component goods that enhance a knowledge-based economy; and government is involved in the provision of services that leverage innovation by making private-sector R&D more effective. By perceiving opportunity and acting on that perception to provide such technology infrastructure—institutions, goods, and services—and assuming the entrepreneurial risk associated with it, government acts as entrepreneur.

1.5. Overview of the Book

While government as entrepreneur is a concept that transcends national innovation and technology policies, the remainder of the book has a distinct, and somewhat exclusive, U.S. policy focus. It builds on this proem and is outlined as follows.

In chapter 2 we discuss background interrelated concepts upon which we later build. These concepts are: innovation and the innovation process, public/private partnerships, research partnerships, and the productivity slowdown. Each of these becomes a building block for the six examples in subsequent chapters, as summarized in table 1.3.

Chapters 3 through 8 illustrate our concept of government as entrepreneur. Each chapter contains significant institutional history and descriptions of relevant technologies associated with the six public/private partnerships, with most of the technical descriptions of the technologies appended in the notes to the chapters. Our prior assumption is that such sufficient background is a prerequisite for understanding our conceptualization of government as entrepreneur and using that understanding to apply the concept to other situations. Also, our examples are both retrospective and prospective. The retrospective examples are intended to ground our concept of government as entrepreneur; the prospective examples are intended to underscore the importance of viewing government policy actions through an entrepreneurial lens.

The examples in each of these chapters illustrate government changing the rules and, in a Baumol-like manner, bringing about a reallocation of entrepreneurial resources that lessen barriers to innovation. Extrapolating, then, from Baumol's view of entrepreneurship, we believe that these

Table 1.3. Examples of Government as Entrepreneur

Public/Private Partnership	Technology Infrastructure	Innovative Policy Action	Entrepreneurial Risk
RJV structure	Legal environment conducive for cooperative research	National Cooperative Research Act of 1984: use of antitrust laws to stimulate private-sector R&D	If the benefits to firms from participating in an RJV outweigh the costs
Advanced Technology Program	Cost-sharing environment conducive for cooperative research	Omnibus Trade and Competitiveness Act of 1988: use of public resources to leverage private-sector R&D that would otherwise not have been undertaken through cooperative research	If the jointly funded research will be successful and if so, whether it will accelerate the development of generic technology
National Institute of Standards and Technology	Voluntary industrial standards	Organic Act of 1901: use of public resources to promulgate voluntary standards to reduce the technical and market risk of private-sector R&D	If the promulgated voluntary standard will be accepted by industry, and if accepted in a timely manner, whether it will enhance competitiveness
Biomass Research and Development Initiative	Cost-sharing environment conducive for developing domestic biofuels that are cost competitive with gasoline	Biomass Research and Development Act of 2000 as amended by the Food, Conservation, and Energy Act of 2008: use of public resources to accelerate the development of biofuels	If the publicly supported research will be successful in generating advanced biofuels to meet the renewable fuel standard

(continued)

Table 1.3. (*continued*)

Public/Private Partnership	Technology Infrastructure	Innovative Policy Action	Entrepreneurial Risk
University research park	Environment conducive for industry/university research collaboration and academic entrepreneurship	The Building a Stronger America Act: use of public resources to establish and/or expand existing parks	If the new or expanded park will attract tenants, and if so, whether they will actively participate in the two-way flow of knowledge between the university and the park
Small Business Innovation Research program	Funded environment conducive for commercializable research	Small Business Innovation Development Act of 1982: use of public resources to target and support research in small firms	If the funded research will result in a commercializable product, process, or service

examples are indeed examples of government as entrepreneur that have a positive impact on the economy and society.

In chapter 3 we discuss research partnerships, in general, and research joint ventures (RJVs) in particular. The RJV organizational structure is the public/private partnership through which government's innovative policy action of using antitrust laws to stimulate private-sector R&D occurs. The technology infrastructure is the legal environment conducive for cooperative research. This action is subject to the uncertainty of whether the benefits to firms from participating in an RJV outweigh the costs. In this chapter we provide an overview of the history of innovative U.S. policies, and we characterize trends over the past two decades of participation in RJVs. The RJV structure is germane to many of the examples that follow.

In chapter 4 we discuss the Advanced Technology Program (ATP). ATP is the public/private partnership through which government's innovative policy action of using public resources to leverage private-sector R&D that would otherwise not have been undertaken through cooperative research occurs. The technology infrastructure is the cost-sharing environment conducive for the cooperative research. This policy action is subject to the uncertainty of whether the jointly funded research will be successful, and if so, whether it will accelerate the development of the generic technology being researched.

In chapter 5 we discuss the National Institute of Standards and Technology (NIST). NIST is the public/private partnership through which government's innovative policy action of using public resources to promulgate voluntary standards to reduce the technical and market risk of private-sector R&D occurs. The technology infrastructure is the voluntary industrial standards. This policy action is subject to the uncertainty of whether the promulgated standard will be accepted by industry, and if accepted in a timely manner, whether it will enhance competitiveness.

In chapter 6 we discuss biofuels and the renewable fuel standard (RFS). The Biomass Research and Development Initiative (BRDI) is the public/private partnership through which government's innovative policy action of using public resources to accelerate the development of biofuels occurs. The technology infrastructure is the cost-sharing environment conducive for developing domestic biofuels that are cost competitive with gasoline. This policy action is subject to the uncertainty of whether the publicly supported research will be successful in generating advanced biofuels to meet the most recent renewable fuel standard.

In chapter 7 we discuss university research parks (URPs). The URP is the public/private partnership through which government's innovative policy action of using public resources to establish and/or expand existing parks occurs. The technology infrastructure is the environment conducive for industry/university research collaboration and academic entrepreneurship. This policy action is subject to the uncertainty of whether the new or expanded park will attract tenants, and if so, whether they will actively participate in the two-way flow of knowledge between the university and the park.

In chapter 8 we discuss the Small Business Innovation Research (SBIR) program. The SBIR program is the public/private partnership through which government's innovative policy action of using public resources targets and supports research in small firms. The technology infrastructure is a funded environment conducive for undertaking research that will eventually be commercialized. This policy action is subject to the uncertainty of whether the funded research will result in a commercializable product, process, or service.

Finally, in chapter 9 we reemphasize, in a circumspect manner, the potential importance of viewing selected public policy actions through the lens of government as entrepreneur.

Notes

1. According to Holcombe (2002, p. 55), "[p]olitical entrepreneurs, like those in the market, discover and act on unexploited profit opportunities. In many ways, there are parallels between political exchange and market exchange, and the political marketplace is, indeed, a market." This book is descriptive in its pedagogy; we neither hypothesize an objective function for government, nor do we formalize the entrepreneurial actions of government. Other scholars will surely do that. Rather, we posit an entrepreneurial dimension for government and illustrate through example that this dimension is realistic and one that should be considered when studying public-policy formation and implementation.

2. Of course, firms within markets must contend with a wide-ranging and often complex set of standards, legal issues, and regulatory bodies, all of which they not only live with but also are entrepreneurially active in shaping.

3. We are aware of the public-choice argument that governmental officials do respond to price-like incentives.

4. We first used the term *government as entrepreneur* narrowly in chapter 10 in Link and Siegel (2007).

5. Inefficient government involvement in market activities, both in terms of timing and level, is often referred to as government failure.

6. United States policy actions are the primary focus of this book because of our previous policy experiences, as illustrated in many of the examples in the later chapters. Certainly, our entrepreneurial view of government is conceptually applicable across nations.

7. Fligstein (1991) and others have argued within the institutional entrepreneurship literature that many nonmarket actors, including government, serve this role.

8. One could argue that supply management policies are both innovative and characterized by entrepreneurial risk. We agree that some innovative supply management policies could be representative of government as entrepreneur, especially if they involve new and innovative means of providing technology infrastructure. But a supply management policy that

affects innovation is not necessarily an innovative policy. The 1981 research and experimental (R&E) tax credit is one such example. For a firm that qualifies for the tax credit, the marginal cost of innovation decreases, and if its innovation is successful and diffuses as a technology, aggregate supply will increase. The R&E tax credit was not innovative; in fact a number of other countries had implemented such a credit long before the United States did (Leyden and Link 1993).

9. This section draws directly from Hébert and Link (1988, 2006a, 2006b).

10. Modern practice has refined Knight's distinction in the following way. Things once considered uninsurable because of a lack of a measurable probability distribution have, in fact, been insured. Recent literature therefore makes three distinctions where Knight made two. *Risk* refers to the situation where the probability distribution of possible outcomes is calculable and known. *Uncertainty* refers to a situation where the possible outcomes are identifiable but the probability distribution of outcomes is not known. *Radical uncertainty* refers to a situation in which the possible outcomes of a given event are unknown and unknowable.

11. Tuttle (1927, pp. 507–8) claimed that prevailing business practices of the era account for Smith's failure to differentiate the function of the capitalist from that of the entrepreneur. In England and France at this time the ownership of capital was prerequisite to becoming the independent head of a business.

12. Where Baudeau went beyond Cantillon was in emphasizing and analyzing the significance of ability. Baudeau underscored the importance of intelligence, the entrepreneur's ability to collect and process knowledge and information. Intelligence—knowledge and the ability to act—also gives the entrepreneur a measure of control so that he is not a mere pawn to the capitalist. Baudeau's entrepreneur is an active agent who seeks to increase production and reduce costs.

13. Bator (1958, p. 352) described the causes of market failure differently. He noted as causes "imperfect information, inertia and resistance to change, the infeasibility of costless lump-sum taxes, businessmen's desire for a 'quiet life,' uncertainty and inconsistent expectations, the vagaries of aggregate demand, etc."

14. Related to market failure is government failure. It is a concept that refers to a less-than-efficient response by the government in its intervention into the market place.

15. These arguments were made by Link and Scott (2005a) in connection with an evaluation of the intramural research program at the Advanced Technology Program within the National Institute of Standards and Technology, a program discussed in chapter 4.

16. Martin and Scott (2000, p. 438) argue that "[l]imited appropriability, financial market failure, external benefits to the production of knowledge, and other factors suggest that strict reliance on a market system will result in underinvestment in innovation, relative to the socially desirable level. This creates a prima facie case in favor of public intervention to promote innovative activity."

17. Arrow (1962) explained that investments in knowledge entail uncertainty to two types, technical and market. The technical and market

results from technology could be very poor, or perhaps considerably better than expected. Thus, a firm could justifiably be concerned about the risk that its R&D investment will fail, technically or for any other reason. Or, if technically successful, the R&D investment output could not pass the market test for profitability. Further, the firm's private expected return typically falls short of the expected social return as previously defined. This concept of downside risk is elaborated upon in Link and Scott (2001).

18. Although technically sufficient, the market might not accept the innovation. Reasons can include imitation or competing substitutes or interoperability issues.

19. See David (1987), for example.

20. See Martin and Scott (2000) for a discussion of similar sources of technological market failure (they use the term "innovation failure"). They relate such sources to particular sectors and posit policy actions.

21. See Tassey (2007) for an alternative taxonomy of factors or barriers associated with underinvestment in R&D. He lists as barriers: technical complexity, timing, economies of scope, spillovers, and infratechnologies and standards. And, he notes (p. 153), "Any one of these five barriers can have serious negative impacts on private-sector R&D investment."

22. For some firms, these barriers are like an impenetrable palisade that prevents them from entering the market.

23. Recall that Cantillon argued that uncertainty is a pervasive fact of everyday life, and likely, we suggest, a pervasive fact of many public policies.

24. For a more luculent explanation, there is likely a family of relationships between innovativeness and entrepreneurial risk, thus the line in figure 1.1 is analogous to an expansion path. In the figure, for a given level of entrepreneurial risk, government's innovativeness can change.

25. Greater entrepreneurial risk implies that more dimensions of the expected outputs and outcomes from a given policy action are characterized by uncertainty and less by measurable risk for which some probability of occurrence could be estimated. Just the reverse is true for lesser entrepreneurial risk.

26. Perception and action characterize much of the Austrian School's thought about the entrepreneur. Both are required.

2

Overview of Fundamental Concepts

Setting the Stage

2.1. Introduction

Several fundamental concepts are reviewed in this chapter to set the stage for later chapters. Emphasis here is more on the concepts per se rather than on their relationship to government as entrepreneur. That integration occurs in each of the subsequent chapters. These interrelated concepts are: the innovation and the innovation process, public/private partnerships, research partnerships, and the productivity slowdown. Our discussion in this chapter is general, yet selected mathematical relationships are developed for completeness in the notes to this chapter because it is these mathematical relationships that drive much of the related academic literature.[1]

Some basic definitions are set forth in section 2.2. In section 2.3 we provide an overview of alternative concepts of innovation and the related models of the innovation process. Section 2.4 introduces public/private partnerships as the relevant mechanism through which government acts as entrepreneur in the provision of technology infrastructure. Research partnerships and research joint ventures (RJVs) are the subject of section 2.5, and the productivity slowdown is discussed in section 2.6. These fundamental concepts are summarized in section 2.7.

2.2. Basic Definitions

Following Bozeman and Link (1983, p. 4): "Invention is the creation of something new. An invention becomes an innovation when it is put in use." When innovation is conceptualized in a static sense, as in the above definition, an innovation put into use is a new technology. When the innovation is the final marketable result, it is called a *product innovation*; when the innovation is applied in subsequent production processes, both in the innovative firm and in adopting firms, it is called a *process innovation*.

More interesting, as a foundation for government as entrepreneur, is a dynamic view of innovation because we conceptualize government's entrepreneurial actions through the provision of technology infrastructure as removing innovation barriers and restoring, in part, efficiency in market activities. That is, we conceptualize government's entrepreneurial actions as removing innovation barriers that had brought about market failure. A dynamic view of innovation is a process whereby an invention becomes an innovation—the innovation process. The entrepreneurial aspects of the innovation process are less related to the starting invention and ending innovation per se, but rather on the transcending process itself.

Related to the innovation process, especially from a policy perspective, are the concepts of technology and technological change. In a narrow sense, technology refers to a specific physical or tangible tool—an innovation. In a broader sense, technology refers to intangible tools such as technological ethic or organizational technology; technological change describes an entire social process. Alternatively, it is useful to think of technology as a physical representation of knowledge.

The information embodied in a technology varies according to its source, its type, and its application. For example, one source of information is science, although scientific knowledge is rarely sufficient for the more particular needs entailed in constructing, literally, a technological device. It could be useful in this regard to think of science as focusing on the understanding of knowledge and technology as focusing on the application of knowledge.[2]

Other sources of knowledge include information from controlled and random experimentation—information that philosophers refer to as ordinary knowledge—and finally, information of the kind that falls under the rubrics of creativity, perceptiveness, and inspiration. This informational view of technology implies that technology per se is an output that arises from a formal, rational, purposefully undertaken process. Such an idea—the production of technology—highlights the role of knowledge, and research produces knowledge in the generation of technology.

The concept of research underscores the myriad sources available from which knowledge can be acquired. Thus, technologies can be distinguished, albeit imperfectly, by the amount of embedded information. More concretely, R&D activities and related investments play a large role in creating and characterizing new technologies.

2.3. Models of the Innovation Process

Vannevar Bush is credited for first using the term *basic research*. In his 1945 report to U.S. President Roosevelt, *Science—the Endless Frontier*, Bush used that term and defined it to mean research conducted without thought of practical ends. Since that time, policymakers have been concerned about definitions that appropriately characterize the various aspects of scientific inquiry that broadly fall under the label of R&D and that relate to the linear model that Bush proffered, as discussed below.

Definitions are important to international and national statistical organizations, like the National Science Foundation (NSF) in the United States and the broadly supported international Organization for Economic Co-operation and Development (OECD), because such agencies collect expenditure data on R&D and on other science and technology indicators. For those data to reflect accurately investments in technological advancement, to be comparable over time within a nation, and to have a degree of comparability across nations, there must be a set of reporting definitions that remain consistent over time.

The classification scheme used by the NSF for reporting purposes was developed for its first industrial R&D survey in 1953–54, as documented in Link's (1996b) history of the classification scheme.[3] While minor definitional changes were made in the survey instrument in the early years of data collection, namely to modify the category originally referred to as basic or fundamental research to simply basic research, the concepts of basic research, applied research, and development have remained much as they were implicitly contained in Bush's 1945 so-called linear model:[4]

Basic Research → Applied Research → Development

The objective of basic research is to gain more comprehensive knowledge or understanding of the subject under study, without specific applications in mind. Basic research is defined as research that advances scientific knowledge but does not have specific immediate commercial objectives, although the research may be in fields of present or potential commercial interest.[5] Much of the scientific research that takes place at universities is basic research.[6]

Applied research is aimed at gaining the knowledge or understanding to meet a specific recognized need. Applied research includes investigations oriented to discovering new scientific knowledge that has specific commercial objectives with respect to products, processes, or services.[7]

Development is the systematic use of the knowledge or understanding gained from research directed toward the production of useful materials, devices, systems, or methods, including the design and development of prototypes and processes.[8]

Bush's linear model is often referred to more broadly as a linear model of the innovation process, and in that context we reinterpreted it four alternative ways in table 2.1. Regardless of the model, the source of innovation is

Table 2.1.   Alternative Linear Models of the Innovation Process

- R&D → Innovation → Economic Growth
- R&D → Knowledge → Innovation → Technological Advancement → Economic Growth
- Basic Research → Applied Research → Development → Innovation → Economic Growth
- Basic Research → Applied Research → Development → Innovation → Production → Diffusion → Economic Growth

investment in new knowledge represented by investments in R&D, in total or by character of use.[9]

Tassey (1992, 1997, 2007) was among the first, if not the first economist or policymaker, to illustrate a nonlinear model of innovation, and Gallaher, Link, and Petrusa (2006) extended his model from a manufacturing firm, discussed below, to a service sector firm. We illustrate in figure 2.1, based on these works, especially on Tassey's work, a nonlinear model for the purpose of emphasizing in later chapters the leveraging role of technology infrastructure in the innovation process and its role as a policy tool.[10]

At the root of the nonlinear model in figure 2.1 is the science base, referring to the accumulation of scientific and technological knowledge. The science base resides in the public domain. Investment in the science base comes through basic research, primarily funded by the government and primarily performed globally in universities and federal laboratories.

For an integrated technology-based manufacturing firm—and the model is similar for a service-sector firm (Gallaher, Link, and Petrusa 2006) except that technology is generally purchased rather than induced through own

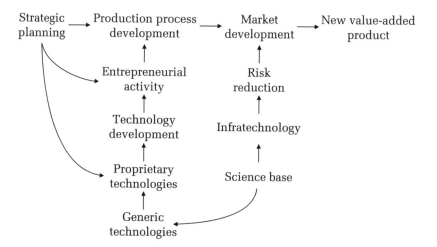

Figure 2.1. Nonlinear Model of Innovation: A Manufacturing Firm

R&D—technology development in the form of basic and applied research generally begins within its laboratory. There, R&D involves the application of scientific knowledge toward the proof of concept of a new technology. Such fundamental research, if successful, yields a prototype or generic technology.[11] If the prototype technology has potential commercial value, follow-on applied research takes place followed by development. If successful, a proprietary technology will result. Basic research, applied research, and development occur within the firm as a result of its strategic planning and guide the firm's market-oriented entrepreneurial activities. Generally, strategic planning involves the formulation of road maps for developing new emerging technologies. A manufacturing firm targets discrete technology jumps, creating new technologies that make its competition obsolete; its strategic plans are long term and not closely linked to current competitive planning.

Entrepreneurial activity then drives the firm toward the production of the new product or process. With entrepreneurial activity, a causal element in this model, the overall innovation process exhibits hysteresis because of the lagging impact of such entrepreneurship. Thus, the relationship between investment in proprietary technology and market development might not be as predictable as the firm's strategic planners would like.

Infratechnologies (i.e., infrastructural technologies) emanate from the science base and from various technology infrastructures such as national laboratories. These technologies, such as test methods or measurement standards, reduce the market risk associated with the introduction of a new product or process. Once a new product has been designed and tested, technical risk could be low, but market risk could be significant until the product is accepted and integrated into existing systems (e.g., in a service-sector firm). The nonlinearity of this system is, literally, in the fact that there are multiple influences on both innovation and technology development, thus underscoring the existence of a need for broad-based and multitargeted public-sector policy actions, not all of which are necessarily entrepreneurial.[12]

Mathematical models relating investments in knowledge, approximated by R&D, to innovation and economic growth have been more modest representations of that process than that suggested by the nonlinear model in figure 2.1. Conceptualizing a general production function that relates (at any level of aggregation ranging from a line of business; to a firm; to an industry, sector, or the economy) output, Q, to inputs—the stock of capital, K; the stock of labor, L; and the stock of technical capital, T—economists have relied on general representations like the following:

$$2.1 \quad Q = A(t)\ F(K, L, T)$$

where $A(t)$ is a time, t, related shift factor meaning that over time the nature of the entire production relations could change.

$A(t)$ represents, in a Schumpeterian sense (1939, p. 62) an entrepreneurial lever related to innovation: "[The production function] describes the way in which quantity of product varies if quantities of factors vary. If, instead of quantities of factors, we vary the form of the function, we have an innovation."

From the specification in equation 2.1, another estimable equation results from which the relationship between investments in the stock of technical capital, R&D, and total factor productivity growth (i.e., the growth in output not attributable to the growth in capital and labor) could be estimated. As reviewed in Link (1987) and Link and Siegel (2003), there is a voluminous literature that documents the positive impact that R&D has on productivity growth, presumably through some underlying yet not specified innovation process.[13]

2.4. Public/Private Partnerships

Public/private partnerships are the relevant programmatic mechanism or organizational structure discussed in this book through which government acts entrepreneurially.

We use the term *public* to refer to any aspect of the innovation process that involves the use of governmental resources, be they federal, state, or local in origin. *Private* refers to any aspect of the innovation process that involves the use of private-sector resources, mostly firm-specific resources. And, *resources* are broadly defined to include all resources—financial resources, infrastructural resources, research resources, and the like—that affect the general environment in which innovation occurs. Finally, the term *partnership* refers to any and all innovation-related relationships, including but not limited to formal and informal collaborations or partnerships in R&D.[14]

A framework that defines our view of the focus of public/private partnerships is in table 2.2.[15] The first column of the table describes the nature

Table 2.2.   Taxonomy of Public/Private Partnership Mechanisms and Structures

Government Involvement	Economic Objective	
	Leverage Public-Sector R&D	Leverage Private-Sector R&D
Indirect	...	...
Direct		
Financial Resources	...	...
Infrastructural Resources	...	...
Research Resources	...	...

Sources: Link (1999, 2006).

and scope of government involvement in a public/private partnership. Government involvement could be indirect or direct, and if direct there is then an explicit allocation of resources including financial, infrastructural, and research. The second and third columns in the table relate to the economic objective of the public/private partnership. Of course, with any innovation-related activity there are spillovers of knowledge and thus economic objectives are multidimensional and they occur over time, but for illustrative purposes herein a single overriding economic objective is assumed. Broadly, the objectives are to leverage public-sector R&D activity, or to leverage private-sector R&D activity.

Our grounding for the argument that a public/private partnership framework is the relevant mechanism for conceptualizing government as entrepreneur is based on extant technology policies. The Office of Technology Policy (1996) classifies public/private partnerships in the United States along a time spectrum in order to illustrate and emphasize that public/private partnerships have evolved from a relationship wherein the government was merely a customer of private-sector research to a relationship wherein the government is a partner in that research. In other words, the Office of Technology Policy's taxonomy is one that stresses the evolution of the public sector's role in partnerships. Specifically the Office of Technology Policy (1996, pp. 33–34) wrote:

> By the late 1980s, a new paradigm of technology policy had developed. In contrast to the enhanced spin-off programs—enhancements that made it easier for the private sector to commercialize the results of mission R&D—the government developed new public-private partnerships to develop and deploy advanced technologies. . . . [T]hese new programs . . . incorporate features that reflect increased influence from the private sector over project selection, management, and intellectual property ownership. Along with increased input, private sector partners also absorb a greater share of the costs, in some cases paying over half of the project cost. . . . The new paradigm has several advantages for both government and the private sector. By treating the private sector as a partner in federal programs, government agencies can better incorporate feedback and focus programs. Moreover, the *private sector as partner* [emphasis added] approach allows the government to measure whether the programs are ultimately meeting their goals: increasing research efficiencies and effectiveness and developing and deploying new technologies.

And figure 2.2 illustrates this Office of Technology Policy view. There are several salient and subtle features in figure 2.2. First, the federal government has changed from being a customer for the technology output of industry programs, which it often financed, to a partner, and often a research partner, in the programs. And second, not only does this role change increase the ability of industry to focus its efforts more efficiently on government needs, but also it speeds up the technology diffusion process.

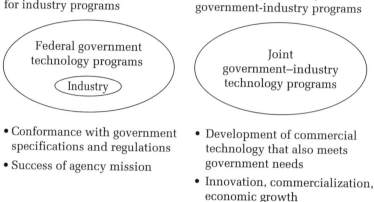

Federal government as customer for industry programs

Industry as partner in joint government-industry programs

- Conformance with government specifications and regulations
- Success of agency mission

- Development of commercial technology that also meets government needs
- Innovation, commercialization, economic growth
- Leadership, competitiveness, jobs

Figure 2.2. Innovative Paradigm for Technology Partnerships
Source: Office of Technology Policy (1996, p. 34)

2.5. Research Partnerships and Research Joint Ventures

The terms *research partnership, strategic partnership* and *strategic alliance* were introduced to the academic and professional literatures in the early 1980s to describe the multitude of forms of agreements between firms, universities, and a variety of other research organizations that analysts had already begun to observe.[16] Research partnerships, and this is the term we use herein, refer to agreements whereby two or more partners share their commitment to reach a common goal by pooling their resources and coordinating their activities.

Research partnerships denote some degree of operational coordination that could or could not involve equity investments. Partnerships can occur vertically across the value chain, from the provision of raw materials and other factors of production; through research, design, production and assembly of parts, components and systems; to product/service distribution and servicing. They can also occur horizontally between partners at the same level of the value chain.[17] Partners can be based in one country; they could also be dispersed across several countries, thus establishing an international partnership.[18] A subset of partnerships can be characterized as innovation-based, focusing primarily on the generation, exchange, adaptation and exploitation of technical advances.

Evid3ence from the popular presses clearly indicates an explosion of partnerships since the early 1980s; a clear dominance of non-equity partner ships since that time; a focus shift from low- and medium-technological to high-technological activities; a significant proportion of research partnerships in the overall population of alliances; and a rapid growth in the proportion of international, high-technology research partnerships in the 1980s that had flattened in the 1990s but continues strongly now. This trend is discussed in chapter 3.

The majority of research partnerships in the industrialized world focus on information technology (IT), biotechnology, and advanced materials, in that order. The set of IT research partnerships is by far the largest. Given that research partnerships involve both users as well as producers of products and services and given that these technologies have infrastructural character-istics, the set of observed research partnerships involves both producers of products and services embodying such technologies.

One major distinction of partnerships is between formal and informal. Very little is known about informal partnerships, apart from anecdotal evi-dence that many firms (and other organizations) frequently partner infor-mally with one another in short-term endeavors, and informal partnerships could account for the vast majority of all partnerships. Informal partnerships are almost impossible to track systematically.

There are several dichotomous distinctions between formal research partnerships. They include: equity versus non-equity partnerships; subsi-dized versus nonsubsidized partnerships; national versus international partnerships; and horizontal versus nonhorizontal (vertical, conglomerate) partnerships.

An obvious research partnership classification scheme is one that emphasizes the type of research partners. Roughly, there are four kinds of partners: firms, universities, other research institutes, and government enti-ties. An alternative classification scheme characterizes research partnerships in terms of their organizational structure and the broad research and tech-nological focus of the relationship. One needs to distinguish between two sets, one involving research partnerships with direct industrial participation or sponsorship, and the other without.[19]

The primary observable formal agreements established by firms in order to produce, acquire, and/or commercially exploit technology in common can be categorized into three groups, involving cooperation in precompetitive research, downstream technology development, and production and/or marketing as well as technology development. All four dichotomous dis-tinctions mentioned above can work their way into each of these three groups.

The preceding classification excludes research partnerships with no industry involvement either as a partner or a sponsor. To the best of our knowledge, there have been no widely available, systematic classifications of such research partnerships besides simple listings on the basis of the type of partners.[20]

The lack of synthetic classifications probably reflects a presumption that these partnerships focus primarily on basic and/or generic research. This need not be the case, of course, as in the situation of government research laboratories specializing on defense work, much of which can be classified as

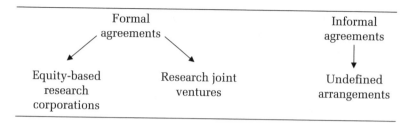

Figure 2.3. Taxonomy of Research Partnerships by Organizational Structure
Source: Hagedoorn, Link, and Vonortas (2000, p. 569)

applied research and development. This example implies the possibility of a basic grouping on the basis of aggregate research orientations such as basic research, applied (or precompetitive) research, and technology development.

Research joint ventures (RJVs) are a formal collaborative research arrangement through which firms jointly acquire technical knowledge. RJVs are a subset of formal research partnerships as emphasized by the term *joint*, and they are the focus of chapter 3 and, through illustration, chapter 4. The term *venture* connotes that there is a sharing of the research outputs from the partnership among the venture's members. Sufficient to note here, as background, the academic literature is clear that participation in research partnerships, in general, and RJVs, in particular, increases the performance of member firms and participation leverages the efficiency of R&D both at the time of involvement and in subsequent periods.[21, 22]

Figure 2.3 is a taxonomy of research partnerships, and RJVs therein.

2.6. The Productivity Slowdown

Productivity growth is a fundamental contributor to overall economic well-being. Because of this, the persistent slowdown in productivity growth that began in the mid-1960s in some industrialized countries, that increased in the early 1970s in most industrialized countries, and that then lasted into the 1980s, caused considerable concern at that time and, upon reflection, its lasting impact is revealed even today through public policies.

An understanding of the causes and correlates of the slowdown is important for several reasons. First, it has historical economic significance, and for that alone it should remain in focus for those who study innovation, technology, and public policy. Second, the research at that time made important discoveries about the linkage between technological change and productivity growth, emphasizing the fundamental role of R&D activity. See table 2.1. Third, the findings from that body of literature set the stage for many subsequent policy actions, several of which are discussed in this book as examples of government as entrepreneur. Finally, fourth, as important as this productivity-slowdown literature is to the evolution of the field, its limitations have brought about a provocative body of thought specifically related to government as entrepreneur, namely to alternative sources of knowledge and their relationship to technological change.

Critical questions, and ones that puzzled economists and policymakers at that time, were: Why did productivity growth decline? When did it begin to decline? Was there a structural change that biased traditionally measured productivity indices? Had the work ethic of the labor force deteriorated during the 1960s? Was it by chance that the productivity slowdown appears to have coincided with the world energy crisis in 1973–74? Had the pool of potential productivity-enhancing innovations dried up? Is the productivity slowdown part of a longer-run cycle? Or: Is the measured slowdown nothing more than a statistical artifact?

As a general rule, the post-productivity-slowdown literature attempted to explain the post-1965 or post-1973 productivity slowdown.[23] This was accomplished mainly by correcting total factor productivity growth estimates to account for changes in efficiency-related factors that are embodied in inputs, but were instead relegated statistically into the residual. These authors also attempted to control for exogenous shocks to the economy that presumably altered the form of the underlying production function. The fact that so many corrections to the conventional productivity statistics have been attempted by so many researchers underscored then and underscores now the importance of fully understanding the simplifying assumptions behind a productivity growth index before interpreting the index for what it is or what it is not.

Several factors related to the productivity growth slowdown are discussed below. Although most researchers agree that each of these factors was important, there still remains some disagreement as to the degree of importance of each. This disagreement results in part from different statistical models and techniques, and from differences in data measurement. The following discussion focuses heavily on the U.S. productivity slowdown. This emphasis characterizes the scope of the literature at that time.

Many suggested at the time of the slowdown that it was nothing more than a cyclical shock and shocks are to be expected from time to time when one takes a long-run view.[24] Others agreed at that time that there are cyclical patterns in productivity estimates, but these authors did not denigrate the importance of the then-recent slowdown. The fundamental issue hinged on whether the causes of the slowdown were cyclical—that is, due to changes in the composition of demand or to the utilization of inputs—or secular in nature—that is, due to inter-sectorial or demographic changes in inputs and technology-related investment behavior.

Cyclical activity in an economy indirectly affects productivity growth by affecting capital investment. Changes in the growth of capital were frequently cited as an independent causal factor explaining the productivity slowdown. With respect to the U.S. economy, the size of capital's role in explaining the labor productivity growth slowdown changed after 1973. Prior to 1973, there was general agreement that the slowdown was due less to a weakness in capital formation than to a decline in total factor productivity growth. For example, the growth rate of labor productivity decreased by 1.0 percentage point in the private business sector between the time periods 1948–65 and 1965–73, declining from an annual rate of growth of 3.3 percent to 2.3 percent.[25]

Some economists documented a strong negative correlation between the inflation rate and labor productivity rate in the U.S. economy as far back as the early 1940s.[26] While this relationship could be spurious, there are sound theoretical reasons for expecting inflationary tendencies to have a dampening impact on measured productivity growth. First, during periods of unanticipated and prolonged inflation there is less certainty about the meaning and interpretation of price signals than during periods of stable prices. Because managerial decisions are made in an uncertain climate, there could be efficiency losses as planning horizons shorten. Moreover, forecasting and decision making in the shortened time frame could be misguided. For example, as input prices rise during inflationary periods, it becomes increasingly difficult to determine what portion of the increase is general and inflation-induced, as opposed to reflecting changes in relative factor costs.

Second, managerial talent may be diverted toward short-run decision making as a result of increased factor price uncertainty. The ramifications of this could show up in an inability to estimate hurdle rates for investments (i. e., minimum rates of return to justify an investment in a project) correctly and also in an altered attitude on the part of managers toward risk taking.

Third, in addition to affecting the choice of an optimal input mix, inflationary tendencies can directly affect capital investments. Depreciation of plant and equipment is based on historical costs. As a result, prolonged periods of inflation will lead to a widened gap between historical costs and economic or effective replacement costs. Thus, current profits and taxes on profits are too high vis-à-vis the level requisite for financing required investments.

One obvious phenomenon linked to the worldwide inflation in the 1970s was the 1973 energy crisis. Some policy scholars contended that the 1973 crisis was the primary influence bringing about the post-1973 productivity slowdown. It was suggested that the energy shock represented a structural change in production relationships.[27]

Comparing productivity growth rates among OECD countries between the two time periods 1960–73 and 1973–79, there were dramatic macroeconomic disturbances between 1972 and 1974 that were important for explaining the post-1973 slowdown, namely the OPEC oil crisis and the input reallocation adjustments that followed. See table 2.3.

It was also suggested at the time that government regulations, environmental and work safety program regulations in particular, reduced measured productivity growth because the compliance costs in the industries affected

Table 2.3.   Average Annual Growth Rates in Productivity-Related Variables: Selected Countries, 1960–73 and 1973–81 (In Percentages)

Country	GDP per man–hour	Capital stock per employee	Adjusted capital stock per employee
France			
1960–1973	5.5	4.8	...
1973–1981	3.0	4.5	3.9
West Germany			
1960–1973	5.4	6.2	...
1973–1981	3.7	4.7	4.1
Japan			
1960–1973	9.3	10.6	...
1973–1981	3.1	5.8	5.2
Netherlands			
1960–1973	5.4	5.9	...
1973–1981	2.6	3.4	2.9
United Kingdom			
1960–1973	3.9	4.2	–
1973–1981	2.9	3.4	2.8
United States			
1960–1973	2.6	2.1	–
1973–1981	1.1	1.0	0.4

Source: Maddison (1984).

were absorbed by diverting real financial, technical, and human resources from activities that would otherwise increase output.[28] The adjective "measured" is critical when speaking about the impact of regulation on productivity growth. It is important to note that there are benefits from regulations, such as improvements in the value and quality of life, that are not likely to be captured in the conventionally measured indices.[29]

One view of unionism predicts that unions will decrease labor productivity by reducing management's flexibility, introducing inefficient work rules, and limiting compensation based on individual production. Another view is that unionism, a form of collective organization, could increase the level of labor productivity. Unions are hypothesized to act as agents for workers by providing a collective voice. Productivity is enhanced through decreased worker turnover and the establishment of grievance procedures, work rules, seniority systems, and the like. In addition, unionization shocks management to reduce inefficiency. The influence of unions in the post-1965 slowdown is rather opaque.[30]

Although there have been many conceptualizations of who the entrepreneur is and what he does, as we summarized in chapter 1, one important characteristic of entrepreneurship is an ability to create or deal with disequilibria. In an environment as dynamic as an economy is, constraints are constantly changing. To requote Schultz (1980, p. 443)

> ...disequilibria are inevitable in [a] dynamic economy. These disequilibria cannot be eliminated by law, by public policy, and surely not by rhetoric. A modern dynamic economy would fall apart if not for the entrepreneurial actions of a wide array of human agents who reallocate their resources and thereby bring their part of the economy back into equilibrium.

This constant readjustment toward equilibrium stimulates productivity growth. Did the productivity slowdown stem from a lack of perception or ability by leaders to exercise entrepreneurial talents? The empirical evidence remains wanting. Hayes and Abernathy (1980, p. 70) suggested that the rules of the game might have changed in the United States in the 1960s and 1970s; what could be referred to as managerial myopia may simply be a rational response to either short-run profit incentives or to a market of managers that is in flux: "[W]e believe that during the past two decades, American managers have increasingly relied on principles which prize analytical detachment and methodological elegance over insight, based on experience, into the subtleties and complexities of strategic decisions. As a result, short-run financial returns have become the overriding criteria for many companies."

In the early 1980s, there was great concern among economists and policymakers in the United States and in other industrialized nations regarding the pervasive slowdown in productivity growth and the concomitant decline in the global competitiveness of firms in key high-technology industries, American firms in particular. One of the alleged culprits of this productivity slowdown was a decline in the rate of technological innovation, which is a reflection of declining entrepreneurship.

The following excerpt from a U.S. House of Representatives hearing on November 18, 1983 (U.S. Congress 1983), aptly reflects the mindset of policymakers at that time:

> A number of indicators strongly suggest that the position of world technology leadership once firmly held by the United States is declining. The United States, only a decade ago, with only five percent of the world's population, was generating about 75 percent of the world's technology. Now, the U.S. share has declined to about 50 percent and in another ten years, without fundamental changes in our Nation's technological policy... the past trend would suggest that it may be down to only 30 percent. [In Committee hearings] many distinguished scientific and industry panels had recommended the need for some relaxation of current antitrust laws to encourage the [entrepreneurial] formation of R&D joint ventures.... The encouragement and fostering of joint research and development ventures are needed responses to the problem of declining U.S. productivity and international competitiveness.

Not only does this passage motivate the examples of government as entrepreneur in the following chapters, specifically in chapter 3, but also it charges government to act in certain instances as entrepreneur.

Notes

1. Relegation of the mathematics to the notes for this chapter and for other chapters should not be interpreted to mean that we view these formulations to be of secondary importance. On the contrary; these formulations are the tools of many economists and lead to relationships that can be estimated to inform public policy. However, the mathematics per se do not enrich our arguments about government as entrepreneur, but they are included for completeness.

2. Science, in a broad sense, is the search for knowledge, and that search is based on observed facts and truths. Thus, science begins with known starting conditions and searches for unknown end results (Nightingale 1998). Technology is the application of new knowledge, learned through science, to some practical problem. Technological change is the rate at which new knowledge is diffused and put into use in the economy.

3. Other scholars who have proffered alternative schemes within the history of this literature, as ably reviewed by Godin (2006, p. 650), include Huxley (1934)—background research, basic research, ad hoc research, and development; Bernal (1939)—pure and fundamental research and applied research; and Anthony and Day (1952)—uncommitted research, applied research, and development.

4. According to Godin (2006, p. 640), "One would be hard-pressed, however, to find anything but a rudiment of this [linear] model in Bush's [1945] manifesto. Bush talked about causal links between science (namely basic research) and socioeconomic progress, but nowhere did he develop a full-length argument based on a sequential process broken down into its elements or that suggests a mechanism whereby science translates in socioeconomic benefits." And Godin goes on to opine that the "model owes little to Bush. It is rather, a theoretical construction of industrialists, consultants, and business schools, seconded by economists." We do not oppugn his perceptions in this regard.

5. The first definition of basic research was developed by Dearborn et al. (1953) based on industrial interviews, although the term *basic research* traces to Vannevar Bush (1945), where he proffered the characterization that basic research is performed without thought of practical ends. The Dearborn et al. definition, used in the NSF 1953–54 survey, was (NSF 1956) the following: Basic or fundamental research—projects that are not identified with specific products or processes applications, but rather have the primary objective of adding to the overall scientific knowledge of the firm. However, NSF expressed concern about the appropriateness of the reporting definition. Thus, in NSF's 1955–56 survey, the word "fundamental" was deleted. The Frascati Manual, which guides data collection throughout the European

Union (EU), defines basic research as work done to acquire new knowledge, without any particular application or use in view.

6. For a firm, investments in basic research are not likely to have an appropriable salutary impact on its innovative activity. Thus, relative to applied research and development, the underinvestment in basic research, from a social perspective, is the greatest.

7. The Frascati Manual (OECD 2005) defines applied research as original investigation to acquire new knowledge directed towards a practical objective or a single product, operation, method, or system.

8. The Frascati Manual defines development as experimental development—systematic work, drawing on existing knowledge aimed at producing new, or to improving substantially, existing products.

9. There is a rich literature related to sources of innovation. Within the taxonomy of Godin (2006, p. 658), the following sources have been identified: Mees (1920)—pure science, development, manufacturing; Stevens (1941)—fundamental research, applied research, test-tube or bench research, pilot plant, production (improvement, trouble shooting, technical control of process and quality); Bichowsky (1942)—research, engineering, factory activities; Furnas (1948)—exploratory and fundamental research, applied, research, development, production; Mees and Leermakers (1950)—research, development (establishment of small-scale use, pilot plan and models, adoption in manufacturing); Brozen (1951)—research, engineering development, production, service; Myers and Marquis (1969)—problem solving, solution, utilization; and Utterback (1974)—generation of an idea, problem solving, implementation.

10. See also Tassey (2005, 2007).

11. Generic research is more germinal than applied research.

12. See Tassey (2007) for an excellent discussion of infratechnologies with reference to biotechnology.

13. Starting with:

$$Q = A(t)\ F(K, L, T)$$

and assuming a specific functional form for $F(\cdot)$ that is known as a Cobb-Douglas production function, then it follows that:

$$Q = A\,e^{\lambda t}\,K^{\alpha}\,L^{\beta}\,T^{\gamma}$$

where λ is a disembodied rate of growth parameter and α, β, and γ are the relative input shares. Constant returns to scale are assumed with respect to K and L, but not with respect to T:

$$(\alpha + \beta + \gamma) = (1 + \gamma) > 1 \text{ for } \gamma > 0.$$

Using logarithmic transformations and differentiating with respect to t yields:

$$\{(\partial Q/\partial t)/Q\} = \lambda + \alpha\{(\partial K/\partial t)/K\} + \beta\{(\partial L/\partial t)/L\} + \gamma\{(\partial T/\partial t)/T\}.$$

Residually measured total factor productivity growth, $\acute{A}/A$, is defined as:

$$\acute{A}/A = \{(\partial Q/\partial t)/Q\} - \alpha\{(\partial K/\partial t)/K\} - \beta\{(\partial L/\partial t)/L\} = \lambda + \gamma\{(\partial T/\partial t)/T\}.$$

The parameter γ is both the relative share of T and the output elasticity of T:

$$\gamma = (\partial Q/\partial T)(T/Q).$$

Substituting this expression for γ into the expression for $\acute{A}/A$ results in:

$$\acute{A}/A = \lambda + \rho(\acute{T}/Q), \text{ where } \acute{T} = (\partial T/\partial t) \text{ and where } \rho = (\partial Q/\partial T).$$

The parameter ρ is the marginal product of technical capital and $\acute{T}$ is the decision making unit's net private investment in the stock of technical capital. It was generally assumed in the early empirical work, that the stock of R&D-based technical capital does not depreciate, or if it does depreciate it does so very slowly. Thus $\acute{T}$ is reasonably approximated by the flow of self-financed R&D expenditures in a given period of time, RD, as

$$\acute{A}/A = \lambda + \rho(RD/Q)$$

and thus ρ is interpreted as the marginal private rate of return to R&D.

While the equation just above has been the econometric foundation for volumes of research related to the return to private-sector or self-financed R&D, as well as to public-sector R&D and to R&D by its character of use (Mansfield 1980, Link 1981a, Griliches 1986), the underlying production function model ignores the transformation process between R&D as an investment in the stock of technical capital, T, and the resulting induced innovation because it simply assumes proportionality between investment as an input and innovation as a technical output. Reliance on the three-factors in equation (2.1) has been guided in large part because of limited available data on investments in the stock of technical capital. Estimable ease aside, an alternative and theoretically more appealing approach to the three-factor production function—based on Link (1978) and the references therein—the following linearly homogonous two-factor augmented produc-tion function is:

$$Q = H(B_1 K, B_2 L)$$

where B_1 and B_2 are factor augmenting coefficients assumed to result from R&D investments. Let m_1 be the dollar amount of R&D devoted to K-aug-mentation, B_1 and let m_2 be the dollar amount of R&D devoted to L-aug-mentation, B_2, such that $B_1 = B_1(m_1)$ and $B_2 = B_2(m_2)$.

Associated with the production function $H(\cdot)$ above is a linearly homogeneous cost function:

$$C(Q; r/B_1, w/B_2) = Q\,G(r/B_1, w/B_2)$$

for r and w constant unit factor costs of K and L, respectively. It follows that the shares of each factor in total costs are:

$$rK/C = H_1 B_1 K/H = G_1 r/GB_1 \text{ and } wL/C = H_2 B_2 L/H = G_2 w/GB_2$$

where the subscript notation on H and G denotes partial derivative with respect to factor inputs. Also, the effect of factor augmentation is to reduce the cost of production at any given rate, $\partial C/\partial B_1 < 0$ and $\partial C/\partial B_2 < 0$.

Assuming that the firm maximizes net revenue for specific values of B_1 and B_2, the following conditions hold:

$$N(B_1, B_2) = \max | Q[p(Q)Q - C(Q; r/B_1, w/B_2)] = [p(Q^*)Q^* - C^*(B_1, B_2)]$$

where Q^* is the output level providing this maximum, where C^* is the associated cost, and where $p(Q^*)$ is an inverse demand function assumed to be stable.

$N(B_1, B_2)$ can be viewed as a level of potential net revenue given that uncertainty exists in the transformation between the R&D investment and the resulting factor augmentation. Realistically, this uncertainty can be related to the unknown success of any R&D project or to the time lag between the initial investment and its impact on production. Thus, it follows that the potential change in net revenue is:

$$\partial N(B_1, B_2)/\partial B_1 > 0 \text{ and } \partial N(B_1, B_2)/\partial B_2 > 0.$$

The expected rate of change in net revenue is thus:

$$P(m)[\partial N(B_1, B_2)/\partial B_1 + \partial N(B_1, B_2)/\partial B_2]$$

for a finite probability of success of completing a particular R&D project, $P(m)$, and for $m = m_1 + m_2$.

The firm is also assumed to select levels of R&D so as to maximize the expected rate of increase in profits in each time period defined as the expected rate of increase in net revenue less the R&D costs to achieve that increase. The objective function thus becomes:

$$\max \{P(m)[\partial N(B_1, B_2)/\partial B_1 + \partial N(B_1, B_2)/\partial B_2] - m\}$$

Based on first order maximizing conditions and assuming that induced technology is neutral, $B_1 = B_2 = B$, then the optimal value of B^* is:

$$B^* = e^{-\int (W/S)dm} [k + \int (-S)^{-1} e^{\int (W/S)dm} dm]$$

where $S = (-(rK + wL)) P(m)$, and $W = (-(rK + wL)) dP(m)/dm$, and where k is a constant of integration. See Link (1978) for an empirical estimate of B^* and for correlations between B^* and R&D expenditures.

14. The above definitions of the terms *public* and *private* are straightforward, but some might pause over the definition of the term *partnership*. Surprisingly, there is not a generally accepted definition for that term in the economics or policy literatures, especially with reference to innovation. Coburn (1995, p. 1), for example, used that term synonymously with cooperation by defining cooperative technology programs as "public-private initiatives involving government and industry—and often universities—that sponsor the development and the use of technology and improve practices to measurably benefit specific companies." The National Research Council (Wessner 2003, p. 7) offered an explanation of a public/private partnership in terms of what it is and what it does: "Public-private partnerships involving cooperative research and development among industry, government, and universities can play an instrumental role in introducing key new technologies to the market...[Partnerships] often contribute to national missions in health, energy, the environment, and national defense and to the [N]ation's ability to capitalize on its R&D investments."

15. This framework was developed by Link (1999, 2006).

16. This section draws directly from background information jointly developed with Nicholas Vonortas under the sponsorship of the NSF.

17. A partnership can have both horizontal and vertical elements.

18. An important issue in geographical classification has been the national attribution of partners fully-, majority-, or partially-controlled by foreign entities (e.g., multinational corporations).

19. The following ten subcategories, adapted from Alic (1990), describe the breadth of activity that falls under the rubric of research partnerships: (1) university-based co-operative research funded jointly by industry (with or without public support); (2) research and technology development (RTD) performed or sponsored by industry associations/contract RTD for multiple clients by nonprofit organizations; (3) jointly funded government-industry RTD (these are co-operative RTD projects with strong government backing and, frequently, with the participation by universities and other research institutes); (4) research corporations (private, equity-based joint venture firms focusing on generic, yet proprietary, R&D); (5) corporate venture capital in small firms by one or more firms (this is a form of equity strategic investment by large firms in smaller high-technology firms sometimes used in combination with R&D contracts); (6) non-equity co-operative RTD agreements between firms in selected areas (flexible agreements that involve a small number of firms, usually only two, typically well focused on projects to develop specific products and/or production processes, and usually of limited duration); (7) inter-firm agreements regarding proven technologies developed independently (non-equity agreements can include technology-sharing agreements of complementary technologies, second-sourcing agreements involving access to proprietary technology, cross-licensing agreements of complementary technologies, technology swaps, etc.); (8) industrial comprehensive joint ventures (equity-based agreements referring to consortia with comprehensive R&D, manufacturing and marketing activities); (9) customer-supplier agreements (agreements including co-production, equity affiliations linking vertically related firms, joint development of products or production equipment, shared engineering databases, subcontracting, etc.); and (10) one-way licensing and/or marketing agreements (traditional technology transfer agreements forming part of long-term relationships between firms, as in OEM agreements). Taken together, these ten categories include the vast majority of observed, formal partnerships that have attracted most attention by policy and business analysts.

20. The one exception is Leyden and Link (1999).

21. This literature is reviewed in Link and Siegel (2007).

22. In terms of the mathematical representations above, a firm involved in either a research partnership or an RJV could have a production function represented as

$$Q = A(t)\ F(K, L, B(t)T)$$

where the augmentation of T is through $B(t)$, and where $B(t)$ characterizes the nature of the research partnership. See Link (1978) for a theoretical and Link and Rees (1990) for an empirical representation of this type of model.

23. Much of the productivity-slowdown literature is reviewed in Link (1987) and Link and Siegel (2003).

24. See for example Nordhaus (1980).

25. See for example Norsworthy, Harper, and Kunze (1979).

26. See for example Clark (1981, 1982).

27. See for example Rasche and Tatom (1977a, 1977b), but some disagreed; see for example Berndt (1980, 1984).

28. See for example Abramovitz (1981).

29. See Link (1982) for empirical evidence.

30. See Hirsch and Link (1987) for empirical support of this argument.

3

Research Partnerships

Organizational Structures for Innovative Efficiency

3.1. Introduction

The research joint venture (RJV) organizational structure is the public/private partnership described in this chapter through which government acts as entrepreneur. Public and private organizations participate in RJVs, and public resources are indirectly used to encourage the partnership formation.[1] See table 3.1. The use of public resources, meaning the lessening of prevailing antitrust laws, creates a legal environment conducive for cooperative research. It is this legal environment that is the technology infrastructure. The so-called legitimization of RJVs (i.e., the relaxation of antitrust laws to stimulate private-sector R&D) was the innovative policy action. It removed the innovation barriers that were suspected of causing an underinvestment in private-sector R&D. The entrepreneurial risk is if the benefits to firms from participating in an RJV outweigh the costs. See table 3.2.

Through RJV activity, firms potentially benefit from the opportunity to capture knowledge spillovers from other members of the venture, reduce innovation costs due to a lessening of duplicative research, realize faster commercialization because the fundamental research stage is shortened, and realize the opportunity to develop an industrywide competitive vision.[2] These listed potential benefits are based on the theoretical literature, anecdotal evidence from the successful Japanese experience with research collaborations in the mid- to late-1970s and early 1980s, and a few limited empirical studies.

Table 3.1.   Public/Private Partnerships: Research Joint Venture

Government Involvement	Economic Objective	
	Leverage Public-Sector R&D	Leverage Private-Sector R&D
Indirect	...	research joint venture structure
Direct		
Financial Resources	...	...
Infrastructural Resources	...	...
Research Resources	...	...

Table 3.2.   Government as Entrepreneur: Research Joint Venture

Public/Private Partnership	Technology Infrastructure	Innovative Policy Action	Entrepreneurial Risk
RJV structure	Legal environment conducive for cooperative research	National Cooperative Research Act of 1984: use of antitrust laws to stimulate private-sector R&D	If the benefits to firms from participating in an RJV outweigh the costs

The realization of these potential benefits is subject to entrepreneurial risk because, in fact, they might not be realized, and if they are realized, the benefits will not likely be appropriable without a cost. This cost includes appropriability loss because research results are shared among participants in the venture, and it includes the inevitable managerial tension among venture participants before each learns to trust the others and work in concert. Anticipation of such categories of cost could deter initial participation in the venture.

The following section discusses the first formal research collaboration in the United States,[3] the Semiconductor Research Corporation (SRC) and SEMATECH (SEmiconductor MAnufacturing TECHnology). This historical overview sets the stage for section 3.3, which summarizes innovative U.S. policies that created the environment (technology infrastructure) conducive for the formation of research partnerships. This section is then followed by a discussion of entrepreneurial risk couched in terms of the potential net benefits associated with research cooperation.

As emphasized in chapter 1, our goal is not to present evidence, statistical or anecdotal, that any particular innovative policy action was or was not successful. Rather, our goal is to offer a lens through which to view government policy actions that have specific characteristics. When government provides technology infrastructure through an innovative policy action characterized by entrepreneurial risk, we say that government is acting entrepreneurially.

Trends in U.S. RJV activity are discussed in section 3.4 based on information published in the *Federal Register*, and in section 3.5 based on a new, unique NSF database. Section 3.6 summarizes and concludes the chapter.

3.2. Semiconductor Research Corporation and SEMATECH

One of the first formal research collaborations in the United States was the SRC. A brief history of the SRC will serve to illustrate that many research collaborations or partnerships are influenced by entrepreneurial governmental policy actions. In the case of the SRC, government involvement was predicated on the belief that competitive industrywide technological issues were facing a sizeable segment of the U.S. semiconductor industry, yet U.S. policymakers were in uncharted waters as to how best to respond.

In the late 1950s, an integrated circuit (IC) industry emerged in the United States. The fledgling industry took form in the 1960s and experienced rapid growth throughout the 1970s. In 1979, when Japanese firms captured 42 percent of the U.S. market for 16 kbit DRAMs (memory devices) and converted Japan's IC trade balance with the United States from a negative $122 million in 1979 to a positive $40 million in 1980, the U.S. industry became painfully aware, in the midst of a domestic and global productivity slowdown, that its dominance of the IC industry was being challenged. It was clear to all in the U.S. industry at that time that it was in their collective best interest to invest in an organizational structure that would strengthen the industry's position in the global semiconductor marketplace.

The Semiconductor Industry Association (SIA) was formed in 1977 to collect and assemble reliable information on the industry and to develop mechanisms for addressing industrywide issues with the federal government. In a presentation at an SIA Board Meeting in June 1981, Erich Bloch of IBM described to the IC industry the nature of the growing competition with Japan and proposed the creation of a semiconductor research cooperative to assure continued U.S. technology leadership. This event witnessed the birth of the SRC, both in concept and in form.

To place the activities surrounding the formation of the SRC in a broader context, there was growing domestic concern in the late 1970s and early 1980s regarding the pervasive slowdown in productivity growth throughout the industrial sector, as discussed in chapter 2. More specifically, policymakers were troubled by the declining global market shares of leading American firms, especially those in the semiconductor industry.[4]

In December 1981, Robert Noyce, then SIA chairman and vice chairman of Intel, announced the establishment of the SRC for the purpose of stimulating joint research in advanced semiconductor technology by industry and U.S. universities and to reverse the declining trend in semiconductor research investments. The SRC was formally incorporated in February 1982 with a stated purpose: to provide a clearer view of technology needs, fund research to address technology needs, focus attention on competition, and reduce research redundancy.[5]

Policymakers soon noticed the virtues of cooperative research, in part because such organizational structures had worked well in Japan and in part because the organizational success of the SRC demonstrated that cooperation among competitive firms at the fundamental research level was feasible and apparently effective.

In 1986, when the SIA and the SRC began to explore the possibility of joint industry/government cooperation, the U.S. semiconductor industry was not in a favorable economic position. During 1986, Japan overtook the United States for the first time in terms of its share of the world semiconductor market. Japan had about 45 percent of the world market compared to about 42 percent for the United States. The U.S. semiconductor industry expected Japan's share to grow at the expense of that of the United States.

In January 1987, President Reagan recommended $50 million in matching federal funding for R&D related to semiconductor manufacturing, and this was to be part of the Department of Defense's 1988 budget. Soon thereafter, the SIA approved the formation of SEMATECH and the construction of a world-class research facility.[6] In September 1987, Congress authorized $100 million in matching funding for SEMATECH.

SEMATECH and its members had, and still have, a mission to create a shared competitive advantage by working together to achieve and strengthen manufacturing technology leadership. This shared vision was to be accomplished by joint sponsorship of leading-edge technology development in equipment supplier firms. As these firms became world-class manufacturers, so would the members of SEMATECH.

By 1988, Japan's world market share reached over 50 percent, and that of the United States fell to about 37 percent. The U.S. share again declined in 1989 and then began to increase at the expense of Japan's. Early in 1992, the United States regained parity with Japan at about 42 percent, and stayed slightly ahead of Japan until 1995 when the gap began to widen in favor of the United States.

The mid-1990s saw increasing cooperation between U.S. and Japanese semiconductor firms, and in fact, in 1998 International SEMATECH began operations with Hyundai (Japan) and Philips (Amsterdam) as important international members. Also, beginning in 1998, all funding came only from member firms.

Table 3.3 shows selected early U.S. public/private partnership legislation to encourage an environment conducive for cooperative research in general.

Table 3.3.   Selected Public/Private Partnership Legislation to Encourage
Cooperative Research

Enabling Legislation	Characteristics of the Program
Stevenson-Wylder Technology Innovation Act of 1980	Act predicated on the premise that federal laboratories embody industrially useful technology. Federal laboratories mandated to establish an Office of Research and Technology Application to facilitate transfer of public technology to the private sector.
University and Small Business Patent Procedure Act of 1980	Known as Bayh-Dole Act. Reformed federal patent policy by providing increased incentives for diffusion of federally funded innovation results. Universities, nonprofit organizations, and small businesses permitted to obtain titles to innovations developed with governmental funds; federal agencies to grant exclusive licenses to their technology to industry.
Small Business Innovation Development Act of 1982	Act required federal agencies to provide special funds to support small business R&D that complemented the agency's mission. Programs called Small Business Innovation Research (SBIR) programs. Act reauthorized in 1992 and 2000.
National Cooperative Research Act of 1984	NCRA encouraged formation of joint research ventures among U.S. firms. Amended by the National Cooperative Research and Production Act of 1993, thereby expanding antitrust protection to joint production ventures.
Trademark Clarification Act of 1984	Act set forth new licensing and royalty regulations to take technology from federally funded facilities into the private sector. Specifically permitted government-owned, contractor-operated (GOCO) laboratories to make decisions regarding which patents to license to the private sector, and contractors to receive royalties on such patents.
Federal Technology Transfer Act of 1986	Act amended the Stevenson-Wylder Act. Made technology transfer an explicit responsibility of all federal laboratory scientists and engineers. Authorized cooperative research and development agreements (CRADAs). Amended by the National Competitiveness Technology Transfer Act of 1989 to include contractor-operated laboratories.
Omnibus Trade and Competitiveness Act of 1988	Act established Advanced Technology Program (ATP) and Manufacturing Extension Partnership (MEP) within the renamed National Institute of Standards and Technology (NIST).

Source: Link (2006).

3.3. Entrepreneurial Policies Toward Research Joint Ventures

3.3.1. An Institutional Perspective

From an historical U.S. perspective, an important result of the productivity slowdown–induced White House Domestic Policy Review of Industrial Innovation in 1978 and 1979 was President Carter's innovative charge to the Department of Justice to clarify its position on collaboration among firms in the area of research. It was his belief that antitrust laws should not be "mistakenly understood to prevent cooperative activity, even in circumstances where it would foster innovation without harming competition" (U.S. Department of Justice 1980, p. i). In response, in November 1980, the Department of Justice issued the *Antitrust Guide Concerning Research Joint Ventures* that included several important premises upon which the legislation leading to the passage of the National Cooperative Research Act of 1984 (discussed below) was based. The *Guide* states that (1980, pp. 1–3):[7]

> Research itself presents a broad spectrum of activity, from "pure" basic research into fundamental principles, on the one hand, to development research focusing on promotional differentiation of a product or market issue on the other extreme. In general, basic research is undertaken with less predictability of outcome, and thus more risk, than developmental research. Moreover, the outcomes of basic research are less likely to be appropriable and thus more likely to be widely diffused in the economy, with the possibility of there being the basis of future advance and competitive opportunity for all.... In general, the closer the joint activity is to the basic end of the research spectrum ... the more likely it is to be acceptable under the antitrust laws.

Several bills focused explicitly on RJVs were introduced in the 98th session of Congress as part of a purposeful response to the productivity slowdown. The Thurmond Bill would have excused all RJVs from existing provisions of antitrust law related to the award of treble damages in successful suits. The Glenn Bill and the Rodino Bill were aimed at relaxing all antitrust regulations serving as barriers to the formation and actions of RJVs. The Mathias Bill was even more comprehensive and included measures for sharing patent and royalty rights coming from cooperative ventures. Much of this thought found its way into the Research and Development Joint Ventures Act of 1983.

In an April 6, 1984, House report on competing legislation, the Joint Research and Development Act of 1984, the supposed benefits of joint research and development were for the first time clearly articulated (recall that at this time it was still too soon for there to be visible benefits coming from the SRC's activities on behalf of the IC industry): "Joint research and development, as our foreign competitors have learned [i.e., Japan], can be pro-competitive. It can reduce duplication, promote the efficient use of scarce technical personnel, and help to achieve desirable economies of scale [in R&D].... [W]e must ensure to our U.S. industries the same economic opportunities as our competitors, to engage in joint research and development, if we are to compete in the world market and retain jobs in this country."

The National Cooperative Research Act (NCRA) of 1984, after additional revisions in the initiating legislation, was passed, "to promote research and development, encourage innovation, stimulate trade, and make necessary and appropriate modifications in the operation of the antitrust laws."

The NCRA of 1984 created a registration process, later expanded by the National Cooperative Research and Production Act (NCRPA) of 1993 and the Standards Development Organization Advancement Act of 2004 (SDOAA), under which RJVs can voluntarily disclose their research intentions to the U. S. Department of Justice; all disclosures are then made public in the *Federal Register*.[8]

RJVs gain two significant benefits from filing with the Department of Justice. One, if the venture was ever subjected to criminal or civil antitrust action, the courts would evaluate the alleged anticompetitive behavior under a rule of reason rather than presumptively ruling that the behavior constituted a per se violation of the antitrust law. For RJVs that have filed, the Act stated: "In any action under the antitrust laws ... the conduct of any person in making or performing a contract to carry out a joint research and development venture shall not be deemed illegal *per se*; such conduct shall be judged on the basis of its reasonableness, taking into account all relevant factors affecting competition, including, but not limited to, effects on competition in properly defined, relevant research and development markets." And two, if the venture was found to fail a rule-of-reason analysis it would be subject to actual damages rather than treble damages.[9]

One of the more notable RJVs formed and made public through the NCRA disclosure process was SEMATECH. It was thought that SEMATECH would be the U.S. semiconductor industry's/U.S. government's technology policy response to the Japanese government's targeting of their semiconductor industry for global domination.

Japan was a pioneer in supporting cooperative R&D in the post–World War II period.[10] The objectives and organization of Japanese cooperative R&D organizations have changed over time. The idea of research associations was imported from the United Kingdom after the war, but the use of formal associations was transformed from an instrument for assisting declining firms and industries to an instrument for gathering, adapting, and distributing technological information more efficiently in high technology industries. Following the activities of the Mining and Manufacturing Technology Research Association of 1961, a large number of Japanese Engineering Research Associations (ERAs) were established. In the mid-1970s, the focus of ERAs changed from generating and adapting specific technologies to assisting sectors catch up with world technologies. ERAs represent only one form of collaborative R&D in Japan. Such cooperation has also included trade associations, joint research institutes, collaboration with large firm networks, and private-sector formal and informal collaborative agreements.

Similar to the United States, the European Community (EC) entered the 1980s facing the productivity slowdown and embracing concerns over the loss of competitiveness in high-technology industries. In response to the continued expansion of the EC and the disparities between the industrial and technological capabilities of member firms, the differences in the science and technology infrastructure among member firms and the lack of an appropriate legal framework and institutions at the EC level for supporting a consistent technology policy, the pilot ESPRIT program was established in 1981, led by the EC with the endorsement of the twelve largest European producers of electronics. ESPRIT served as the progenitor of the European Framework Program on R&D to which it lent many features including the support of cooperative R&D.[11]

The NCRA was later expanded by the National Cooperative Research and Production Act (NCRPA) of 1993 and then by the Standards Development Organization Advancement Act of 2004 (SDOAA). The former expanded antitrust-related coverage to production joint ventures and the latter indemnified cooperation related to the promulgation of standards.

3.3.2. A Theoretical Perspective

There is a vast theoretical literature to explain why firms enter into formal research partnerships and what the coadjutant results are to the partners, industry, and society.[12] Scholars have approached this question from three perspectives, and here we discuss these perspectives, which characterize the entrepreneurial risk of RJVs, under the literature headings of transaction costs, strategic management, and industrial organization theory. The rationale for these three categories rests on the division of labor between the schools of theorists. Management theorists have traditionally focused on the firm and its interorganizational activities; industrial organization theorists have focused on the firm as well but have emphasized the effect of its actions on efficiency, industry structure, and spillovers to society; and transaction-costs theorists have focused on a blend of the above two loci of interests.

According to transaction-costs theorists, entrepreneurs attempt in different ways to organize a transaction, including arm's length markets and market displacements through internal administrative hierarchies. The boundary between the market and the firm is then determined by the relative cost of carrying out a transaction using each organizational structure. Over the past decade, this literature has shifted its focus to examining cooperation among firms, and research partnerships that fall within that scope. Briefly, to determine if a research partnership would form, one must determine why such an organization structure would have a cost advantage over either the market or a hierarchal organization form of operation for the specific type of activity.

According to management theorists—and this is a heterogeneous group of scholars—there are several ways to think about research partnerships.

A competitive-force approach views collaboration as a means of shaping competition by improving the firm's comparative competitive position, be it through an offensive or defensive strategy. A strategic-network approach views networks—and networks result from research partnerships—as a new organizational form. Networks can achieve efficiencies though economies of scale and scope because members can pursue their comparative advantage. The resource-based view of the firm argues that a firm's sustainable competitive advantage is related to the resources that it owns. Firm performance, therefore, is based on the unique and differentiable capabilities of the firm, and through partnerships the firm can acquire complementary resources to indemnify its advantages. A dynamic-capabilities view of research partnerships focuses on the mechanisms through which a firm accumulates and exploits new skills and capabilities. These capabilities facilitate the firm reconfiguring its competencies to adapt to a changing competitive environment. Finally, a strategic approach to research partnership considers how managers can prospectively determine the resources and capabilities needed for future performance in an uncertain market. Participation in partnerships can assist a firm in gaining requisite experience, and through participation the firm increases its exposure to related markets and new opportunities.

Industrial organization scholars have viewed membership in a research partnership as a game.[13] Nontournament models of the game assert that the firm invests in R&D to decrease costs and thus compete in terms of price or output quality in the market. Therefore, there is a tradeoff between competition in R&D and cooperation in R&D especially in terms of the social spillovers of each approach. Tournament models assume a single path to technological advancement and then focus on the emulous behavior of the winner of the race, and the winner is determined by such factors as timing, the number of firms in the race, each firm's level of R&D investment, and each firm's market power.

Table 3.4 summarizes these literatures.[14]

3.4. Trends in U.S. Research Joint Ventures

3.4.1. An Institutional Perspective

Through 2006, there have been 962 formal RJVs filed and disclosed under the NCRA, as reported in the CORE (COoperative REsearch) database.[15, 16] Certainly, this number is a lower bound on the total number of research partnerships in the United States, even since 1984, as was previously noted in chapter 2 (and which is discussed below). Not all RJVs are as publicly visible as SEMATECH. Most are quite small, with only two or three members, and others are quite large with hundreds of members.[17] The average (mean) size of these joint ventures is thirteen members, and the median size is five members.

Figure 3.1 shows the trend in RJVs from 1985 through 2006 based on the year of the disclosure of the filing in the *Federal Register*. Certainly, the trend

Table 3.4. Arguments to Basic Questions about Research Partnerships, by Theoretical Area

Question	Transaction Costs	Strategic Management	Industrial Organization
Incentives to form a research partnership	• Minimize costs of transactions involving intangible assets • Circumvent incomplete contracts • Avoid opportunistic market behavior • Avoid high costs of internalizing partnership activities	• Share R&D costs • Pool risks • Economies of scale and scope • Co-opt competition • Coordinate value chains with coalition partners • Increase efficiency, synergy, power through networks • Access complementary resources to exploit own resources • Use collaboration as learning vehicle to accumulate and deploy new skills and capabilities • Learn from partners; transfer knowledge • Create new investment options	• Share R&D costs • Pool risks • Economies of scale and scope • Co-opt competition • Accelerate returns on investments • Access complementary resources • Decelerate rate of innovation • Increase market power
Results expected from research partnerships • To partners	• Successfully meet incentives	• Successfully meet incentives • Interdependency	• Successfully meet incentives • Interdependency

- To industry, society
  - Better resource allocation
  - Industrial competitiveness
    - Increase R&D efficiency
    - Increase flow of information
    - Increase overall R&D expenditures when spillovers are high
    - Increase social welfare
    - Subsidize on certain occasions

Source: Hagedoorn, Link, and Vonortas (2000, p. 575).

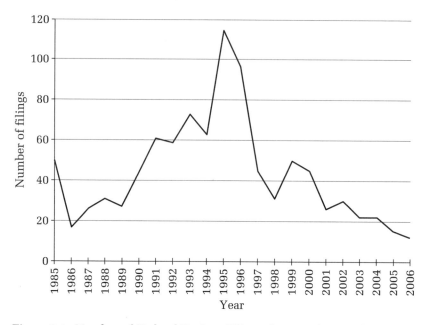

Figure 3.1. Number of *Federal Register* Filings, by Year (n = 962)

in RJV disclosures was upward until the mid-1990s, and since then it has generally declined.[18] While informal cooperation in research could have been prevalent in the United States for decades, formal RJV relationships are new and it could take longer than two decades to detect meaningful trends.

Figure 3.2 shows the percent of RJVs disclosed in the *Federal Register*, by technology area. Collaboration occurs most often when the research area is related to computer software and materials R&D.

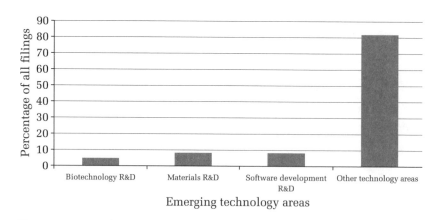

Figure 3.2. Distribution of RJVs by Emerging Technology Areas (n = 962)

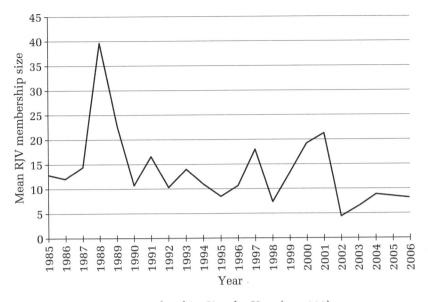

Figure 3.3. Mean RJV Membership Size, by Year (n = 962)

Figure 3.3 shows the trend in the mean membership size of RJVs. Between 1985 and 2006, the mean membership size is about thirteen, but, mean membership size has fluctuated by year of disclosure. More important than the year-by-year variability in mean membership size is the fact that the RJVs are relatively small as shown by the overall median member size of five in figure 3.4.

Figure 3.5 shows the trend in the product innovation versus process innovation mix of RJVs. Noticeable in the figure is that the percentage of RJVs focused on process innovations did not dramatically decrease in favor of product innovations after the passage of the NCRPA in 1993, which specifically encouraged production-oriented collaboration.

3.4.2. Partners in U.S. Research Joint Ventures

Noticeable among the RJVs filed with the Department of Justice and disclosed in the *Federal Register* is the presence of federal government agencies (federal laboratories and/or governmental agencies) and universities as research partners.[19] Over the past two decades, the number of RJVs with at least one federal government agency has generally increased; 2006 is a notable exception, although very few RJVs were noticed in the *Federal Register* in that year. See figure 3.6. Through 2006, the annual mean percentage of all RJVs that had at least one federal government agency as a research partner was thirteen.

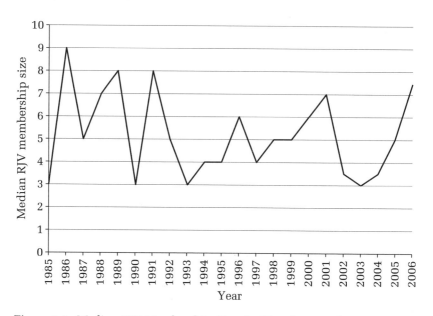

Figure 3.4. Median RJV Membership Size, by Year (n = 962)

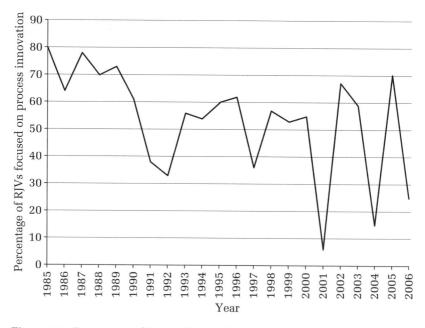

Figure 3.5. Percentage of Research Joint Ventures in Manufacturing Focused on Process Innovations (n = 962)

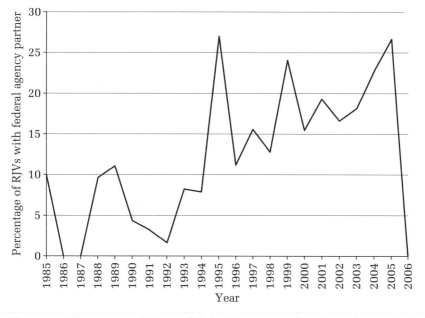

Figure 3.6. Percentage of Research Joint Ventures with a Federal
Government Agency as a Member (n = 962)

Leyden and Link (1999) argued that federal agencies, federal laboratories in
particular, are invited to join an RJV, especially a large RJV, because they take
on the role of an honest broker. Larger RJVs are likely to generate economies of
technological scope that come from the larger number of participants; larger
venture size also results in a greater cost of monitoring the RJV's activities, and
in a reduced ability of member firms to appropriate individually the research
output of the RJV. Government agency participation, which reduces still
further the ability of members to appropriate research results, could also
reduce the cost of monitoring the RJV. For smaller RJVs, the loss in appropriability associated with government agency participation could be too great
and the saving in monitoring costs could be too low to justify to the members
inviting the agency to participate. However, for a large RJV, the additional loss
in appropriability could be sufficiently small and the savings in monitoring
costs sufficiently high that a government agency's participation becomes
desirable—at least this is theoretically the case.

Universities are also members of RJVs, although less prevalent than government agencies. Figure 3.7 shows the percentage of RJVs that have had at
least one university as a member. Clearly, the percentage has fallen steadily
over the past decade.

A university has a financial incentive to partner with industry in its
applied research especially if commercial technologies are expected to result.

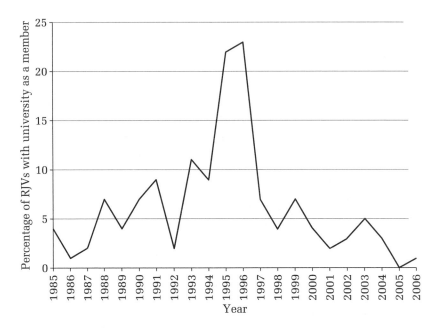

Figure 3.7. Percentage of Research Joint Ventures with a University as a Member (n = 962)

Industry also has a research efficiency incentive to partner with a university; efficiencies are gained through access to complementary activities and research results. As Rosenberg and Nelson (1994, p. 340) noted: "What university research most often does . . . is to stimulate and enhance the power of R&D done in industry, as contrasted with providing a substitute for it." Relatedly, Hall, Link, and Scott (2003, p. 490) argued:[20] "Universities are included (invited by industry) in those research projects that involve what we have called "new" science. Industrial research participants perceive that the university could provide research insight that is anticipatory of future research problems and could be an ombudsman anticipating and translating to all the complex nature of the research being undertaken. Thus, one finds universities purposively involved in projects that are characterized as problematic with regard to the use of basic knowledge."

Generalizations aside, some stylized conclusions can be drawn from the limited empirical evidence there is in the literature: firms that interact with universities generally have greater R&D productivity (Link and Rees 1990) and greater patenting activity; a key motive for firms to maintain joint research relationships with universities is to have access to key university personnel—faculty as well as students as potential employees (Hall, Link, and Scott 2003); and larger RJVs are more likely to invite a university to join the venture than smaller RJVs because larger RJVs are less likely to expect substantial additional appropriability problems to result because of the addition of a university partner, and because the larger ventures have both a lower marginal cost and a higher marginal value from the university R&D contributions to the venture's innovative output (Baldwin and Link 1998, Link and Scott 2005c).

Many commentators have predicted that university participation in such collaboration will increase in the future. According to the Council on Competitiveness (1996, pp. 3–4), for example: "Over the next several years, participation in the U.S. R&D enterprise will have to continue experimenting with different types of partnerships to respond to the economic constraints, competitive pressures and technological demands that are forcing adjustment across the board . . . [and in response] industry is increasingly relying on partnerships with universities, while the focus of these partnerships is shifting progressively toward involvement in shorter-term research." And (Council on Competitiveness 1996, p. 11): "For universities, cutbacks in defense spending have resulted in a *de facto* reallocation of funding away from the physical sciences and engineering and shifted the focus of defense research away from the frontiers of knowledge [e.g., basic science] to more applied efforts. . . . Although defense spending is clearly not the only viable mechanism to support frontier research and advanced technology, the United States has yet to find an alternative innovation paradigm to replace it." Given this spending trend, and the increasing ease of global technology transfer, it is conceivable, at least according to the Council, that the United States may lose its technological leadership in some important areas, such as health and advanced materials, because innovation in these fields is closely linked to improvements in basic science.

There is some indication that scholars are beginning to think more deeply and more broadly about the social, economic, and technological consequences of university involvement in private-sector research partnerships (Siegel, Thursby, Thursby, and Ziedonis 2001). This thinking reflects some major concerns about the impact of these relationships on the research university's mission to conduct basic research. Unfortunately, there is a void of information that can be studied by researchers to examine the ramifications of this trend from a wide variety of disciplinary perspectives.

It is likely that the increasing trend toward university and private-sector research partnerships will continue. A 1993 national survey of U.S. biology, chemistry, and physics faculty revealed that many academic scientists desired more of such involvement. An earlier survey of engineering faculty members reached the same conclusion. However, one of the authors (Morgan 1998, p. 169) of the surveys was quick to point out one area of major concern:

> [A major concern is the] diminution of the role of the university as an independent voice to help look out for the broader societal good and to guard against industrial as well as other excesses. An independent science, engineering and public policy role is essential to ensure an adequate supply of well educated scientists and engineers prepared to

work with the public sector in public interest groups. Having industry assume a more central role as customer and client for university-based scientific and engineering research, while in some way a natural and desirable step, needs to be balanced against the need for independence, oversight and service to society and the larger public good.

Other evidence of the increasing desire on the part of both parties to enhance the partnership between university and private-sector research is the growth of university research or science parks. This is the subject of chapter 7.

3.4.3. A New Look at Research Joint Venture Activity

As discussed above, the entrepreneurial risk associated with the use of antitrust law to stimulate private-sector R&D through RJVs as a public/private partnership is whether firms will respond to the collaborative incentives in the NCRA and its follow-on legislation, and if so, will they realize the expected net benefits from research partnerships. Certainly, the descriptive evidence in the *tour des la figures* above is insufficient to address this question at more than a superficial level, but it is worth noting that since the mid-1990s the number of *Federal Register* filings has dramatically decreased.[21] One could suggest, especially from the patterns in figure 3.1 and figure 3.3, that firms initially embraced the legislation and formed and participated in RJVs, but then experience in such ventures suggested that the net benefits from such partnerships were small or even negative.

Alternatively, one could argue that the *Federal Register* filings are an incomplete picture of formal research relationships in the United States because the cost of filing with the Department of Justice and having the venture then disclosed in the *Federal Register* outweighed the antitrust indemnification benefits. And the government has yet to file an antitrust-violation suit based on research collaborations. While the direct cost of filing with the Department of Justice is likely small, perhaps only a few person-hours of effort, the indirect cost could be enormous if the public disclosure of research partners sent a signal to the firm's rivals about the direction of its future innovation strategies.

To address the issue of the representativeness of *Federal Register* filings, in general, and the representativeness of the precipitous decline in RJVs activity in recent years, in particular, we, under the sponsorship of the NSF, collected survey data from partnership-active firms. Our methodology was as follows. We identified all publicly traded firms that were listed as research partners in at least one *Federal Register* filing during the five year interval of 2000 through 2004. From this sampling population of 2,319 firms, we segmented the firms by 2004 sales and by primary industry (based on *Register of Corporation* information), and then selected a balanced survey sample of one hundred firms.

The point of contact in each firm was the general council. This point of entry into the firm was successfully used in other research (Hertzfeld, Link, and Vonortas 2006). We asked for count information on all formal research partnerships in which the firm had been engaged over the period 2000 to 2004, and we compared that count to the number of such partnerships that were listed in the *Federal Register* (taking into account up to a one-year lag in filing).[22] We found that the sample of firms surveyed had been involved, on average (mean), in up to seven times as many research partnerships as were reported in the *Federal Register* and the number of such partnerships increased nearly 23 percent, on average (mean), between 2000 and 2004, inclusive.

3.5. Conclusions

The relaxation of antitrust law to stimulate private-sector R&D is the innovative U.S. policy action emphasized in this chapter. Such a use of antitrust laws to stimulate competitiveness was certainly innovative. At first blush this use of antitrust laws could be viewed as paradoxical because the relaxation of antitrust laws was used to create an environment conducive for cooperative research to stimulate innovation-based competition. The legislative establishment of these same laws at the turn of the last century was argued on the basis of a need to stimulate competition in markets. But, as the previous quotation from President Carter made clear, innovation can be fostered through a relaxation of antitrust laws without harming competition. The public/private partnership mechanism that facilitates this action was and still is the RJV structure.

Trends in U.S. RJVs were illustrated in an effort to underscore the entrepreneurial risk (i.e., if the benefits from participating in a research partnership outweigh the costs) that surrounds the NCRA policy action even today. The jury is still out as to whether the benefits to all firms from participating in an RJV outweigh the costs. *Federal Register* filings suggest that the entrepreneurial risk associated with the passage of the NCRA remains; but the NSF-sponsored survey data, albeit not in the public domain, suggest that the firms affected by the NCRA were not inhibited by partnership participation—if not for all firms then certainly some.

In the following chapter we discuss two specific RJVs, the printed wiring board RJV and the flat panel display RJV. Both of these joint ventures were funded through the Advanced Technology Program (ATP).

Notes

1. The development and evolution of the material in this chapter is discussed in Link (1999, 2006).

2. These benefits are elaborated upon in Hagedoorn, Link, and Vonortas (2000) and Combs and Link (2003). See also Belderbos, Carree, and Lokshin (2004).

3. Although not formal, in 1879, Thomas A. Edison, the founder of the General Electric Company, teamed up with Corning Glass Works to make the first incandescent light bulb (Levine and Byrne 1986).

4. The declining U.S. position in the semiconductor industry was well known, and in other industries there was growing concern. However, when the U.S. Department of Commerce (1990) released its 1990 report on emerging technologies, it was apparent to all that the concerns expressed in the late 1970s and early 1980s were quite valid.

5. The twelve founding members were Advanced Micro Devices, Control Data Corporation, Digital Equipment Corporation, General Instruments, Honeywell, Hewlett-Packard, IBM, Intel, Monolithic Memories, Motorola, National Semiconductor, and Silicon Systems.

6. The thirteen charter members of SEMATECH were Advanced Micro Devices, AT&T, Digital Equipment Corporation, Harris Corporation, Hewlett-Packard, IBM, Intel, LSI Logic Corporation, Micron Technology, Motorola, National Semiconductor Corporation, Rockwell International Corporation, and Texas Instruments.

7. See Bozeman, Link, and Zardkoohi (1986) for a theoretical model of RJV activity based on this Department of Justice opinion.

8. In practice, the mean time lag between filing with the Department of Justice and disclosure in the *Federal Register* is three to seven months.

9. Notwithstanding section 4 of the Clayton Act of 1914.

10. This discussion draws from Hagedoorn, Link, and Vonortas (2000). See also Caloghirou, Ioannides, and Vonortas (2003).

11. As Hagedoorn, Link, and Vonortas (2000) note, European policies for cooperation in R&D go beyond the EC level: they spread to all EU states.

12. This section draws from Hagedoorn, Link, and Vonortas (2000) and Combs and Link (2003).

13. As described in Hertzfeld, Link, and Vonortas (2006), the workhorse model in industrial organization theory assumes a two-stage game in which firms choose levels of innovative activity in the first stage and compete in the output market in the second stage. Innovative activity is measured in terms of investments in R&D. Firm 1's, for example, first-stage objective is to incur the optimum level of R&D to maximize its profits from its output choices in the second stage of the game. The first-stage objective function to be maximized is:

$$\max \pi_1 |_{x_1} = p[q(x)]q_1(x) - C_1(x)q_1(x) - x_1$$

where q is the vector of outputs, x is the vector of R&D of all firms in the industry, C is the unit cost of production, and the subscript 1 (i.e., $1 \ldots n$ firms) refers to the firm in question. In this problem it is assumed that the innovation expenditures of a firm always lower its own marginal cost of production and could lower the cost of its rivals. In other words, intellectual property protection is not complete, and spillovers of knowledge do occur. A standard result of such models is that, in a noncooperative situation, a firm's own investment in R&D in a nonperfectly appropriable environment is likely to be suboptimal. The equilibrium solution can often be brought closer to the social optimum by allowing firms to collaborate in R&D. Assuming that firms collaborate in the first stage in a research partnership, but compete in the second stage of the game, the objective of the partnership will be to maximize all partner's profits, Π, with respect to the level of collaborative R&D, X:

$$\max \Pi(X)|_X = \sum_i p[q(X)q_i(X) - \sum_i C_i(X)q_i(X) - X$$

for $i = 1 \ldots n$ firms.

14. Table 3.4 addresses from a theoretical perspective two questions: What are the incentives to form a research partnership? And: What are the expected results from a research partnership? Combs and Link (2003) have summarized the theoretical literature related to related policy questions: Do research partnerships improve efficiency? Do research partnerships increase competition in the marketplace? Do research partnerships increase consumer surplus through improved products of faster introduction of new products? Link and Siegel (2007) have summarized the Combs and Link findings in the context of the entrepreneurial firm.

15. The CORE database was constructed by A. Link under the sponsorship of the NSF. Its resource base is information contained in public domain filings published in the *Federal Register*. The unit of observation in the CORE database is the U.S. RJV. The CORE database is maintained by A. Link at the University of North Carolina at Greensboro, and it is available on request; NSF support expired at the end of 2006. Other important databases related to research partnerships are the MERIT-CATI (*Cooperative Agreements and Technology Indicators*) database and the NCRA-RJV database. The MERIT-CATI database is an international relational database covering cooperative agreements involving different parent firms. It contains information on each agreement and selected information on those firms participating. This database is maintained by J. Hagedoorn and his colleagues at MERIT. The NCRA-RJV database also used information from the *Federal Register* on U.S. RJVs. The particular characteristic of this database is that its unit of observation is the research partner (whereas the CORE database, which relies on the same information set, uses the RJV itself). The NCRA-RJV database is maintained by N. Vonortas at The George Washington University.

16. After the passage of SDOAA in 2004 there have been 261 filings under that Act. These filings are not included in the total of 962 because their research focus is cooperative in the sense of developing standards and not cooperative research in the sense of the RJVs in all of the previous years.

17. As an illustration of the research activity that can successfully occur through a small, less-visible research partnership, consider the Southwest Research Institute Clean Heavy Diesel Engine II joint venture, noticed in the *Federal Register* in early-1996. The eleven member companies, from six countries including the United States, joined together to solve a common set of technical problems. Diesel engine manufacturers were having difficulties, on their own, meeting desired emission control levels. The eleven companies were coordinated by Southwest Research Institute, an independent, nonprofit contract research organization in San Antonio, Texas, to collaborate on the reduction of exhaust emissions. The joint research was successful, and each member company took with it fundamental process technology to use in their individual manufacturing facilities to meet desired emission

control levels. The joint venture was formally disbanded in mid-1999 after completing its technical objectives.

18. Brod and Link (2001) identified selected correlates with the trend in RJVs over time. In particular, the annual number of filings of RJVs changed, on average, in a countercyclical manner and in relationship to industrial development (as opposed to research) activity.

19. The federal government can enter directly into research partnerships with firms through the federal laboratory system. This relationship can take various forms ranging from informal relationships whereby a firm(s) inter-acts with a federal laboratory scientist, or more formal relationships whereby a firm(s) utilizes federal laboratory facilities and is jointly involved with the laboratory scientists in the research. Or, the relationship can be nothing more than an informational transfer whereby the firm utilizes public information that was generated within a government agency. While very few studies have systematically looked at the economics of federal laboratories as research partners, two generalizations can be made (Leyden and Link 1999): federal laboratories are generally associated with research joint ventures that are large in terms of other member companies, and one key advantage to part-nering with a federal laboratory is access to specialized technical equipment.

20. See also, Hall, Link, and Scott (2000, 2001) and Link and Scott (2005c).

21. See Reuer and Zollo (2005) for a pioneering study of successful versus failed research partnerships.

22. If a firm declined to participate in the survey, another comparable size/industry firm was contacted.

4

Advanced Technology Program

Stimulating Competitiveness through Cooperative Research

4.1. Introduction

The Advanced Technology Program (ATP) is the public/private partnership described in this chapter through which government acts as entrepreneur. ATP's public financial resources leverage private-sector R&D.[1] See table 4.1. The use of public resources, legislated through the innovative policy action of the Omnibus Trade and Competitiveness Act of 1988, to leverage private-sector R&D that would not otherwise have been undertaken lessens barriers to innovation (see table 1.2) and creates a cost-sharing environment conducive for cooperative research. It is this cost-sharing environment conducive for cooperative research that is the technology infrastructure. The entrepreneurial risk associated with the activities of the ATP is if the jointly funded research will be successful, and if so, whether it will accelerate the development of generic technology. See table 4.2.

4.2. A Brief History of the Advanced Technology Program

The ATP was established within the National Institute of Standards and Technology (NIST, discussed in chapter 5) through the Omnibus Trade and Competitiveness Act of 1988 and modified by the American Technology Preeminence Act of 1991.[2] The goals of ATP, as stated in its enabling legislation, are to assist U.S. businesses in creating and applying the generic

Table 4.1.   Public/Private Partnerships: Advanced Technology Program

Government Involvement	Economic Objective	
	Leverage Public-Sector R&D	Leverage Private-Sector R&D
Indirect	. . .	. . .
Direct		
Financial Resources	. . .	Advanced Technology Program
Infrastructural Resources	. . .	. . .
Research Resources	. . .	. . .

Table 4.2.   Government as Entrepreneur: Advanced Technology Program

Public/Private Partnership	Technology Infrastructure	Innovative Policy Action	Entrepreneurial Risk
Advanced Technology Program	Cost-sharing environment conducive for cooperative research	Omnibus Trade and Competitiveness Act of 1988: use of public resources to leverage private-sector R&D, that would otherwise not have been undertaken, through cooperative research	If the jointly funded research will be successful and if so, whether it will accelerate the development of generic technology

technology and research results necessary to commercialize significant new scientific discoveries and technologies rapidly, and refine manufacturing technologies.

These same goals were restated in the *Federal Register* on July 24, 1990: "The ATP . . . will assist U.S. businesses to improve their competitive position and promote U.S. economic growth by accelerating the development of a variety of pre-competitive generic technologies by means of grants and cooperative agreements."

As discussed in chapter 2, total factor productivity declined significantly in the United States in the early to mid-1970s, and then again in the early 1980s. While it recovered in the mid-1980s, the U.S. position in critical technologies, relative to Japan and to Europe, was not strong. Table 4.3 shows the technologies where, in 1989 and likely even before, the United States

Table 4.3.   Critical Technology Report Card, Relative Position in 1989

Relative Position	United States vs. Japan	United States vs. Europe
Behind	Advanced Materials	Digital Imaging Technology
	Advanced Semiconductor	
	Devices	
	High-Density Data Storage	
	Optoelectronics	
Even	Superconductors	Flexible Computer-Integrated
		Manufacturing
		Superconductors
Ahead	Artificial Intelligence	Artificial Materials
	Biotechnology	Advanced Semiconductor
	Flexible Computer-Integrated	Devices
	Manufacturing	Artificial Intelligence
	High-Performance	Biotechnology
	Computing	High-Density Data Storage
	Medical Devices and	High-Performance Computing
	Diagnostics	Medical Devices and Diagnostics
	Sensor Technology	Optoelectronics
		Sensor Technology

Source: Department of Commerce (1990).

was, from a market-share and technology-competitiveness position (i.e., behind, even, ahead), still behind Japan and Europe. Table 4.4 shows the relative trend (i.e., gaining, holding, losing, losing badly) in the technologies. In general, computer-based operating and processing technologies were, at that time, no longer an international market strength of the United States.

The ATP received its first appropriation from Congress in fiscal year 1990. The program funded research, not product development. Commercialization of the technology resulting from a project might overlap the research effort at a nascent level, but generally full translation of the technology into products and processes was expected to take a number of additional years. ATP, through cost sharing with industry, invested in risky technologies that were thought to have the potential for spillover benefits to the economy.

Appropriations to ATP increased from $10 million in 1990 to a peak level of $341 million in 1995. Funding decreased in 1996 to $221 million, and it has averaged about $200 million per year until 2004 when it fell to just under $150 million. In 2007, ATP was eliminated by Congress with President Bush's signing of the America COMPETES Act, and the Technology Innovation Program (TIP) was created.[3] While operating, ATP funded through competitive processes 824 research projects (from a total of 7,530 proposals) involving more than 1,600 organizations. In total, ATP awarded over $2.4 billion with industry allocating nearly that same amount in the form of research matching funds.[4]

Table 4.4.   Critical Technology Report Card, Relative Trend in 1989

Relative Trend	United States vs. Japan	United States vs. Europe
Losing Badly	Advanced Materials Biotechnology Digital Imaging Technology Superconductors	Digital Imaging Technology Flexible Computer-Integrated Manufacturing

Losing	Advanced Semiconductor
	    Devices
	High-Density Data Storage
	High-Performance Computing
	Medical Devices and
	    Diagnostics
	Optoelectronics
	Sensor Technology
		Medical Devices and
		    Diagnostics

Holding	Artificial Intelligence
	Flexible Computer-Integrated
	    Manufacturing
		Advanced Materials
		Advanced Semiconductor
		    Devices
		High-Density Data Storage
		Optoelectronics
		Sensor Technology
		Superconductors

Gaining		Artificial Intelligence Biotechnology High-Performance Computing

Source: Department of Commerce (1990).

Two examples of ATP-funded collaborations are discussed in this chapter to illustrate the extent to which ATP funding overcame entrepreneurial risk.[5] In section 4.3 we discuss the printed wiring board joint venture, and in section 4.4 we discuss the flat panel display joint venture. These are only two of the 227 joint ventures supported by ATP. They are certainly not the most or least important ventures in terms of economic impacts, but, they are two joint ventures for which we have some unique insights (Link 1996a, 1997). Thus, we discuss these two RJVs not for the purpose of characterizing ATP's portfolio of projects, but for the purpose of illustrating in detail the innovative nature of ATP and the entrepreneurial risk that characterized funded projects.[6]

4.3. Printed Wiring Board Joint Venture

4.3.1. Early History of the Industry

Paul Eisler, an Austrian scientist, is credited for developing the first printed wiring board (Flatt 1992). After World War II he was working in England on a

Table 4.5.   World Market Share for Printed Wiring
Boards, 1980–94

Year	United States	Japan	Rest of the World
1980	41%	20%	39%
1981	40	22	38
1982	39	23	38
1983	40	21	39
1984	42	24	34
1985	36	25	39
1986	34	32	34
1987	29	30	41
1988	28	27	45
1989	28	31	41
1990	26	35	39
1991	27	34	39
1992	29	31	40
1993	26	28	46
1994	26	26	48

Sources: Link (1997) and Link and Scott (1998).

concept to replace radio tube wiring with something less bulky. What he developed is similar in concept to a single-sided printed wiring board.

A printed wiring board (PWB) or printed circuit board (PCB) is a device that provides electrical interconnections and a surface for mounting electrical components. While the term PWB is more technically correct because the board is not a circuit, the term PCB is more frequently used in the popular literature.

Based on Eisler's early work, single-sided boards were commercialized during the 1950s and 1960s, primarily in the United States. As the term suggests, a single-sided board has a conductive pattern on only one side. During the 1960s and 1970s, technology was developed for plating copper on walls of drilled holes in circuit boards. This advancement allowed manufacturers to produce double-sided boards with top and bottom circuitry interconnections through the holes. From the mid-1970s throughout the 1980s there was tremendous growth in the industry. In the same period, PWBs became more complex and dense, and multilayered boards were developed and commercialized.

4.3.2. Competitiveness of the Printing Wiring
Board Industry at the Time of Funding

As shown in table 4.5, the United States dominated the world PWB market in the early 1980s. However, Japan steadily gained market share from the United States. By 1985, the U.S. share of the world market was, for the first time, less than that of the rest of the world excluding Japan; and by 1987 Japan's world market share surpassed that of the United States and continued to grow until 1990. By 1994, the U.S. share of the world market was approximately equal to that of Japan, but considerably below the share of the rest of the world, which was nearly as large as the two combined.[7]

In 1991, the Council on Competitiveness issued a report on American technological leadership. Motivated by evidence that technology has been the driving force for economic growth throughout American history, the report documented that as a result of intense international competition, America's technological leadership had eroded. In the report, U.S. technologies were characterized in one of four ways: "strong," meaning that the U.S. industry is in a leading world position and is not in danger of losing that lead over the next five years; "competitive," meaning that the U.S. industry is leading, but this position is not likely to be sustained over the next five years; "weak," meaning that the U.S. industry is behind or likely to fall behind over the next five years; and "losing badly or lost," meaning that the U.S. industry is no longer a factor or is unlikely to have a presence in the world market over the next five years. The 1991 Council on Competitiveness report characterized the U.S. PWB industry as "losing badly or lost." However, in 1994, the Council updated its report and upgraded its assessment of the domestic industry to "weak" in large part because of renewed R&D efforts by the industry.

Table 4.6 shows the value of U.S. PWB production from 1980 through 1994 based on data collected by the Institute for Interconnecting and Packaging Electronic Circuits (IPC 1992, 1995a). While losing ground in relative terms in the world market, the PWB industry grew in nominal terms over those fifteen years. In 1994, production in the domestic market was $6.43 billion, nearly 2.5 times the 1980 level, without adjusting for inflation, and approximately 1.5 times the 1980 level in real terms.

There are two types of PWBs that account for the value of U.S. production: rigid and flexible. Rigid PWBs are reinforced. For most panels, this reinforcement is woven glass. Rigid PWBs can be as thin as two millimeters or as thick as five hundred millimeters. Generally, rigid boards are used in subassemblies that contain heavy components. Flexible PWBs do not have any woven-glass reinforcement. This allows them to be flexible. These boards are normally made from thin film materials around one to two millimeters thick, typically from polyimide.[8]

As shown in table 4.7, Japan dominated the flexible PWB world market in 1994; but North America, the United States in particular, about equaled Japan in the rigid PWB market (IPC 1995b).

Most U.S. produced rigid and flexible PWBs are used in the computer market. Rigid boards are used more frequently in communication equipment than flexible boards, whereas military equipment utilizes relatively more flexible boards (IPC 1995b).[9] PWB producers are divided into two general groups: manufacturers that produce PWBs for their own end-product use and manufacturers that produce boards for sale to others. Those in the first group

Table 4.6. Value of U.S.
Production of Printed Wiring
Boards

Year	Value ($millions)
1980	$2,603
1981	2,816
1982	2,924
1983	4,060
1984	4,943
1985	4,080
1986	4,033
1987	5,127
1988	5,941
1989	5,738
1990	5,432
1991	5,125
1992	5,302
1993	5,457
1994	6,425

Sources: Link (1997) and Link and Scott (1998).

Table 4.7. 1994 World Production of Printed Wiring Boards, by Board Type

Region	Rigid	Flexible
Japan	27%	48%
Taiwan	6	...
China/Hong Kong	6	...
Rest of Asia	9	6
Germany	5	...
Rest of Europe	13	...
Europe	...	14
Africa/Mid-East	4	...
N. America	29	30
S. America	1	...
Rest of World	...	2
Total	100% or $21.2 billion	100% or $1.65 billion

Sources: Link (1997) and Link and Scott (1998).

are original equipment manufacturers (OEMs) or captives, and those in the second group are referred to as independents or merchants. In 1994, independents accounted for 83 percent of all PWBs in the United States (IPC 1992).[10]

4.3.3. Roles and Relationships among Members of the RJV

In April 1991, ATP announced that one of its initial eleven awards was to a joint venture led by the National Center for Manufacturing Sciences (NCMS) to research aspects of PWB interconnect systems. The five-year, $28.5 million project (with $13.8 million coming from ATP), was expected to benefit the entire U.S. PWB industry.

The original members of the joint venture were Digital Equipment Corporation (DEC), AT&T, Texas Instruments, and Hamilton Standard Interconnect. DEC participated in the project for only eighteen months. Its decision to withdraw was, according to NCMS, strictly because of the financial condition of the corporation at that time. DEC's financial condition did not improve, ultimately leading to the closing and sale of its PWB facilities. Three firms joined the joint venture to assume DEC's research responsibilities: AlliedSignal in 1993, and Hughes Electronics and IBM in 1994. Also, Sandia National Laboratories became involved in the joint venture during 1992, as anticipated when NCMS submitted its proposal to ATP for funding. Sandia subsequently obtained an additional $5.2 million from the Department of Energy to support the research effort of the joint venture.[11]

The PWB research joint venture can be described in economic terminology as a horizontal collaborative research arrangement (see chapter 2). Economic theory predicts, and empirical studies to date support, that when horizontally related firms form a joint venture, research efficiencies will be realized in large part because of the reduction of duplicative research and the sharing of research results (Link 1997). This was precisely the case, as evidenced both by the quantitative estimates of cost savings reported by the members and by the case examples provided in support of the cost-savings estimates.[12]

A Steering Committee, with a senior technical representative from each of the participating organizations, worked collectively to direct and control the four research teams to ensure that each was meeting the technical goals of the project. NCMS provided the program management, coordination, facilitation, and interface with ATP for the PWB project. NCMS coordinated and scheduled activities and provided the interface between the administrative functions of accounting, contracts, and legal activities related to intellectual property agreements.[13]

The joint venture's research activities were divided into four components: materials, surface finishes, imaging, and product (research not product development).[14] Given the generic research agenda of the joint venture at the beginning of the project, the organizational structure conceptually seemed to be appropriate for the successful completion of all research activities. At the close of the project, this also appeared to be the case in the opinion of the members. NCMS released to ATP a summary statement of the technical progress of the joint venture at the conclusion of the project. The PWB Research Joint Venture Project accomplished all of the originally proposed research goals and the project exceeded the original expectations of the members.[15]

Regarding entrepreneurial risk, participants in the joint venture were asked to quantify a number of metrics that compared the current end-of-project technological state to the technological state that would have existed at this time in the absence of ATP's financial support of the joint venture. Additional questions were also posed to each team leader in an effort to obtain insights about the results of the joint venture that affect the industry as a whole.

Each member of the PWB research joint venture was asked which of the major research tasks in which they were involved would have been started by their firm in the absence of the ATP-funded joint venture. Aggregate responses suggested that only one-half would have begun in the absence of ATP funding. The other one-half would not have been started either because of the cost of such research or the related risk. And, of those tasks that would have been started without ATP funding, the majority would have been delayed by at least one year for financial reasons.

4.4. Flat Panel Display Joint Venture

4.4.1. Background Information

According to Link and Scott (1998, p. 136), referring to an untitled U.S. Department of Defense report: "Flat panel displays represent a technological and business area of great concern worldwide. This is because these devices are recognized as the critical human interface device in many military and industrial systems and commercial products in an increasingly information intensive world."

Given this view, the widespread belief that flat panel displays (FPDs) will replace the cathode ray tube (CRT) in most American weapon systems before the turn of the century, and the realization that Japan's share of the world flat panel market dwarfed that of the United States and will likely continue to do so for at least the near term, it is not surprising that governmental support for the industry was forthcoming.

Government support took a number of forms. One form of direct support came in the form of a defense-oriented initiative. The National Flat Panel Display Initiative was announced in 1994. This program provided direct funding to the then very thin domestic flat panel industry. A second form of support came through a partnership between ATP and a research joint venture of flat panel display manufacturers. A group of small, flat panel firms took the initiative to form a research joint venture and apply to the ATP's initial competition. And the joint venture received funding.

4.4.2. Flat Panel Display Technology

FPD describes technology for displaying visual information in a package that has a depth significantly smaller than its horizontal or vertical dimensions. This technology was first developed in the United States at the University of Illinois in the early 1960s. Soon thereafter, RCA, Westinghouse, and General Electric were researching the feasibility of flat panels operating on liquid crystal technology. By the early 1970s, IBM was researching an alternative— plasma display technology. However, none of these firms continued their research in FPDs.

At RCA, flat panel technology was seen as a commercial alternative to the television CRT, but because RCA's management at that time viewed this technology as a threat to its existing business, flat panel technology was never exploited to its commercial potential. Research at Westinghouse successfully led to the development of active matrix liquid crystal displays and electro-luminescent displays, but because of the firm's weak position in the television market, financial support for the development of prototypes was canceled. And similarly, changes in the corporate strategy at General Electric (e.g., the divestiture of their consumer-electronics group in the early 1970s) effectively stopped the firm's research related to FPDs. Finally, IBM, which had completed some pioneering research in plasma display technology and actually established and operated a plasma-panel manufacturing plant for several years, became convinced that liquid crystal display technology was more promising. They divested their plasma operation, but were not able to find a U.S. partner for liquid crystal research.[16]

Japanese firms, Sharp in particular, began to specialize in flat panels in the early 1970s in response to the demand for low-information content displays (e.g., watches and portable calculators). Research in Japan progressed rapidly, and by the mid-1980s a number of Japanese firms were producing portable television screens based on active matrix liquid crystal displays. By the end of the 1980s, aided in part by the investment support that the Japanese firms received from the Ministry of International Trade and Industry (MITI), Japan had established itself as the world leader in flat panel technology.

In the most general sense, a FPD consists of two glass plates with an electrically optical material compressed between them. This sandwiched material responds to an electrical signal by reflecting or emitting light. On the glass plates are horizontal and vertical rows of electrical conductors that form a grid pattern, and it is the intersection of these rows and columns that define picture elements, called pixels. The modulation of light by each pixel creates the images on the screen.

There are three broad types of commercially available FPDs: liquid crystal displays, electroluminescent displays, and plasma display panels. A liquid crystal display (LCD) consists of two flat glass substrates with a matrix of indium tin oxide on the inner surfaces and a polarized film on the outer surfaces.[17] The light source for a LCD is generally a cathode, florescent, or halogen bulb placed behind the rear plate. The most common flat panel display is a passive matrix LCD (PMLCD). These panels were first used in watches and portable calculators as early as the 1970s. Characteristic of PMLCDs are horizontal electrodes on one plate and vertical electrodes on the other plate. Each pixel is turned on and off as voltage passes across rows and columns. Active matrix LCDs (AMLCDs) rely on rapidly responding switching elements at each pixel (as opposed to one signal on the grid) to control the on-off state. This control is achieved by depositing at least one silicon transistor at each pixel on the inner surface of the rear glass. The advantages associated with AMLCDs are color quality and power efficiency; hence, they are dominant in the notebook computer and pocket television markets. The disadvantages of AMLCDs is their small size and high cost.

Whereas LCDs respond to an external light source, electroluminescent displays (ELDs) generate their own light source. Sandwiched between the glass substrate electrodes is a solid phosphor material that glows when exposed to an electric current. The advantages of ELDs are that they are rugged, power efficient, bright, and can be produced in large sizes; but ELDs were in the development stage for color capabilities at the time of the ATP award. ELDs are primarily used in industrial process control, military applications, medical and analytical equipment, and transportation.

Like ELDs, plasma display panels (PDPs) rely on emissive display technology. Phosphors are deposited on the front and back substrates of glass panels. In response to a plasma or florescent lamp, inert gas is discharged between the plates of each cell to generate light. While offering a wide viewing angle and being relatively inexpensive to produce, PDPs are not power efficient and their color brightness is inferior to that of LCDs for small displays. PDPs are used in industrial and commercial areas as multiviewer information screens and are being developed for HDTV.

In the early 1990s, the demand for laptop computers increased dramatically. Then, U.S. producers of FPDs were small, research-based firms capable of only producing small volumes of low-information content displays. U.S. producers—Apple, Compaq, IBM, and Tandy in particular—were soon in a position of needing thousands of flat panels each month. However, the domestic FPD industry was unable to meet this demand or to increase its production capabilities rapidly. On July 18, 1990, in response to the huge increase in FPD imports, U.S. manufacturers filed an anti-dumping petition with the U.S. Department of Commerce's International Trade Administration (ITA) and with the International Trade Commission (ITC). While duties were placed on Japanese AMLCDs from 1991 to 1993, the end result of the anti-dumping case was not to bolster U.S. FPD manufacturers but rather to drive certain domestic manufacturers offshore.

In 1993, the National Economic Council (NEC) and President Clinton's Council of Economic Advisors concluded that the U.S. FPD industry illustrated the need for coordination between commercial and defense technology. As a result of a NEC-initiated study, the National Flat Panel Display

Table 4.8. World Flat Panel
Display Market

Year	Value of Shipments ($billions)
1983	$ 0.05
1984	0.08
1985	0.12
1986	1.66
1987	2.03
1988	2.58
1989	3.23
1990	4.44
1991	4.91
1992	5.51
1993	7.14
1994	9.33
1995	11.50
1996 (est.)	13.04
1997 (est.)	14.55
1998 (est.)	16.12
1999 (est.)	17.73
2000 (est.)	19.51
2001 (est.)	22.46

Source: Link and Scott (1998).

Initiative was announced in April 1994. This initiative was "A five-year, $587-million program to jump-start a commercial industrial base that will be able to meet DOD's needs in the next century" (Flamm 1994, p. 27).

Even with the National Flat Panel Display Initiative, U.S. flat panel producers were clearly a minor player in the global market at the time of ATP funding (Krishna and Thursby 1996). Table 4.8 shows the size of the world FPD market beginning in 1983, with 1995 projections to 2001. Noticeable in table 4.8 is the greater than tenfold increase in the nominal value of shipments between 1985 and 1986 in large part because of the successful introduction of a variety of new electronic products into the market by the Japanese.

4.4.3. Roles and Relationships among Members of the RJV

In April 1991, ATP also announced that one of its initial eleven competitive awards was to a joint venture managed by the American Display Consortium (ADC). The five-year, $15 million project (with $7.3 million from ATP) was expected to advance and strengthen the basic materials and manufacturing process technologies needed for U.S. flat panel manufacturers to become world-class producers of low-cost, high-volume, state-of-the-art advanced display products.

The two lead firms were relatively small. The larger of the two is Planar Systems, Inc. Planar is a public firm, and it is the leading domestic developer, manufacturer, and marketer of high-performance electronic display products. Its technological base is electroluminescent technology. Photonics Imaging is a very small investor-owned research firm. Its expertise relates to control technology as applied to automation of the production process. The other firms are small and had minor roles.

The primary motivations for these two firms to organize under the umbrella of the ADC were: the availability of government funding would supplement internal budgets so that the proposed research could be undertaken in a timelier manner; and the belief that the proposed research could be more effectively undertaken cooperatively (see chapter 3 regarding the NCRA).

The Advanced Display Manufacturers of America Research Consortium (ADMARC) submitted the original research proposal to ATP. The ADMARC was formed for the specific purpose of participating in the ATP competition. As initially structured, the head of Photonics Imaging acted as the Program Manager. Optical Imaging Systems (OIS) was to be the third member.

Initially, Photonics was to lead the automated inspection and automated repair research, Planar the flip chip-on-glass research, and OIS the poly-silicon on-glass research. During the first year of the project, OIS was sold and could not at that time continue with its research obligations. Initially, Photonics and Planar undertook OIS's research commitments. The poly-silicon on-glass effort was broadened to silicon on-glass, but the scope of the research was lessened. Throughout the research project, the membership of the ADC has changed, but not all new members in the research consortium participated in the ATP-funded joint venture. In the second year of the project, Electro Plasma, Inc.; Northrop Grumman Norden Systems; Plasmaco, Inc.; and Kent Display Systems began to share research costs. Still, Photonics and Planar remained as the research leaders of the joint venture. Each of these firms brought to the project specific expertise related to sensor and connector technology as applied to flat panels.[18]

The goals of the project were achieved. Research to automatically inspect and repair flat panels demonstrated that such a system could be designed. Also, research showed that flip chip-on-glass could be a viable technology to achieve interconnect density between a flat screen display panel and the integrated circuit, but it was not cost effective at the time the project ended.[19]

Regarding entrepreneurial risk, the unanimous opinion of the participants was that the research would not have occurred by either of them or by anyone else in the industry in the absence of ATP funds. It was also their opinion that, counterfactually, if some firm attempted to undertake this research it would have taken them more money than was allocated to the project plus an additional three years of research.

4.5. Conclusions

The two examples in this chapter—and there are many more similar examples (Link 1996a, Link and Scott 1998)—clearly indicate that the R&D activity of firms recipient of ATP's public resources to leverage their R&D were not swayed by the entrepreneurial risk inherent in RJVs.

Most of the participants in the PWB RJV and all of the participants in the flat panel display RJV agreed that in the absence of ATP funding, industry would not have undertaken the research. And, in response to counterfactual questions, all agreed that if industry had undertaken the research it would have taken longer to conduct and would have been more expensive. Thus, ATP's funding of RJVs did accelerate the development of the two generic technologies.

Notes

1. The development and evolution of the material in this chapter is discussed in Link (1999, 2006) and Link and Scott (2005a).

2. This section draws, in part, on Link (2006).

3. At the time of writing this book, the exact goals, objectives, and structure of TIP had not been finalized.

4. These statistics are at http://www.atp.nist.gov/eao/statistics.htm.

5. A number of recipients of ATP support view it almost as a palatine public program. We have exercised caution in our description of these two examples so not to exaggerate their social impact.

6. And, our detailed discussion illustrates significantly more about RJV activity that can be gleaned from filings in the *Federal Register*.

7. While there is no single event that explains the decline in U.S. market share, one very important factor was the decline in R&D by original equipment manufacturers (OEMs). OEMs are manufacturers that produce PWBs for their own end-product use.

8. Rigid boards account for the lion's share of the U.S. PWB market (IPC 1992, 1995a). In 1994, nearly 93 percent of the value of U.S. PWB production was attributable to rigid boards. Of that, approximately 66 percent was multilayer boards. Multilayer boards consist of alternating layers of conductor and insulating material bonded together. In comparison, single-sided boards have a conductive pattern on one side, while double-sided boards have conducting patterns on both.

9. There are eight distinct market segments for PWBs (IPC 1992):

- Automotive: engine and drive performance, convenience and safety, entertainment, and other applications for diagnostic display and security.
- Business/Retail: copy machines, word processors, cash registers, POS terminals, teaching machines, business calculators, gas pumps, and taxi meters.
- Communications: mobile radio, touch tone, portable communication, pagers, data transmissions, microwave relay, telecommunications and telephone switching equipment, and navigation instruments.

- Consumer Electronics: watches, clocks, portable calculators, musical instruments, electronic games, large appliances, microwave ovens, pinball/arcade games, TV/home entertainment, video records, smoke, and intrusion detection systems.
- Computer: mainframe computers, mini-computers, broad level processors, add-on memories, input devices, output devices, terminals, and printers.
- Government and Military/Aerospace: radar, guidance and control systems, communication and navigation, electronic warfare, ground support instrumentation, sonar ordinance, missiles, and satellite-related systems.
- Industrial Electronics: machine and process control, production test measurement, material handling, machining equipment, pollution, energy and safety equipment, numerical control power controllers, sensors, and weighing equipment.
- Instrumentation: test and measurement equipment, medical instruments and medical testers, analytical nuclear instruments, lasers, scientific instruments, and implant devices.

10. Independent's share of the total domestic market for rigid and flexible PWBs increased from 40 percent in 1979 to 83 percent in 1994. In 1994, independents accounted for 93 percent of the rigid PWB market. Independent manufacturers of PWBs, for the most part, are relatively small producers. The vast majority of independent producers had less than $5 million in sales.

11. RJVs are required by the NCRA to re-file with the Department of Justice when the membership of the venture changes. This pattern of membership changes is not uncommon.

12. AT&T, Hughes, IBM, and Texas Instruments were four of the leading domestic captive producers of PWBs when the project began; and they were also members of NCMS, the joint venture administrator. Although in the same broadly defined industry (i.e., they are horizontally related), two of these firms, AT&T and IBM, were not direct competitors because their PWBs were produced for internal use in different applications. AT&T produced PWBs primarily for telecommunications applications while IBM's application areas ranged from laptop computers to mainframes. Although Hughes and Texas Instruments produced for different niche markets, they did compete with each other in some Department of Defense areas.

13. The joint venture was organized to "mimic a company with a chain of command," according to one member of the Steering Committee. As well, according to this member: "If it was not organized this way then no one would be accountable. Most of the people had this project built into their performance review. If they failed on the project, then they failed at work. The structure also allowed ease of reporting. The information flowed up to the team leader as the focal point for information distribution. The team leader would then report to the Steering Committee of senior managers who were paying the bills" (Link 1997).

14. Prior to entering the 1990 ATP General Competition for funding, the members of the research joint venture conducted a systems analysis of the PWB manufacturing process and concluded that fundamental generic technology development was needed in these four components of the PWB

business. Each component consisted of a combination of research areas which provided significant improvements to existing processes, and explored new technology to develop breakthrough advances in process capabilities. A multifirm team of researchers was assigned to each of the four research components. The four research teams were involved in sixty-two separate tasks.

15. The major technical accomplishments of the Materials Team were the following:

- Developed single-ply laminates that have resulted in cost savings to industry and in a change to military specifications that will now allow single-ply laminates.
- Developed new, dimensionally stable thin film material that has superior properties to any other material used by the industry. This material has resulted in a spinoff NCMS project to continue the development with the goal of commercialization by 1998.
- Identified multiple failure sources for "measling". Measling is the separation or delamination at the glass resin interface in a PWB. The findings revealed that PWBs were being rejected, but that the real source for the board's failure was not being correctly identified as a problem with the adhesion of resin to the glass.
- Completed an industry survey that led to the development of a Quality Function Deployment (QFD) model (discussed below). The model defines the specifications of the PWB technology considered most important to customers.
- Completed an evaluation (resulting in a database) of over one hundred high-performance laminates and other selected materials that offer significant potential for improving dimensional stability and plated through-hole (PTH) reliability. Revolutionary materials have also been identified that exhibit unique properties and potentially can eliminate the need for reinforced constructions.
- Developed a predictive mathematical model that allows the user to predict dimensional stability of various construction alternatives.
- Developed, with the Product Team, a finite element analysis model (FEM) that predicts PTH reliability.
- Developed low-profile copper foil adhesion on laminate to the point where military specifications could be revised to allow lower adhesion for copper.
- Developed plasma monitoring tool.
- Filed patent disclosure for a Block Co-polymer replacement for brown/black/red oxide treatments for inner layer adhesion. This substitute will facilitate lower copper profiles and thinner materials.

The major technical accomplishments of the Surface Finishes Team were the following:

- Improved test methods that determine the effectiveness of various materials during the soldering process, concluding that one surface finish (imidazole) is applicable to multiple soldering applications.
- Commercialized imidazole through licensing the technology to Lea Ronal Chemical Company.
- Conducted survey of assembly shops to determine the parameters manufacturers monitor in order to make reliable solder interconnections.

- Evaluated numerous other surface finish alternatives, and presented data at the spring 1995 IPC Expo in San Jose; paper won the Best Paper Award at the conference.
- Filed three patent disclosures: A Solderability Test Using Capillary Flow, Solderability Enhancement of Copper through Chemical Etching, and A Chemical Coating on Copper Substrates with Solder Mask Applications.
- Facilitated the adoption of test vehicles developed by the team for development use, thus saving duplication of effort.

The major technical accomplishments of the Imaging Team were the following:

- Developed and successfully demonstrated the process required in order to obtain greater than 98 percent yields for 3 mil line and space features. When the project began, the industry benchmark was a 30 percent yield. The team obtained more than 50 percent yield for 2 mil line and space features; when the project began the industry benchmark yield was less than 10 percent.
- Developed and now routinely use test equipment and data processing software to evaluate fine-line conductor patterns for defect density, resolution limits, and dimensional uniformity.
- Applied for patent on conductor analysis technology and licensed the technology to a start-up firm, Conductor Analysis Technologies, Inc. (CAT, Inc.), in Albuquerque, New Mexico. CAT, Inc. now sells this evaluation service to the PWB industry. According to NCMS, it is highly unlikely that a private-sector firm would have developed this technology outside of the joint venture. Thus, commercializing this technology through CAT, Inc. has benefited the entire industry.
- Evaluated new photoresist materials and processing equipment from industry providers, and designed new test patterns for the quantitative evaluation of resists and associated imaging processes.
- Developed and proved feasibility for a new photolithography tool named Magnified Image Projection Printing; this tool has the potential to provide a noncontact method of printing very fine features at high yields and thus has generated enough interest to form a spinoff, non-ATP-funded NCMS project to develop a full scale alpha tool. No results are yet available.

The major technical accomplishments of the Product Team were the following:

- Developed revolutionary new interconnect structure called Multilayer Organic Interconnect Technology (MOIT), described as the next generation Surface Laminar Circuit (SLC) technology; demonstrated feasibility of MOIT on 1,000 input/output Ball Grid Array packages and test vehicles using mixed technologies, including flip-chip.
- Completed industry survey related to subtractive chemical processes, additive processes, and adhesion. The results of the survey showed that there was no industry interest in the research area; therefore new tasks were undertaken.
- Identified chemical properties to enhance the understanding of the adhesion of copper to the base material, magnetic-ion plating of metal conductive layers, and the development of PTH models and software that are very efficient and cost effective to run.

- Developed evolutionary test vehicles that simulate Personal Computer Micro Interface Card Adapter (PCMICA) and computer workstation products. These test vehicles have been used to speed the development of new materials, surface finishes, and imaging technology by other teams.
- Performed several small hole drilling studies and minimum plating requirement studies for PTHs.
- Delivered paper on a finite element analysis model (FEM), developed with the Materials Team, which won the Best Paper Award at the fall 1994 IPC meetings in Boston.

16. In the late 1970s and early 1980s other domestic firms considered entering the FPD market, but none did because of the large minimum R&D and production commitment needed. These firms included Beckman Instruments, Fairchild, Hewlett-Packard, Motorola, Texas Instruments, and Timex. The lack of presence of U.S. firms in the global flat panel display market is in part because of the difference between R&D and manufacturing (McLoughlin and Nunno 1995, p. 10): "Several U.S. firms were early inventors and experimenters in FPD technologies and are superb at developing new FPD technologies. However, the U.S. commercial manufacturing base for FPD products is not as developed. A survey of U.S. firms which either closed or sold FPD production facilities prior to 1990 found several common reasons why these firms were no longer in the industry: the belief that advanced displays were not central to the firm's business strategy; the cost of capital for establishing an FPD manufacturing line; the fear that Japanese competition is too strong to overcome; and the belief that the global economy allows purchases of FPD technology from any source, domestic or foreign."

17. The substrates are separated by micron-sized spacers, the outer edges are sealed, and the inner void is filled with a liquid crystal fluid that changes the transmission of light coming through the plates in response to voltage applied to the cell.

18. The research members of the joint venture compete with one another in terms of both technology and markets.

19. The specific goals of the automated inspection project were:

- To design and manufacture an automatic inspection and manual repair station which would be suitable for inspecting patterns on flat display systems and give the capability of manually repairing the indicated defects, and
- To establish a design of systems that could be manufactured and sold to the flat panel display industry.

The specific goals of the flip chip-on-glass project were:

- To evaluate and develop FCOG technologies,
- To evaluate the reliability and performance of the most promising FCOG technologies, and
- To develop cost-effective equipment for the assembly of FCOG.

5

National Institute of Standards and Technology

An Institutional Response to Innovation Barriers

5.1. Introduction

The National Institute of Standards and Technology (NIST) is a public/ private partnership component described in this chapter through which government acts as entrepreneur. NIST leverages public-sector and private-sector R&D through the direct provision of infrastructural and research resources that reduce the technical and market risk of developing infrastructure technologies—infratechnologies—that become the technical basis for standards, voluntary standards in particular.[1] This is necessary because infratechnologies and hence standards are quasi-public goods and they result in underinvestment by the private sector (Tassey 2007). See table 5.1. The innovative policy action of using public resources toward voluntary industrial standards, the technology infrastructure, lessens barriers to innovation (see table 1.2) by reducing both technical risk (e.g., through public-sector research that diffuses through the private sector) and market risk (e.g., through the promulgation of voluntary standards). The entrepreneurial risk associated with the activities of NIST is if the promulgated voluntary standard will be accepted by industry, and if accepted in a timely manner, whether it will enhance competitiveness. See table 5.2.

A standard is a prescribed set of rules, conditions, or requirements concerning: definitions of terms; classification of components; specification of

Table 5.1.   Public/Private Partnerships: National Institute of Standards and Technology

Government Involvement	Economic Objective	
	Leverage Public-Sector R&D	Leverage Private-Sector R&D
Indirect	. . .	. . .
Direct		
Financial Resources	. . .	. . .
Infrastructural Resources	National Institute of Standards and Technology	National Institute of Standards and Technology
Research Resources	National Institute of Standards and Technology	National Institute of Standards and Technology

Table 5.2.   Government as Entrepreneur: National Institute of Standards and Technology

Public/Private Partnership	Technology Infrastructure	Innovative Policy Action	Entrepreneurial Risk
National Institute of Standards and Technology	Voluntary industrial standards	Organic Act of 1901: use of public resources to promulgate voluntary standards to reduce the technical and market risk of private-sector R&D	If the promulgated voluntary standard will be accepted by industry, and if accepted in a timely manner, whether it will enhance competitiveness

materials, their performance, and their operations; delineation of procedures; and measurement of quantity and quality in describing materials, products, systems, services, or practices.

5.2. A Brief History of NIST

The concept of the government's involvement in standards—mandatory standards rather than voluntary standards—traces to the Articles of Confederation signed on July 9, 1778. In Article 9, § 4: "The United States, in

Congress assembled, shall also have the sole and exclusive right and power of regulating the alloy and value of coin struck by their own authority, or by that of the respective States; fixing the standard of weights and measures throughout the United States...." This responsibility was reiterated in Article 1, § 8 of the Constitution of the United States: "The Congress shall have power...[t]o coin money, regulate the value thereof, and of foreign coin, and fix the standard of weights and measures...."[2]

A Joint Resolution on June 14, 1836, provided for the construction and distribution of weights and measures.[3] On July 20, 1866, Congress and President Andrew Johnson authorized the use of the metric system in the United States. This was formalized in the Act of July 28, 1866—An Act to Authorize the Use of the Metric System of Weights and Measures.[4, 5]

Because of the growing use of the metric system in scientific work rather than commercial activity, the French government held an international conference in 1872, which included the participation of the United States, to settle on procedures for the preparation of prototype metric standards. Then, on May 20, 1875, the United States participated in the Convention of the Meter in Paris and was one of the eighteen signatory nations to the Treaty of the Meter.[6]

Then, the Act of July 11, 1890 gave authority to the Office of Construction of Standard Weights and Measures (or Office of Standard Weights and Measures), which had been established in 1836 within the Treasury's Coast and Geodetic Survey: "For construction and verification of standard weights and measures, including metric standards, for the custom-houses, and other offices of the United States, and for the several States...."[7]

Following from a long history of U.S. leaders calling for uniformity in science, traceable at least to the several formal proposals for a Department of Science in the early 1880s, and coupled with the growing inability of the Office of Weights and Measures to handle the explosion of documentary standards in all aspects of federal and state activity, it was inevitable that a standards laboratory would need to be established. The political force for this laboratory came in 1900 through Lyman Gage, then Secretary of the Treasury under President William McKinley. Gage's original plan was for the Office of Standard Weights and Measures to be recognized as a separate agency called the National Standardizing Bureau. This Bureau would maintain custody of standards, compare standards, construct standards, test standards, and resolve problems in connection with standards.[8] Finally, the Act of March 3, 1901, also known as the Organic Act, established the National Bureau of Standards within the Department of the Treasury, where the Office of Standard Weights and Measures was administratively located:[9]

Be it enacted by the Senate and House of Representatives of the United States of America in Congress assembled, That the Office of Standard Weights and Measures shall hereafter be known as the National Bureau of Standards...That the functions of the bureau shall consist in the custody of the standards; the comparison of the standards used in scientific investigations, engineering, manufacturing, commerce, and educational institutions with the standards adopted or recognized by the Government; the construction, when necessary, of standards, their multiples and subdivisions; the testing and calibration of standard measuring apparatus; the solution of problems which arise in connection with standards; the determination of physical constants and the properties of materials, when such data are of great importance to scientific or manufacturing interests and are not to be obtained of sufficient accuracy elsewhere.

In the post–World War I years, the Bureau's research focused on assisting in the growth of industry. Research was conducted on ways to increase the operating efficiency of automobile and aircraft engines, electrical batteries, and gas appliances. Also, work was begun on improving methods for measuring electrical losses in response to public utility needs. This latter research was not independent of international efforts to establish electrical standards similar to those established over fifty years before for weights and measures.

After World War II, significant attention and resources were given to the activities of the Bureau. In particular, the Act of July 21, 1950 established standards for electrical and photometric measurements.[10] Then, as a part of the Act of June 20, 1956, the Bureau moved from Washington, D.C., to Gaithersburg, Maryland.

The responsibilities listed in the Act of July 21, 1950, and many others, were transferred to the National Institute of Standards and Technology when the National Bureau of Standards was renamed under the guidelines of the Omnibus Trade and Competitiveness Act of 1988:[11]

The National Institute of Standards and Technology [shall] enhance the competitiveness of American industry while maintaining its traditional function as lead national laboratory for providing the measurement, calibrations, and quality assurance techniques which underpin United States commerce, technological progress, improved product reliability and manufacturing processes, and public safety . . . [and it shall] advance, through cooperative efforts among industries, universities, and government laboratories, promising research and development projects, which can be optimized by the private sector for commercial and industrial applications . . . [More specifically, NIST is to] prepare, certify, and sell standard reference materials for use in ensuring the accuracy of chemical analyses and measurements of physical and other properties of materials . . .

NIST's mission is to promote U.S. economic growth by working with industry to develop and apply technology, measurements, and standards. It carries out this mission through three major programs: measurement and standards laboratories that provide technical leadership for vital components of the nation's technology infrastructure needed by U.S. industry to continually improve its products and services;[12] a grassroots Manufacturing Extension Partnership with a network of local centers offering technical and business assistance to smaller manufacturers; and a highly visible quality outreach program associated with the Malcolm Baldrige National Quality Award that recognizes continuous improvements in quality management by U.S. manufacturers and service companies.[13]

5.3. The Economics of Standards

An industry standard is a set of specifications to which all elements of products, processes, formats, or procedures under its jurisdiction must conform. The process of standardization is the pursuit of this conformity, with the objective of increasing the efficiency of economic activity.

The complexity of modern technology, especially its system characteristics, has led to an increase in the number and variety of standards that affect a single industry or market. Standards affect the R&D, production, and market penetration stages of economic activity and therefore they have a significant collective effect on innovation, productivity, and market structure. (See table 2.1.) Thus, a concern of government policy is the evolutionary path by which a new technology, or more accurately certain elements of a new technology, becomes standardized.

Standardization, according to Tassey (2000), can and does occur without formal promulgation as a standard. This distinction between de facto and promulgated standards—that is through a process of voluntary standards generally initiated by industry—is important more from an institutional process than an economic-impact perspective.

In one sense, standardization is a form rather than a type of infrastructure because it represents a codification of an element of an industry's technology or simply information relevant to the conduct of economic activity. And, because the selection of one of several available forms of a technology element as the standard has potentially important economic effects, the process of standardization is important. While economics is increasingly concerned with standards due to their proliferation and pervasiveness in many new high-technology industries, the economic roles of standards are unfortunately poorly understood.

Standards can be grouped into two basic categories: product-element standards, and nonproduct-element standards. This distinction is important because the economic role of each type is different.

Product-element standards typically involve one of the key attributes or elements of a product, as opposed to the entire product. In most cases, market dynamics determine product-element standards. Alternative technologies compete intensely until a dominant version gains sufficient market share to become the single de facto standard. Market control by one firm can truncate this competitive process. Conversely, nonproduct-element standards tend to be competitively neutral within the context of an industry. This type of standard can impact an entire industry's efficiency and its overall market penetration rate.[14]

Industry organizations often set nonproduct-element standards using consensus processes. The technical bases (infrastructure technologies or infratechnologies) for these standards have a large public-good content. Examples include measurement and test methods, interface standards, and standard reference materials.

From both the positions of a strategically focused firm as well as of a public policymaker, standardization is not an all-or-nothing proposition. In complemented system technologies, such as distributed data processing, telecommunications, or factory automation, standardization typically proceeds in an evolutionary manner in lock step with the evolution of the technology. Complete standardization too early in the technology's lifecycle can constrain innovation.

The overall economic value of a standard is determined by its functionality (i.e., interaction with other standards at the systems level) and the cost of implementation (i.e., compliance costs). Standards should be competitively neutral, which means adaptable to alternative applications of a generic technology over that technology's lifecycle.

There has been limited empirical research to quantify the impact of standards, and other infrastructure technologies, on firm performance. Link and Tassey (1993) showed that firms that invest in infrastructure technologies, meaning formulate greater internal capabilities to utilize NIST's output, are more efficient in their in-house R&D than firms that do not. Their study, albeit the only one of its kind, follows logically from a theoretical understanding of the role of standards, or more generally, infrastructure technology or infratechnology, in the innovation process. (See figure 2.1.)

There have been a number of economic impact evaluations of standards.[15] In the following sections we describe three historical instances of NIST's standards activities, and for each we offer an opinion about NIST's success in overcoming the entrepreneurial risk implicit in each standards-related activity. As in the previous chapter, we emphasize that the examples of government as entrepreneur are historical, meaning that the examples are dated at least to the previous decade. This must be the case for us to look retrospectively to determine how effective the innovative policy actions were in overcoming the inherent entrepreneurial risk.

Optical fiber standards are described in section 5.4. Integrated Services Digital Network (ISDN) standards are discussed in section 5.5, alternative refrigerants are discussed in section 5.6, and Internet protocol standards are the subject of section 5.7. Each of these four examples represents NIST's entrepreneurial involvement to remove barriers to innovation.[16]

5.4. Optical Fiber Standards

5.4.1. Optical Fiber Technology

Voice transmission using light pulses is not a new technology. As early as 1880 Alexander Graham Bell reported such speech transmission.[17] Many inventors in the early 1900s also experimented with this technology, but they had only limited success. The problems hindering the development and early use of optical communications were two: the lack of a suitable light source and the lack of a suitable transmission medium because the atmosphere was plagued with many sources of interference.

Three critical technologies in the optical fiber system are a transmitter to convert electrical impulses to optical impulses, that is, electrons into photons; a transmission medium; and a receiver to recode the light impulses into electrical impulses. Photodiodes (receivers) were widely used in physics-related research in the early 1950s. However, the major technological breakthrough associated with optical communication systems came in the late 1950s, spurred in large part by research at the Bell Laboratories in the form of the laser (Light Amplification by Stimulated Emission of Radiation). With the laser also came the realization (in the 1950s) that optical communication would be a reality. The only missing element was a suitable transmission medium.

Although the U.S. American Optical Company and the U.K. Standard Telecommunications Laboratories were early developers of optical fiber, significant technical problems remained. The critical technical barrier to commercialization was overcome in 1966; academic research led to the specification of the maximum signal loss for commercially viable long-distance transmission (20 dB/km, or lower).[18] The industrial research community knew that the key factor in commercializing optical communication technology would be the fiber core, specifically the development of a glass with minimal absorption of light pulses due to impurities. Corning made the breakthrough in the summer of 1970. The company developed a core that registered an attenuation rate of 16 decibels per kilometer (dB/km).[19]

Although the optical fiber technology evolved in the 1970s to the point of allowing commercial communication applications, the market for the technology remained small. Yet the optical fiber industry maintained its faith in the technology.[20] The 1982 deregulation of the telecommunications industry and MCI's plan to build an optical communications network to compete with AT&T provided the market with the competitive push it needed. MCI ordered over 100,000 kilometers of fiber from Corning in that year.[21]

There are two general types of optical fiber: multimode fiber and single-mode fiber. These two types of fiber differ primarily in terms of the size of the core, with multimode fiber having the larger one. Multimode fiber was first developed for use with a light-emitting diode (LED). It was thought that LEDs would have a significant cost advantage over lasers. However, as lasers became more reliable and less expensive to manufacture, the use of single-mode fiber increased. Lasers and LEDs are both appropriate as light sources. However, LEDs are less powerful and operate at slower speeds, thus making them more suitable for short-hauls and for transmissions with lower information carrying requirements.[22, 23]

During the 1980s, NIST was involved in providing basic measurement technology; evaluating test procedures through interlaboratory comparisons;

Table 5.3.   Optical Fiber Standards Evaluated or Written by the National Institute of Standards and Technology

Fiber Characteristic	Single-Mode (Year Issued)	Multimode (Year Issued)
Attenuation	FOTP 78 (2002)	FOTP 46 (1983)
Cut-off Wavelength	FOTP 80 (1988)	. . .
Mode-Field Diameter	FOTPs 164, 167 (1986, 1987)	. . .
Core Diameter	. . .	FOTPs 29, 43, 44, 58 (1981, 1984, 1984, 1984)
Chromatic Dispersion	FOTP 168, 169, 175 (1987, 1988, 1989)	FOTPs 168, 169, 175 (1987, 1988, 1989)
Bandwidth	. . .	FOTPs 30, 51, 54 (1982, 1983, 1982)
Numerical Aperture	. . .	FOTPs 29, 44, 47, 177 (1981, 1984, 1983, 2003)
Geometry	FOTP 176 (1993)	FOTP 176 (1993)

Note: A higher numbered FOTP could be issued in an earlier year than a lower numbered one because the evaluation period was longer. FOTPs are numbered when the evaluation process begins.

Sources: Link (1991, 1996a) and subsequent personal correspondence with NIST scientists.

and offering technical assistance, or helping to write twenty-two significant fiber optic test procedures in cooperation with the then Electronics Industries Association (EIA).[24] Table 5.3 summarizes this standard-based technology infrastructure by Fiber Optic Test Procedure (FOTP) numbers.

5.4.2. Economics of Fiber Optic Standards

Based on an economic-impact assessment of the role of NIST-supported optical fiber standards beginning in the early 1980s, Link's (1991, 1996a) 1990 survey-based counterfactual analysis of optical fiber manufacturers and users concluded that NIST's involvement in optical fiber standards was accepted by the industry and was timely enough to stimulate the development of the fiber industry. Link's analysis found that the optical fiber industry would have developed significantly slower—two to three times as slow—in the absence of NIST's involvement in the promulgation of relevant standards.

During the 1980s, manufacturers and users reported that the primary economic benefit they received, other than realizing the industry developed faster than it otherwise would have developed, thus ensuring the health of the U.S. industry, was reduced transactions costs. With NIST-supported standards, fewer resources were needed to resolve technical disputes related to the sale or purchase of fiber than would have been expended in the absence of the standards. The entrepreneurial activity by NIST resulted in more rapid market penetration of optical fiber, which, in turn, accelerated capacity growth in domestic and international communications markets.

5.5. Integrated Services Digital Network (ISDN) Technology

5.5.1. ISDN Technology

During the 1970s and 1980s, the once-separate disciplines of computer processing and communications merged in a new discipline called information processing.[25] Combining the intelligence of the processing discipline with the transmission resources of the communications discipline was at that time the goal of the information-processing network. Such a network would be able to serve the needs of a variety of users and would be capable of processing vast amounts of information in digital form. One architecture for such information processing is the ISDN.

In early 1988, NIST solicited (i.e., intervened into the market in an innovative way) broad industry contacts to investigate the development of ISDN in concert with users and implementers or vendors, ISDN conformance testing methodologies, and standards-based ISDN implementation agreements. Respondents to these surveys reported that users generally had both a lack of awareness of ISDN and a paucity of representation in the ongoing development of the technology. The consensus was that the market-pull forces of direct user involvement in the development of standardized applications would stimulate the then-expected widespread demand for ISDN. Respondents therefore sought to establish a forum that would allow users to provide continuous input into and influence on the development of ISDN with vendors, service providers, and other groups interested in the promotion of the technology. As a result, the North American ISDN Users Forum (NIUF)—a joint effort among NIST, the user community, and the ISDN industry—was created in late 1988. This effort represented a technology infrastructure championed by NIST in the belief that ISDN technology was the next generation of communication networks.

The goal of ISDN, in the late 1980s, was a worldwide network communications infrastructure that was expected to provide end-to-end digital connectivity of a vast array of information through a limited set of standard, multipurpose user-to-network interfaces. ISDN had evolved from the digital-based public telephone system designed to transport and integrate information on a common network. With ISDN, computer and communications technologies converge to speed and simplify the flow of information between sender and receiver.

The total communication environment from the sender to the receiver comprised two types of network domains: access and wide area. The ISDN-access network was at that time primarily the domain of the users and was physically composed of customer premises equipment (CPE), which included terminals (e.g., computer, facsimile), other ancillary communications equipment, and a transmission line that connects to an exchange located within the wide area network.[26] The wide area network (WAN) is the domain of the telephone companies. It includes the local exchange companies and their interexchange or long-distance companies.[27] Several specialized technological methods are necessary to achieve ISDN functionality within the WAN.[28]

ISDN was expected to allow users to send, receive, and modify information using existing telephone lines in ways that were not previously possible.[29] ISDN had the potential to provide enhanced telecommunications performance, efficiency, options, and affordability to individual users who have access to basic telephone service (POTS).[30]

Advancements in ISDN concepts and deployment could further benefit society. ISDN had been identified as a likely component for the future National Information Infrastructure (NII).[31] The NII envisioned a seamless information infrastructure interconnecting individual residences, businesses, and government entities with high information bandwidths on a peer-to-peer basis. Transmission technologies to achieve this goal would exist if there was a proliferation of high bandwidth fiber optic systems.[32]

Created in 1988 with NIST as the catalyst, NIUF had the purpose of creating a strong user voice in the implementation of ISDN and ISDN-application needs. NIST served the role of a funder and nonpartisan facilitator. The key to interoperability is agreement on both the use and the interpretation of standards. ISDN standards developed by national and international standards-making organizations—the American National Standards Institute (ANSI) and the International Telecommunications Union–Telecommunications Standardization Sector (ITU-TSS)—are broadly designed to meet many requirements. Mere compliance with a standard is not sufficient to guarantee interoperability. Differing interpretations of these standards by vendors in isolation from each other often resulted in incompatible services and products.[33]

5.5.2. Economics of ISDN Standards

Based on an economic impact assessment of the role of NIST in the NIUF in 1995 (Marx and Link 1995, Link 1996a), a survey-based counterfactual analysis of the then Regional Bell Operating Companies (RBOCs) concluded that absent NIST's involvement in promulgating standards and coordinating the activities of NIUF, expectations of future growth in ISDN customers over to the end of the century were between 10 percent and 50 percent of current expectations.[34]

However, as well-intentioned as NIST's efforts were in the early 1990s, expectations about ISDN technology and users were not realized. Part of the reason was that RBOCs could not agree on interoperability standards, even with NIST's assistance, and competing technologies developed, such as broadband Internet services, and DSL and cable modem services. Thus, while the NIST-encouraged NIUF was an innovative approach to promulgating standards, the entrepreneurial risk associated with industry acceptance was too great to bring about a market realization of the technology.

5.6. Alternative Refrigerants

5.6.1. Refrigerant Technology

Historically, chemical compounds known as chlorofluorocarbons (CFCs) were used extensively as aerosol propellants, refrigerants, solvents, and industrial foam blowing agents. Refrigerants are chemicals used in various machines, such as air-conditioning systems, that carry energy from one place to another. Until the 1970s, most refrigerants used throughout the world were made of CFCs because of their desirable physical and economic properties. However, research showed that the release of CFCs into the atmosphere could possibly damage the ozone layer of the earth. In response to the accumulation of such findings, an international treaty was drafted that resulted in the signing of the Montreal Protocol in 1987, a global agreement to phase out the production and use of CFCs and replace them with other compounds that would have a lesser impact on the environment.[35] The Protocol outlined a phase-out period for substances such as CFCs.[36]

In order to meet the phase-out schedule in the Protocol, research was needed to develop new types of refrigerants, called alternative refrigerants, which would retain the desirable physical properties of CFCs, but would pose little or no threat to the ozone layer. Possible candidates for replacement had to have a number of properties and meet specific criteria to be judged as feasible replacements. Since 1987, the United States and other nations have forged international environmental protection agreements in an effort to replace CFCs with alternative, more environmentally neutral chemical compounds in order to meet the timetable imposed by the Protocol.

NIST became involved in alternative refrigerant research in 1982 and has continued to support U.S. industry in its development and use of CFC replacements. The Physical and Chemical Properties Division of NIST's Chemical Science and Technology Laboratory (CSTL) has been the focal point for this research effort.[37]

The results from NIST's properties research were made available to industry in various forms. Undertaking this research was certainly an innovative policy action, but it was an action subject to entrepreneurial risk characterized by finding an alternative refrigerant to comply with the Montreal Protocol, finding it in a timely manner, and ensuring industry compliance. The most effective form for dissemination of information was through the REFPROP program, a computer package that is available through NIST's Standard Reference Data Program. The REFPROP program could be used by both manufacturers and users of alternative refrigerants in their respective manufacturing processes. A particular benefit of the REFPROP program was its ability to model the behavior of various refrigerant mixtures, and this had proven to be a key method in developing CFC replacements.[38]

Refrigeration is a process by which a substance is cooled below the temperature of its surroundings. Objects can be cooled as well as areas and spaces. The type of refrigeration that relates to the research at NIST is mechanical refrigeration, as opposed to natural refrigeration.

A number of components are required for mechanical refrigeration. The vapor compression cycle of refrigeration requires the use of a compressor, a condenser, a storage tank, a throttling valve, and an evaporator. These elements, when working together, produce the desired cooling effect. The refrigerant is sent through the compressor, which raises its pressure and temperature. The refrigerant then moves into the condenser, where its heat is released into the environment, then through the throttling valve and into the evaporator where its pressure and temperature drop. At this point, the cycle begins again. The conduit for this heat exchange is the refrigerant.[39]

During most of the history of mechanical refrigeration, CFCs have been the most widely used refrigerants. The term chlorofluorocarbons refers to a family of chemicals whose molecular structures are composed of chlorine (Cl), fluorine (F), and carbon (C) atoms. Their popularity as refrigerants has been in no small part because of their desirable thermal properties as well as their molecular stability.[40]

The link between chlorofluorocarbons and ozone depletion has been debated for decades. Much of the impetus for international environmental treaties, such as the Montreal Protocol and legislation such as the Clean Air Act, has come from studies that assert that CFCs released into the atmosphere react with the earth's ozone layer and eventually destroy it.[41]

The alternative refrigerant industry consists of two types of companies: refrigerant manufacturers that produce the alternative refrigerants; and heating, ventilating, and air-conditioning (HVAC) equipment manufacturers in whose machines the alternative refrigerants are used. These are the two industry groups that are considered the first-level users of NIST's research.

Refrigerant manufacturers consist of the group of firms that manufacture a wide range of chemicals, including alternative refrigerants. The two major manufacturers of alternative refrigerants in the early 1990s were DuPont and AlliedSignal. These and other firms had purchased multiple versions of the REFPROP program since its inception.[42]

5.6.2. Economics of the REFPROP Program

Based on an economic-impact assessment of the role of NIST in its development and support of REFPROP in 1998, a survey-based counterfactual analysis of the major manufacturers of alternative refrigerants reported that, in the absence of NIST's materials' properties' database, they would likely have responded to the Montreal Protocol timetable by hiring additional research scientists and engineers to attempt to provide the materials' characterization and analysis needed by their in-house alternative refrigerant research programs or through their participation in research consortia. Smaller manufacturers reported that they would have relied on others' (in the industry) research, and in the interim would have looked for alternative uses of the refrigerants they produced. Thus, not only was NIST intervention timely, it was successful in terms of its cost effectiveness for the industry. The entrepreneurial actions by NIST basically bailed out the U.S. domestic industry that was facing potentially costly stretching out of new product development and significantly greater costs.

5.7. Internet Protocol Standards

5.7.1. Cyber Security

Cyber security refers to measures for protecting computer systems, networks and information from disruption or unauthorized access, use, disclosure, modification, or destruction.[43] Cyberspace is a nation's information technology (IT) infrastructure; it is the nervous system of a country (and of the global economy). Cyberspace links a nation's critical infrastructures across both public and private institutions in sectors ranging from agriculture to transportation. This information control system is composed of hundreds of thousands of interconnected computers, servers, routers, switches, and fiber optic cables that allows this critical infrastructure to work.

The Internet and computing infrastructure used by private and public organizations consists of three categories of resources: computing resources, such as central processing units and memory; storage resources, such as disk drives and storage area networks; and network resources, including routers, wireless access points and hubs that connect multiple storage and computing resources. Physical security breaches are typically well-defended under lock and key; network components must be compromised for an attacker to access any computing or data-storage resources. Thus, network components are the most common target because they provide access and allow attackers to threaten applications, operating systems, or storage or computing resources once inside.[44]

Common security tools and procedures include firewalls, content filters, intrusion detection systems, access control, stronger user identification, cryptography,[45] hardening,[46] auditing, and end-user and administrator training.[47]

The Cyber Security Research and Development Act of 2002 amended the National Institute of Standards and Technology Act "to establish a program of assistance to institutions of higher education that enter into partnerships with for-profit entities to support research to improve the security of computer systems." The Act also authorized NIST "to identify emerging issues, including research needs, related to computer security, privacy and cryptography."[48]

Another possibility is that the government could underwrite the research and implementation costs for organizations that are pilot-testing new innovations related to cyber security. This direct approach might increase private investments in innovative cyber security strategies, moving them toward a socially desirable level.

A subset of Internet standards, called communications protocols, supports the most basic functionality of the Internet.[49] One such communications protocol that lies at the heart of the Internet, is Internet protocol (IP).[50] The IP enables data and other traffic to travel through the Internet and to arrive at the desired destination. It provides a standardized envelope for the information sent; specifically, the IP contains headers that provide addressing, routing, and message-handling information that enables a message to be directed to its final destination over the various media that comprise the Internet.

The current generation of the IP, version 4 (IPv4), has been in use since the 1980s and has supported the Internet's worldwide growth over the last decade. With the transformation of the Internet in the 1990s from a research network to a commercialized network, concerns were raised about the ability of IPv4 to accommodate emerging demand, especially the anticipated demand for unique Internet addresses. As a result, the Internet Engineering Task Force (IETF) began work on a new generation IP, which became IP version 6 (IPv6).[51, 52]

The redesigned header structure in IPv6, including new flow labels, and the enhanced capabilities of the new protocol could provide significant security benefits to Internet users, network administrators, and software applications developers. Further, some experts believe that widespread IPv6 adoption could spur increased research and development of and interest in transitioning to a new network security model, in which techniques such as Internet protocol security (IPsec) could be more commonly and effectively used.

Based largely on these perceived security benefits, in June 2003 the U.S. Department of Defense (DoD) announced that all hardware and software being developed, procured, or acquired for its Global Information Grid (GIG) would have to be IPv6-capable by October 1, 2003.[53] In August 2005 the U.S. Office of Management and Budget (OMB) issued a memorandum stating that by June 2008 all federal government agencies' infrastructure must be using IPv6 and agency networks must interface with this infrastructure. This decision of the OMB was based not only on the perceived security and efficiency benefits to the government, but also on the idea that government could help by spurring the demand for new IPv6-enabled products and services, thereby jump-starting the market and providing incentives for start-up companies to develop new enhanced products and services that would be supported by a more advanced IP structure.

5.7.2. Economics of IPv6

Industry stakeholders and Internet experts generally agree that IPv6 networks would be technically superior to IPv4 networks. This belief motivated the 2005 OMB memorandum for all government agencies' infrastructure to be IPv6 compatible by 2008. Even with the assistance of NIST, the transition to IPv6 will be costly (Gallaher and Rowe 2005, 2006), and network security could decrease during the transitional periods. Because of lack of penetration by IPv6 at this time, the traditional NIST role of helping to overcome the entrepreneurial risk associated with a transition to IPv6 cannot (yet) be evaluated.

5.8. Conclusions

The examples in this chapter show that NIST activities did in fact reduce the technical and market risk of private-sector R&D related to optical fiber and alternative refrigerant technology in a timely manner, and that action did enhance competitiveness. In these two cases, the entrepreneurial risk associated with the promulgation of standards did not inhibit industry accepting the standards in a timely manner. The adoption of the standards enhanced competitiveness.

The due diligence of NIST did not similarly result in the same economic benefits with respect to ISDN or IPv6 technology. With respect to ISDN, NIST's actions did not remove all market risk; with respect to IPv6, the jury is still out. Nevertheless, NIST, that is government, did act entrepreneurially; it was just the case that the entrepreneurial risk associated with its actions inhibited firm acceptance.

Notes

1. The development and evolution of the material in this chapter is discussed in Link (1999, 2006).

2. This section draws on Link (2006).

3. The resolution stated: "That the Secretary of the Treasury be, and he hereby is, directed to cause a complete set of all the weights and measures adopted as standards, and now either made or in the progress of manufacture for the use of the several custom-houses, and for other purposes, to be delivered to the Governor of each State in the Union, or such person as he may appoint, for the use of the States respectively, to the end that an uniform standard of weights and measures may be established throughout the United States."

4. As background to the Act of July 28, 1866, the origins of the metric system can be traced to the research of Gabriel Mouton, a French vicar, in the late 1600s. His standard unit was based on the length of an arc of 1 minute of

a great circle of the earth. Given the controversy of the day over this measurement, the National Assembly of France decreed on May 8, 1790, that the French Academy of Sciences along with the Royal Society of London deduce an invariable standard for all the measures and all the weights. Within a year, a standardized measurement plan was adopted based on terrestrial arcs, and the term *mètre* (meter), from the Greek word *metron* meaning to measure, was assigned by the Academy of Sciences.

5. The Act stated: "*Be it enacted*..., That from and after the passage of this act it shall be lawful throughout the United States of America to employ the weights and measures of the metric system; and no contract or dealing, or pleading in any court, shall be deemed invalid or liable to objection because the weights or measures expressed or referred to therein are weights and measures of the metric system.... *And be it further enacted*, That the tables in the schedule hereto annexed shall be recognized in the construction of contracts, and in all legal proceedings, as establishing, in terms of the weights and measures expressed therein in terms of the metric system; and said tables may be lawfully used for computing, determining, and expressing in customary weights and measures the weights and measures of the metric system...."

6. In a Joint Resolution before Congress on March 3, 1881, it was resolved that: "The Secretary of the Treasury be, and he is hereby directed to cause a complete set of all the weights and measures adopted as standards to be delivered to the governor of each State in the Union, for the use of agricultural colleges in the States, respectively, which have received a grant of lands from the United States, and also one set of the same for the use of the Smithsonian Institution."

7. The subsequent Act of July 12, 1894, established standard units of electrical measure: "*Be it enacted*..., That from and after the passage of this Act the legal units of electrical measure in the United States shall be as follows:...That it shall be the duty of the National Academy of Sciences [established in 1863] to prescribe and publish, as soon as possible after the passage of this Act, such specifications of detail as shall be necessary for the practical application of the definitions of the ampere and volt hereinbefore given, and such specifications shall be the standard specifications herein mentioned."

8. Although Congress at that time wrestled with the level of funding for such a laboratory, its importance was not debated.

9. The subsequent Act of February 14, 1903, established the Department of Commerce and Labor, and in that Act it was stated that: "...the National Bureau of Standards..., be...transferred from the Department of the Treasury to the Department of Commerce and Labor, and the same shall hereafter remain...." Then, in 1913, when the Department of Labor was established as a separate entity, the Bureau was formally housed in the Department of Commerce.

10. The Act of July 21, 1950, stated: "*Be it enacted by the Senate and House of Representatives of the United States of America in Congress assembled,* That from and after the date this Act is approved, the legal units of electrical and photometric measurements in the United States of America shall be those defined and established as provided in the following sections....The unit of

electrical resistance shall be the ohm ... The unit of electrical current shall be the ampere ... The unit of electromotive force and of electrical potential shall be the volt ... The unit of electrical quantity shall be the coulomb ... The unit of electrical capacity shall be the farad ... The unit of electrical inductance shall be the henry ... The unit of power shall be the watt ... The units of energy shall be the (a) joule ... and (b) the kilowatt-hour ... The unit of intensity shall be the candle ... The unit of flux light shall be the lumen ... It shall be the duty of the Secretary of Commerce to establish the values of the primary electric and photometric units in absolute measure, and the legal values for these units shall be those represented by, or derived from, national reference standards maintained by the Department of Commerce."

11. This Act also created the ATP; see chapter 4.

12. The measurement and standards laboratories constitute the center-piece program at NIST. NIST's organizational structure is laboratory based. The laboratories at NIST provide technical leadership for vital components of the Nation's technology infrastructure needed by U.S. industry to continually improve its products and services. Currently, there are seven research laboratories and two research centers at NIST:

- The Electronics and Electrical Engineering Laboratory (EEEL) promotes U.S. economic growth by providing measurement capability of high impact focused primarily on the critical needs of the U.S. electronics and electrical industries, and their customers and suppliers.
- The Manufacturing Engineering Laboratory (MEL) performs research and development of measurements, standards, and infrastructure technology as related to manufacturing.
- The Chemical Science and Technology Laboratory (CSTL) provides chemical measurement infrastructure to enhance U.S. industry's productivity and competitiveness; assure equity in trade; and improve public health, safety, and environmental quality.
- The Physics Laboratory (PL) supports U.S. industry by providing measurement services and research for electronic, optical, and radiation technologies.
- The Materials Science and Engineering Laboratory (MSEL) stimulates the more effective production and use of materials by working with materials suppliers and users to assure the development and implementation of the measurement and standards infrastructure for materials.
- The Building and Fire Research Laboratory (BFRL) enhances the competitiveness of U.S. industry and public safety by developing performance prediction methods, measurement technologies, and technical advances needed to assure the life-cycle quality and economy of constructed facilities.
- The Information Technology Laboratory (ITL) works with industry, research, and government organizations to develop and demonstrate tests, test methods, reference data, proof of concept implementations, and other infrastructural technologies. (The Computer Systems Laboratory [CSL] and the Computing and Applied Mathematics Laboratory [CAML] were combined on February 16, 1997, to form the ITL.)
- Center for Nanoscale Science and Technology (CNST) enables science and industry by providing essential measurement methods, instrumentation, and standards to support all phases of nanotechnology development, from discovery to production.

- NIST Center for Neuron Research (NCNR) focuses on providing neutron measurement capabilities to the U.S. research community.

In addition to these research laboratories, the Technology Services Laboratory provides a variety of products and services to U.S. industry such as Standard Reference Materials, Standard Reference Data, and Weights and Measures. The Program Office was established within NIST in 1968. Its mission is to support the Director and Deputy Director and to perform program and policy analyses related to the laboratories; articulate and document NIST program plans; generate strategies, guidelines, and formats for long-range planning; analyze external trends, opportunities, and user needs regarding NIST priorities; coordinate, carry out, and issue studies; collect, organize, verify, and present descriptive NIST data; administer multiorganizational processes; provide staff support for key management committees; develop relevant budget documents; implement NIST information policies and standards; and perform economic-impact analyses for NIST as a whole and produce analytical leadership for the laboratories' impact assessment efforts.

13. See Link and Scott (2006a) for an economic evaluation of the social impact of the National Quality Award.

14. See Link (1983).

15. See Link (1996a) and Link and Scott (1998), and see the NIST Program Office website.

16. Based on our previous research experience related to NIST activities, these four examples are representative of the portfolio of NIST standards-related activities.

17. This section draws on Link (1991, 1996a).

18. See Chaffee (1988).

19. See Magaziner and Patinkin (1989) for a more detailed history of Corning's research in this area.

20. In fact, Corning began to build its first factory in 1978 (operable in 1979), even before receiving their first sizeable fiber order. AT&T's commitment to the technology was dramatically revealed in 1980 when they announced their intention to build a 611-mile fiber optic network between Cambridge, Massachusetts, and Washington, D.C. See Chaffee (1988).

21. According to Magaziner and Patinkin (1989, p. 290), "The MCI order caught the world off guard—AT&T, the Japanese, everyone. Corning had the football" and the others would try to take it away.

22. See ITC (1988).

23. Two types of multimode fiber are used commercially. Step index fibers have a core diameter of 50 to 400 millimeters and are best suited for short-haul, limited bandwidth, low-cost applications. In comparison, graded index fibers are best suited for medium-haul and medium to high bandwidth applications, having a core diameter of 30 to 60 millimenters. Single-mode fibers are best suited for long-haul, high-bandwidth applications where a single-mode injection laser source is used. The core diameter of these fibers is 3 to 10 millimeters. Very few technologies can be successfully commercialized and achieve significant market penetration without the availability and use of critical technology infrastructure such as standards. NIST has been very supportive of the optical fiber industry by evaluating, providing technical input, and helping to write relevant standards.

24. After 1997 this association was renamed the Electronics Industries Alliance.

25. This section draws on Marx and Link (1995) and Link (1996a).

26. From a functional perspective, information generated from each of the user's terminals would be multiplexed at a network termination. The network termination would separate information transfer responsibility between the user and the service provider (e.g., local telephone company), and thus would define the boundaries between access and wide area domains. The digital bit streams of information are then transported from the network termination over an access line via the appropriate transmission media to the user's local exchange. ISDN required a separation of terminal-generated information into both user information (e.g., voice, video) and control information. The separation and mapping of these information modes would be performed within the sender's access network, and then they would be extended across the wide area network into the receiver's access network. User information would be configured by the user's communication function and would not subject to ISDN protocols. In comparison, control information would conform to ISDN protocols that were based on international and national ISDN standards.

27. The WAN has two sub-networks: transport and control, and exchanges. The transport and control network provides the wide area transmission user information between originating and terminating exchanges, thereby extending the communication domain beyond the physical limitations of the local access network. The transport network can be either publicly or privately owned. The exchange provides the switching capability with the transport network.

28. ISDN requires end-to-end digital transmission facilities, a sophisticated protocol for network switches known as Stored Program Control, and an advanced signaling capability know as Signaling System 7 in the control network. Other important tools for ISDN include the use of the Open Systems Interconnection (OSI) hierarchical reference electronic devices fabricated by very large-scale integration (VLSI) to support the complex functionality in hardware. International and national standards govern the implementation of these and other technological methods for ISDN. The primary standardization ISDN interfaces are Basic Rate Interface (BRI), Primary Rate Interface (PRI), and Broadband ISDN. Both BRI and PRI are arbitrarily classified as Narrowband ISDN interfaces to distinguish them from Broadband ISDN. See Ronayne (1988).

29. For example, the data transfer speeds of high-speed modems operating at 14.4 kilobits per second (kbps) were too slow to make telecommuting feasible for many users, but a 144.0 kbps data rate with a direct interface into the company local area network allowed efficient access to office-based data and software.

30. The key benefits associated with this technology were increased bandwidth, limited number of access methods for all services, and reduced costs of accessing data.

31. The NII resulted from the High Performance and Communication Act of 1991. President Clinton had proposed an advanced, seamless web of public and private communication networks.

32. The development of standard message protocols necessary for subscriber control of broadband services, a crucial development in achieving NII's goals, could evolve from the current standards in narrowband ISDN. ISDN's ability to support such digital connections on an as-needed bandwidth basis would make ISDN a potential building block for the NII.

33. Selecting options, clarifying ambiguities, explaining applicability to specific equipment and environments, and developing conformance tests are essential activities that lead to interoperability. These functional standardization activities constitute a significant product development cost, and vendors are often unwilling to incur this cost because distributed application environments and multivendor products mandate common protocol implementations.

34. In 1995 there were approximately 300,000 ISDN customers with over 3,000,000 expected by the end of the century (Link 1996).

35. The primary reason for the refrigerant industry's switch from CFCs to alternative refrigerants was the issuance of the Montreal Protocol in 1987, and its subsequent amendments. The Protocol, formally known as "The Montreal Protocol on Substances that Deplete the Ozone Layer," is the primary international agreement providing for controls on the production and consumption of ozone-depleting substances such as CFCs, halons, and methyl bromide. The Montreal Protocol was adopted under the 1985 Vienna Convention for the Protection of the Ozone Layer and became effective in 1989.

36. Each year the parties to the Protocol meet to review the terms of the agreement and to decide if more actions are needed. In some cases, they update and amend the Protocol. Such amendments were added in 1990 and 1992, the London Amendment and the Copenhagen Amendment respectively. These amendments together accelerated the phase-out of controlled substances, added new controls on other substances such as HCFCs, and developed financial-assistance programs for developing countries. The main thrust of the original Protocol was to delineate a specific phase-out period for "controlled substances" such as CFCs and halons. For various CFCs, the original phase-out schedule required production and consumption levels to be capped at 100 percent of 1986 levels by 1990, with decreases to 80 percent by 1994, and to 50 percent by 1999. The 1990 and 1992 amendments, and the U.S. Clean Air Act amendments of 1990, called for an increase in the phase-out so that no CFCs could be produced after 1996. The Copenhagen Amendment called for decreases in HCFCs and for zero production by 2030.

37. That Division had more than forty years of experience in the measurement and modeling of the thermophysical properties of fluids. The Division had been involved with refrigerants for nearly a decade. Early work was performed at NIST in conjunction with the Building Environment Division, and this work led to the development of early computer models of refrigerant behavior. In addition, research performed by Division members serves as a basis for updating tables and charts in reference volumes for the refrigeration industry. Research on alternative refrigerants falls broadly into three areas: effects of man-made chemicals on the atmosphere, chemical and physical properties of alternative refrigerants, and methods to place chemicals in machines. The first area is referred to by NIST scientists as "understanding the problem," and the other two areas are referred to as "solving the

problem." The primary focus of the Physical and Chemical Properties Division was on the properties of refrigerants.

38. NIST's research efforts on characterizing the chemical properties of alternative refrigerants and how these refrigerants perform when mixed with other refrigerants potentially averted a very costly economic disruption to a number of industries. According to interviews with industry and university researchers, NIST served critical functions that were important to the timely, efficient implementation of the Montreal Protocol.

39. For a refrigerant to be effective, it must satisfy the following properties (Shedlick, Link, and Scott 1998, Link and Scott 1998): chemical properties (stable, inert); health, safety, and environmental properties (nontoxic, nonflammable, nondegrading to the atmosphere); thermal properties (appropriate critical point and boiling point temperatures, low vapor heat capacity, low viscosity, high thermal conductivity); and miscellaneous properties (satisfactory oil solubility, high dielectric strength of vapor, low freezing point, reasonable containment materials, easy leak detection, low cost). Not every refrigerant meets these properties. When deciding upon a refrigerant, all properties must be evaluated. For example, a refrigerant that has acceptable thermodynamic properties might be extremely toxic to humans, while one that is nontoxic might be unstable and break down inside the refrigeration machinery.

40. Chlorofluorocarbons have a nomenclature that describes the molecular structure of the CFC. In order to determine the structure of CFC-11, for example, one takes the number (11) and adds 90 to it. The sum is 101. The first digit of the sum indicates the number of carbon atoms in the molecule, the second digit the number of hydrogen atoms, and the third digit the number of fluorine atoms. Any further spaces left in the molecule are filled with chlorine atoms. Of the various chlorofluorocarbons available, CFC-11, CFC-12, and CFC-13 have been used most extensively because of their desirable properties. CFC-11 and CFC-12 are used in refrigeration and foam insulation. CFC-13 is a solvent used as a cleaning agent for electronics and a degreaser for metals. Applications of CFCs, and it is important to note that refrigerants are only one-fourth of the applications, also include solvents, rigid foam, fire extinguishing, and flexible foam.

41. The chemistry advanced by these CFC studies suggests that once a CFC molecule drifts into the upper atmosphere, it is split apart by ultraviolet light. This process releases a chlorine atom, which reacts with an ozone molecule. The reaction produces a chlorine monoxide molecule and an oxygen molecule, neither of which absorb ultraviolet radiation. The chlorine monoxide molecule then reacts with another ozone molecule, and the original chlorine atom is freed to react with additional ozone (Cogan 1988).

42. Each of these firms markets its own brand of refrigerants. For example, DuPont's alternative refrigerants are sold under the Suva brand, while AlliedSignal's are sold under the AZ brand. Precise market shares of the alternative refrigerant market were not publicly available.

43. This section draws on Gallaher, Link, and Rowe (2008).

44. In general, attacks on cyber security infrastructure can be identified as pursuing one or more of the following broad goals, all of which can inflict

economic damages on the target: damaging or diminishing the effectiveness of vital cyber security infrastructure components; gaining unauthorized access to the target's sensitive information; and/or gaining unauthorized access to cyber resources for illegal use. The major types and methods of attacks include: network probing and scanning (through network-mapping tools); distributed denial of service (through a connection generator capable of producing a large amount of legitimate-looking Internet traffic); spam (through focused email software); traffic analysis and sniffing (through focused network software); application or host compromised (through worms, viruses, or Trojans); account and identify information theft (through phishing and social engineering; phishing refers to an attackers attempt to extract private, confidential information from targets by crafting forged emails or websites that pretend to originate from or belong to a trusted target); and zero-day attacks (through viruses released when security analyzes it).

45. Cryptography refers to techniques that allow individuals to conceal data and maintain its integrity.

46. Hardening refers to general improvements in the cyber infrastructure to make it more difficult to attack.

47. Government's role to enhance private investments in cyber security is to remove or lessen the barriers that cause organizations to underinvest in cyber security from a social perspective. From an economic perspective, if a firm's marginal private cost of investing in cyber security decreases (assuming a decreasing marginal private return schedule), it will in turn increase the level of its investments. Government could achieve this goal by, for example, funding the collection, analysis, and dissemination of both reliable and cost-effective information (e.g., performance of software and hardware) related to cyber security. Many trade associations and industry consortia in the United States, for example, attempt to provide such services, but few do so in a productive manner (Gallaher, Link, and Rowe 2008). Furthermore, evaluating the effectiveness and efficiency of potential cyber-security solutions is a complex and costly activity. In many instances, the taxonomy and metrics do not readily exist to facilitate comparisons of competing technologies that make similar claims.

48. The Act states:

Computer security technology and systems implementations lack—

(A) sufficient long term research funding;
(B) adequate coordination across Federal and State government agencies and among government, academic and industry, and;
(C) sufficient numbers of outstanding researchers in the field.

Accordingly, Federal investment in computer and network security research and development must be significantly increased to—

(A) improve vulnerability assessment and technology system solutions;
(B) expand and improve the pool of information security professionals, including researchers, in the U.S. workforce; and
(C) better coordinated information sharing and collaboration among industry, government and academic research projects.

49. This section draws on Gallaher, Link, and Rowe (2008) and Gallaher and Rowe (2005, 2006).

50. The Internet Protocol (IP) is a type of communications protocol. A communications protocol is a set of rules and conventions that control the format and relative timing of message transmission between two points within a computer network.

51. Designed in the mid-1990s, IPv6 has slowly been integrated into most major networking hardware and software sold today. Cameras, cell phones and refrigerators are beginning to be equipped with IPv6 addresses in an effort by vendors to use the characteristics of IP to enhance product features and provide new services. As of 2005, the majority of routers sold are IPv6-capable, and by 2008, most operating systems and application software on the market will be IPv6-capable. IPv6-based networks would be technically superior to IPv4-based networks in many ways. The increased address space available under IPv6 could stimulate development and deployment of new communications devices and new applications. IPv6 also could enable network restructuring to a more hierarchical structure, possibly without network address translation (NAT) devices, to occur more easily. The redesigned header structure in IPv6 (which includes new flow labels) and the enhanced capabilities of the new protocol could provide significant security benefits.

52. For a brief discussion of the reasons for developing a next-generation IP and the IETF's activities in that area, see Huston (2003).

53. See Stenbet (2003).

6

Biofuels

The Renewable Fuel Standard

6.1. Introduction

The Biomass Research and Development Initiative (BRDI) is the public/ private partnership described in this chapter through which government acts as entrepreneur. BRDI's use of public financial resources leverages both public- and private-sector R&D. See table 6.1. The innovative policy action of using public resources to support public- and private-sector R&D lessens barriers to innovation (see table 1.2) and creates a cost-sharing environment conducive for developing domestic biofuels that are cost competitive with gasoline. It is this cost-sharing environment,[1] authorized by the Biomass Research and Development Act of 2000, and later amended by the Food, Conservation, and Energy Act of 2008, which is the technology infrastructure. This technology infrastructure provides a basis for implementing the renewable fuel standard (RFS) set forth in the EISA of 2007. The RFS lays out a schedule for the adoption of advanced biofuels, including some that are not yet commercially viable. The entrepreneurial risk associated with the activities of the BRDI is if the publicly supported research will be successful in leveraging the development of advanced biofuels to meet the renewable fuel standard set forth by the EISA of 2007. See table 6.2.

Table 6.1.   Public/Private Partnerships: Biofuels

Government Involvement	Economic Objective	
	Leverage Public-Sector R&D	Leverage Private-Sector R&D
Indirect	. . .	. . .
Direct		
Financial Resources	Biomass Research and Development Initiative	Biomass Research and Development Initiative
Infrastructural Resources	. . .	. . .
Research Resources	. . .	. . .

Table 6.2.   Government as Entrepreneur: Biofuels

Public/Private Partnership	Technology Infrastructure	Innovative Policy Action	Entrepreneurial Risk
Biomass Research and Development Initiative	Cost-sharing environment conducive for developing domestic biofuels that are cost competitive with gasoline	Biomass Research and Development Act of 2000 as amended by the Food, Conservation, and Energy Act of 2008: use of public resources to accelerate the development of biofuels	If the publicly supported research will be successful in generating advanced biofuels to meet the renewable fuel standard

6.2. A Brief History of the Biomass Research and Development Act of 2000

The Biomass Research and Development Act of 2000, Section III of the Agriculture Risk Protection Act of 2000, created the BRDI to accelerate, among other things, biofuels R&D.[2] The purpose of the BRDI, as stated in the 2000 Act, is:

> . . . to stimulate collaborative activities by a diverse range of experts in all aspects of biomass processing for the purpose of conducting fundamental and innovation-targeted research and technology development; to enhance creative and imaginative approaches toward biomass processing that will serve to develop the next generation of

advanced technologies making possible low cost and sustainable biobased industrial products; to strengthen the intellectual resources of the United States through the training and education of future scientists, engineers, managers, and business leaders in the field of biomass processing; and to promote integrated research partnerships among colleges, universities, national laboratories, Federal and State research agencies, and the private sector as the best means of overcoming technical challenges that span multiple research and engineering disciplines and of gaining better leverage from limited Federal research funds.

The 2000 Act also established a Board and a Technical Advisory Committee. The Board was originally established under the name of The Interagency Council on Biobased Products and Bioenergy, under Executive Order 13134. The membership of the Board includes representatives from eleven government agencies and is co-chaired by representatives of the Department of Energy (DoE) and the Department of Agriculture (USDA). In October of 2008, the Board released their National Biofuels Action Plan, providing a strategy for achieving the renewable fuel standard in the EISA of 2007.[3] The Technical Advisory Committee is a group of thirty representatives from industry, state government, and academia that aids in strategic planning and offers guidance to the Biomass Research and Development Board on the technical priorities of the Biomass R&D Initiative.

The 2000 Act was revised by the Energy Policy Act of 2005 and amended by Section 232 of the Energy Independence and Security Act (EISA) of 2007 as well as by the Food, Conservation, and Energy Act of 2008. The Energy Policy Act of 2005 specified technical areas to be covered by a DoE/USDA joint solicitation that comprises a major part of current funding activity under the BRDI.[4] The EISA of 2007 authorizes the development of analytical tools to conduct more thorough analyses of the lifecycle impacts of existing and emerging biofuel technologies. These tools are particularly important as biofuels counted toward the renewable fuel standard mandated by the EISA must have lifecycle greenhouse gas (GHG) emissions of specified levels. The Food, Conservation, and Energy Act of 2008 requires a multiagency study be conducted on the infrastructure requirements associated with expanding usage of biofuels. It also expands the mandate for Federal agencies to conduct coordinated research and development on biobased products, including biofuels.

6.3. Renewable Fuel Standard

The EISA of 2007 set a new renewable fuel standard (RFS) which mandates a schedule—see table 6.3—for incorporating different classes of biofuels into the U.S. transportation-fuel supply.

The RFS set forth by the EISA of 2007 extended the RFS originally proposed in the Energy Policy Act of 2005. The 2005 schedule required

Table 6.3.   Renewable Fuel Standard from EISA of 2007

Year	Renewable Biofuel	Advanced Biofuel	Cellulosic Biofuel	Biomass-based Diesel	Undifferentiated Advanced Biofuel	Total RFS
2008	9.0	...	...	...	...	9
2009	10.5	0.6		0.5	0.1	11.1
2010	12	0.95	0.1	0.65	0.2	12.95
2011	12.6	1.35	.25	0.8	0.3	13.95
2012	13.2	2	0.5	1	0.5	15.2
2013	13.8	2.75	1	...	1.75	16.55
2014	14.4	3.75	1.75	...	2	18.15
2015	15	5.5	3	...	2.5	20.5
2016	15	7.25	4.25	...	3.0	22.25
2017	15	9	5.5	...	3.5	24
2018	15	11	7	...	4.0	26
2019	15	13	8.5	...	4.5	28
2020	15	15	10.5	...	4.5	30
2021	15	18	13.5	...	4.5	33
2022	15	21	16	...	5.0	36

Source: EISA (2007).

incorporation of over 7.5 billion gallons of bioethanol and biodiesel by 2012. The new schedule (EISA 2007) extends the schedule to 2022 and requires the incorporation of advanced biofuels, such as cellulosic ethanol, which are not yet commercially viable.

6.4. Biofuel Technology

Biofuel technologies include bioethanol, biodiesel, and biopetroleum technologies. Bioethanol, an alcohol, is an alternative fuel made either by biochemical or thermochemical processing. Most of the ethanol currently produced in the United States is made from corn, thus posing an alternative use for the food crop. The corn-ethanol industry is supported in a variety of ways including direct biofuel-production subsidies, tariffs on imported biofuels, and subsidies for distribution, storage, and transport of biofuels.[5]

In addition to corn, ethanol can be produced from sugarcane, cellulosic feedstocks, and a variety of other forms of biomass. The United States has a small-scale domestic sugarcane-ethanol industry, which is limited to a few parts of the country with suitable climates, and it also imports additional sugarcane ethanol from Brazil and other countries. Currently, cellulosic ethanol is neither cost competitive with gasoline nor is it available on a commercial scale; however, subsidies to support this industry may soon emerge. For example, $50 million in new grants for cellulosic-ethanol and biofuels R&D is authorized by the EISA of 2007.[6] There are currently dozens of cellulosic ethanol startup companies in the United States along with several demonstration plants funded by the Department of Energy under a cost-share arrangement with industry.[7]

There are three reasons ethanol is blended with gasoline: to reduce greenhouse-gas emissions, to increase octane content, and to extend gasoline stocks. Though pure ethanol is incompatible with our current gasoline infrastructure,[8] several ethanol and gasoline blends are in use. The most common blend available at pumps in the United States is gasoline blended with 10 percent ethanol (E-10). Also available are E-15 blends and E-85 blends. Blends that incorporate 15 percent ethanol (E-15) are compatible with all vehicles, but blends that incorporate 85 percent ethanol (E-85) are only compatible with flex-fuel engines.

Ethanol has about two-thirds of the energy density of gasoline. The distance a consumer can drive on a tank of E-15 differs only slightly from the distance on a tank of gasoline. Energy density is much more of an issue for drivers using high ethanol blends of flex-fuel vehicles. Because E-85 is presently available at very few pumping stations in the United States, many drivers of flex-fuel vehicles use low ethanol blends.[9]

Table 6.4 chronicles ethanol milestones from 1876 through 1995. Hallmarks of that history include the Energy Tax Act of 1978, which gave a

Table 6.4.   Ethanol Milestones, 1876–1995

Date	Milestone Use	Comment
1876–1908	Ethanol fuel used in automobiles	Otto Cycle (1876) was the first combustion engine designed to use alcohol and gasoline, followed by Henry Ford's Model T (1908), which was designed to use ethanol, gasoline, or any combination of the two fuels.
1940s	First U.S. fuel ethanol plant built	The U.S. Army built and operated an ethanol plant in Omaha, Nebraska, to produce fuel for the army and to provide ethanol for regional fuel blending.
1973	Yom Kippur War, OPEC oil embargo	OPEC raised crude oil prices by 70 percent, embargoed the United States for its support of Israel, and threatened to reduce production by 5 percent per month until Israel withdrew from Palestine.
1974	Oil embargo ends	The embargo and gasoline lines shocked the world, and Project Independence was initiated to review strategic energy options.

Table 6.4. (*continued*)

Date	Milestone Use	Comment
1974	Solar Energy Research, Development, and Demonstration Act	The Act (Public Law 93–473) provided legislative support for research and development for the conversion of cellulose and other organic materials (including wastes) into useful energy or fuels.
1977	Food and Agricultural Act	The Act (Public Law 95–113) authorized U.S. Department of Agriculture (USDA) loan guarantees for the first four biomass pilot plants (none actually built) and expanded USDA research for renewable fuels or fossil substitutes.
1978	Energy Tax Act	The Energy Tax Act of 1978 (Public Law 9–618) gave a 4-cents-per-gallon exemption from federal excise taxes to motor fuels blended with ethanol (minimum 10 percent ethanol) and granted a 10-percent energy investment tax credit for biomass-ethanol conversion equipment (in addition to the 10-percent investment tax credit available).
1979	Fuel ethanol blends marketed	Amoco Oil Company began marketing commercial alcohol-blended fuels, followed by Ashland, Chevron, Beacon, and Texaco, which also owned ethanol production facilities.
1979	Interior and Related Agencies Appropriation Act	The Act (Public Law 96–126) appropriated $19 billion for an Energy Security Reserve to stimulate production of alternative fuels, $100 million for product development feasibility studies, and $100 million for cooperative agreements to support commercial development of alternative fuel plants.
1980	First U.S. ethanol survey	The survey found that fewer than 10 facilities existed, producing approximately 50 million gallons of ethanol per year.
1980	Supplemental Appropriation and Rescission Act	The Act (Public Law 96–304) earmarked another $100 million for further feasibility studies and another $200 million for cooperative agreements. The DoE made 47 feasibility study grants during 1980 and 1981, as well as cooperative agreements with ethanol producers.

(*continued*)

Table 6.4. (*continued*)

Date	Milestone Use	Comment
1980	Crude Oil Windfall Tax Act	The Act (Public Law 96–223) extended the 4-cents-per-gallon federal excise tax exemption to December 31, 1992, and extended the energy investment tax credit to December 31, 1985. An income tax credit was also provided to alcohol fuel blenders—40 cents per gallon for 190-proof alcohol and 30 cents per gallon for 150–90 proof. The excise tax exemption and the income tax credit were either/or alternatives: both could not be used.
1980	Energy Security Act	The Act (Public Law 96–294) offered insured loans for small ethanol producers (less than 1 million gallons per year), loan guarantees that covered up to 90 percent of construction costs on ethanol plants, price guarantees for biomass energy projects, and purchase agreements for biomass energy used by federal agencies. It also established the DoE Office of Alcohol Fuels and authorized $600 million for both USDA and DoE for biomass research. Subsequent rescissions altered this allocation to $20 million for USDA and $800 million for DoE to use for alcohol fuel loans. The Consolidated Farm and Rural Development Act of 1980, which rescinded the $505 million allocated to USDA, appropriated $250 million for alcohol loan guarantees that were used to support 12 firms.
1982	Surface Transportation Assistance Act	The Act (Public Law 97–424) raised the gasoline excise tax to 9 cents per gallon and increased the tax exemption for gasohol to 5 cents per gallon (9 cents for fuels containing 85 percent alcohol or more). The blender's income tax credit was increased to 50 cents per gallon for 190-proof alcohol and 37.5 cents for 150–90 proof.
1984	Tax Reform Act	The Act (Public Law 99–198) raised the gasohol exemption from 5 to 6 cents per gallon, with the overall tax unchanged at 9 cents per gallon of retail fuel. The blender's income tax credit was increased

Table 6.4. (*continued*)

Date	Milestone Use	Comment
		to 60 cents per gallon for 190-proof alcohol and 45 cents for 150–90 proof.
1985	Industry shakeout	Of the 163 commercial ethanol plants existing in 1985, only 74 (45 percent) were operating, producing 595 million gallons per year. The high failure rate was partially the result of poor business judgment and bad engineering.
1988	First use of ethanol as an oxygenate	Denver, Colorado, mandated oxygenated fuels for winter use to control carbon monoxide emissions. Other cities followed.
1990	Omnibus Budget Reconciliation Act	The Act (Public Law 101–508) decreased the gasohol tax exemption from 6 to 5.4 cents per gallon. Tax credits for neat ethanol sales remained unchanged at 6 cents per gallon. The expiration date was extended to 2002.
1990	Clean Air Act Amendments	The Amendments (Public Law 101–549) mandated the winter use of oxygenated fuels in 39 major carbon monoxide nonattainment areas and required year-round use of oxygenates in 9 severe ozone nonattainment areas in 1995.
1990	Ethanol industry changes	Ethanol plants began switching from coal to natural gas and adopting other cost-reducing technologies, estimated to reduce costs as by much as 10 cents per gallon. High-fructose corn syrup prices and markets increased, also encouraging expansion of wet mills and ethanol capacity.
1992	Energy Policy Act	The Act (Public Law 102–486) modified the excise tax exemption to accommodate blends of less than 10 percent ethanol resulting from more sophisticated blending strategies for pollution control. The tax exemption was set at 4.16 cents per gallon for mixtures containing 7.7 percent ethanol and 3.08 cents per gallon for mixtures containing 5.5 percent ethanol.
1994	Favorable Internal Revenue Service ruling	The IRS ruling extended the excise tax exemption and income tax credits to ethanol blenders producing ETBE.

(continued)

Table 6.4. (*continued*)

Date	Milestone Use	Comment
		Previously, the blended ethanol product had to be sold to final consumers for the credits to be received.
1994	EPA Renewable Oxygen Standard (ROS)	The ROS required that 30 percent of the oxygenates contained in fuels be produced from renewable sources—a provision generally considered a boon for the corn-ethanol industry.
1994	Conversion of corn fiber to ethanol achieved in a commercial facility	New Energy Ethanol Company of Indiana, in cooperation with the National Renewable Energy Laboratory, successfully achieved ethanol production from cellulose. Several other cellulosic ethanol conversion facilities have been proposed, using a wide variety of technologies, but none is commercial yet.
1995	American Petroleum Institute and National Petroleum Refining Association vs. EPA	A U.S. court ruled that the EPA's ROS was an unconstitutional constraint on commerce.
1995	Highest U.S. ethanol production capacity ever	U.S. ethanol production capacity has risen to 1.5 billion gallons per year, primarily through expansions in wet milling capacity. Of the existing capacity, 70 percent is wet milling (low cost with high-value coproducts), and 30 percent is from dry mills (higher cost, limited coproducts).

Source: Energy Information Administration, U.S. Department of Energy (1995).

4-cents-per-gallon exemption from Federal excise taxes to motor fuels blended with ethanol (minimum 10 percent ethanol) and granted a 10 percent energy investment tax credit for biomass-ethanol conversion equipment (in addition to the 10 percent investment tax credit available), and the Clean Air Act Amendments of 1990, which mandated the winter use of oxygenated fuels in thirty-nine major carbon monoxide–nonattainment areas and required year-round use of oxygenates in nine severe ozone-nonattainment areas in 1995.

There are several legislative initiatives since 1995 that are worth noting.[10] One is the Farm Security and Rural Investment Act of 2002 that established a Bioenergy Program in response to Executive Order 13134. The Bioenergy

Program issues payments to assist ethanol producers in expanding their ethanol production capacity.

The American Jobs Creation Act of 2004 included a Volumetric Ethanol Excise Tax Credit (VEETC) of 51-cents-per-gallon ethanol for gasoline suppliers producing ethanol-gasoline blends.

In addition to the VEETC, there are additional incentives for small producers. The Energy Policy Act of 2005 expanded on a policy originally introduced in the Omnibus Budget Reconciliation Act of 1990 by setting the credit given to small ethanol producers at 10 cents per gallon for the first fifteen million gallons of ethanol produced each year. Also included in the Energy Policy Act of 2005 was a provision requiring the Federal Trade Commission to address the question of whether sufficient competition exists in the ethanol industry.

The Food, Conservation, and Energy Act of 2008, was passed despite President Bush's veto. Though incentives for corn ethanol were reduced in this act, new incentives for the cellulosic-ethanol industry were implemented in order to assist in the development of cost-effective advanced biofuels to help meet the RFS set forth in EISA 2007. The blender's credit was reduced from 51 cents to 45 cents in January, 2009 per requirements set forth in the act.[11]

The United States is not alone in its pursuit of biofuel technologies. With many nations seeking to reduce petroleum imports, boost rural economies, and improve air quality, world fuel ethanol production was more than thirteen billion gallons in 2007.[12] While traditional ethanol leaders like the U.S., Brazil, Canada and the European Union continue to increase both the production and use of ethanol, new players in the global industry such as China and Japan are beginning to emerge. See table 6.5.

6.5. Examples of R&D Funded through the Biomass Research and Development Initiative

A variety of single as well as multiple-agency solicitations are included under the BRDI. One important initiative is an annual joint solicitation between USDA and DoE which has been in place since fiscal year 2002. The technical focus areas for this solicitation, as modified by the Energy Policy Act of 2005, are as follows:[13]

1. Feedstock Production through the development of crops and cropping systems relevant to production of raw materials for conversion to biobased fuels and biobased products.
2. Overcoming Recalcitrance of cellulosic biomass through developing technologies for converting cellulosic biomass into intermediates that can subsequently be converted into biobased fuels and biobased products.
3. Product Diversification through technologies relevant to production of a range of biobased products (including chemicals, animal feeds,

Table 6.5. World Fuel Ethanol
Production, 2007

Country	Millions of Gallons
United States	6,498.6
Brazil	5,019.2
European Union	570.3
China	486.0
Canada	211.3
Thailand	79.2
Colombia	74.9
India	52.8
Central America	39.6
Australia	26.4
Turkey	15.8
Pakistan	9.2
Peru	7.9
Argentina	5.2
Paraguay	4.7
Total	13,101.7

Source: Renewable Fuels Association (2007).

and cogenerated power) that eventually can increase the feasibility of fuel production in a biorefinery.

4. Analysis that provides strategic guidance for the application of biomass technologies in accordance with realization of improved sustainability and environmental quality, cost effectiveness, security, and rural economic development, usually featuring system-wide approaches.

The program has granted sixty awards since 2002.[14]

The 2007–08 solicitations under the BRDI include a USDA solicitation on Woody Biomass Utilization and joint research solicitation from DoE and USDA on Plant Feedstock Genomics for Bioenergy.

6.6. Conclusions

Renewable fuel standards are targets set by the U.S. government mandating the incorporation of specific volumes of renewable fuels into the transportation fuel supply over time. The RFS set forth by the EISA of 2007 is unique in that it mandates the incorporation of renewable fuels that are not yet commercially available. The Biomass R&D Act, as amended by the Food, Conservation, and Energy Act of 2008, is innovative in that it provides a cost sharing environment conducive for developing new domestic biofuels to meet the requirements of the RFS.

Notes

1. Note that government agencies have long been funding research on biofuels. BRDI created an interagency initiative on the topic and mandated that investments in biofuels be accelerated.

2. The Biomass Research and Development Act was motivated on the following premises: "Congress finds that—

(1) conversion of biomass into biobased industrial products offers outstanding potential for benefit to the national interest through... improved environmental quality [and a]... sustainable resource supply;

(2) the key technical challenges to be overcome in order for biobased industrial products to be cost-competitive are finding new technology and reducing the cost of technology for converting biomass into desired biobased industrial products;

(3) biobased fuels, such as ethanol, have the clear potential to be sustainable, low cost, and high performance fuels that are compatible with both current and future transportation systems and provide near-zero net greenhouse gas emissions;

(4) biobased chemicals have the clear potential for environmentally benign product life cycles;

(5) biobased power can... provide environmental benefits [and]... diversify energy resource options;

(6) many biomass feedstocks suitable for industrial processing show the clear potential for sustainable production...;

(7) ...technologies that result in further diversification of the range of value-added biobased industrial products can meet a key need for the grain processing industry;

(8) ...cellulosic feedstocks are attractive because of their low cost and widespread availability; and research resulting in cost-effective technology to overcome the recalcitrance of cellulosic biomass would allow biorefineries to produce fuels and bulk chemicals on a very large scale...;

(9) research into the fundamentals to understand important mechanisms of biomass conversion can be expected to accelerate the application and advancement of biomass processing technology by... increasing the confidence and speed with which new technologies can be scaled up and... giving rise to processing innovations based on new knowledge;

(10) the added utility of biobased industrial products developed through improvements in processing technology would encourage the design of feedstocks that would meet future needs more effectively;

(11) the creation of value-added biobased industrial products would create new jobs in construction, manufacturing, and distribution, as well as new higher-valued exports of products and technology;

(12) ...because of the relatively short-term time horizon characteristic of private sector investments, and because many benefits of biomass processing are in the national interest, it is appropriate for the Federal Government to provide precommercial investment in fundamental research and research-driven innovation in the biomass processing area and... such an investment would provide a valuable complement to ongoing and past governmental support in the biomass processing area; and

(13) several prominent studies, including studies by the President's Committee of Advisors on Science and Technology and the National Research Council...support the potential for large research-driven advances in technologies for production of biobased industrial products as well as associated benefits; and...document the need for a focused, integrated, and innovation-driven research effort to provide the appropriate progress in a timely manner.

3. See http://www.brdisolutions.com/default.aspx.

4. The Technical Areas specified by the Energy Policy Act of 2005 are as follows:

1. Feedstock Production through the development of crops and cropping systems relevant to production of raw materials for conversion to biobased fuels and biobased products.

2. Overcoming Recalcitrance of cellulosic biomass through developing technologies for converting cellulosic biomass into intermediates that can subsequently be converted into biobased fuels and biobased products.

3. Product Diversification through technologies relevant to production of a range of biobased products (including chemicals, animal feeds, and cogenerated power) that eventually can increase the feasibility of fuel production in a biorefinery.

4. Analysis that provides strategic guidance for the application of biomass technologies in accordance with realization of improved sustainability and environmental quality, cost effectiveness, security, and rural economic development, usually featuring system-wide approaches and Joint Solicitation Awards.

5. In addition to the federal blender's credit, many states offer a blender's credit as well. Though most of the U.S. market for biofuels is supplied by U.S. grown corn ethanol, a small fraction is supplied by imported biofuels. The blender's credit granted to petroleum companies for blending with imported ethanol is offset by a 2.5 percent *ad valorem* tariff as well as a 54-cents-per-gallon tariff established by the Omnibus Reconciliation Act of 1980 and extended to 2010 by the Food, Conservation, and Energy Act of 2008. The ethanol blender's credit applies, regardless of point of origin, but because the import tariffs are higher than the 45-cents-per-gallon blender's credit, they nullify the benefit of the domestic subsidy. Despite the tax disadvantage to producers of blending imported ethanol, the United States still does meet a small part of its demand for ethanol with imports. High blends of ethanol are incompatible with the existing petroleum distribution, storage, and transportation infrastructure in the United States because they mix easily with water and corrode pipelines. New infrastructure is therefore required for the E-85 blends that can be used in flex-fuel vehicles. There exists a 30 percent "fuel property tax credit" to encourage the construction of new E-85 facilities. In addition, mileage from flex-fuel vehicles is calculated liberally under Corporate Average Fuel Economy (CAFE) standards.

6. Section 230 of the EISA of 2007 reads as follows:

(a) Definition of Eligible Entity—In this section, the term "eligible entity" means—

(1) an 1890 Institution (as defined in section 2 of the Agricultural Research, Extension, and Education Reform Act of 1998 (7 U.S.C. 7061));

(2) a part B institution (as defined in section 322 of the Higher Education Act of 1965 (20 U.S.C. 1061)) (commonly referred to as "Historically Black Colleges and Universities");

(3) a tribal college or university (as defined in section 316(b) of the Higher Education Act of 1965 (20 U.S.C. 1059c(b))); or

(4) an Hispanic-serving institution (as defined in section 502(a) of the Higher Education Act of 1965 (20 U.S.C. 1101a(a))).

(b) Grants—The Secretary shall make cellulosic ethanol and biofuels research and development grants to 10 eligible entities selected by the Secretary to receive a grant under this section through a peer-reviewed competitive process.

(c) Collaboration—An eligible entity that is selected to receive a grant under subsection (b) shall collaborate with 1 of the Bioenergy Research Centers of the Office of Science of the Department.

(d) Authorization of Appropriations—There is authorization to be appropriated to the Secretary to make grants described in subsection (b) $50,000,000 for fiscal year 2008, to remain available until expended.

7. In February of 2007, the Department of Energy selected six cellulosic-ethanol plants to receive up to $385 million in federal funding (http://www.doe.gov/news/4827.htm). The six selected projects are described below:

- Abengoa Bioenergy Biomass of Kansas, LLC of Chesterfield, Missouri, up to $76 million.

  The proposed plant will be located in the state of Kansas. The plant will produce 11.4 million gallons of ethanol annually and enough energy to power the facility, with any excess energy being used to power the adjacent corn dry grind mill. The plant will use 700 tons per day of corn stover, wheat straw, milo stubble, switchgrass, and other feedstocks. Abengoa Bioenergy Biomass investors/participants include: Abengoa Bioenergy R&D, Inc.; Abengoa Engineering and Construction, LLC; Antares Corp.; and Taylor Engineering.

- ALICO, Inc. of LaBelle, Florida, up to $33 million.

  The proposed plant will be in LaBelle (Hendry County), Florida. The plant will produce 13.9 million gallons of ethanol a year and 6,255 kilowatts of electric power, as well as 8.8 tons of hydrogen and 50 tons of ammonia per day. For feedstock, the plant will use 770 tons per day of yard, wood, and vegetative wastes and eventually energycane. ALICO, Inc. investors/participants include: Bioengineering Resources, Inc. of Fayetteville, Arkansas; Washington Group International of Boise, Idaho; GeoSyntec Consultants of Boca Raton, Florida; BG Katz Companies/JAKS, LLC of Parkland, Florida; and Emmaus Foundation, Inc.

- BlueFire Ethanol, Inc. of Irvine, California, up to $40 million.

  The proposed plant will be in Southern California. The plant will be sited on an existing landfill and produce about 19 million gallons of ethanol a year. As feedstock, the plant would use 700 tons per day of sorted green waste and wood waste from landfills. BlueFire Ethanol, Inc. investors/participants include: Waste Management, Inc.; JGC Corporation; MECS Inc.; NAES; and PetroDiamond.

- Broin Companies of Sioux Falls, South Dakota, up to $80 million.

  The plant is in Emmetsburg (Palo Alto County), Iowa, and after expansion, it will produce 125 million gallons of ethanol per year, of which roughly 25 percent will be cellulosic ethanol. For feedstock in the production of cellulosic ethanol, the plant expects to use 842 tons per day of corn fiber, cobs, and stalks. Broin Companies participants include: E. I. du Pont de Nemours and Company; Novozymes North America, Inc.; and DOE's National Renewable Energy Laboratory.

- Iogen Biorefinery Partners, LLC, of Arlington, Virginia, up to $80 million.

  The proposed plant will be built in Shelley, Idaho, near Idaho Falls, and will produce 18 million gallons of ethanol annually. The plant will use 700 tons per day of agricultural residues including wheat straw, barley straw, corn stover, switchgrass, and rice straw as feedstocks. Iogen Biorefinery Partners, LLC investors/partners include: Iogen Energy Corporation; Iogen Corporation; Goldman Sachs; and The Royal Dutch/Shell Group.

- Range Fuels (formerly Kergy Inc.) of Broomfield, Colorado, up to $76 million.

  The proposed plant will be constructed in Soperton (Treutlen County), Georgia. The plant will produce about 40 million gallons of ethanol per year and 9 million gallons per year of methanol. As feedstock, the plant will use 1,200 tons per day of wood residues and wood-based energy crops. Range Fuels investors/participants include: Merrick and Company; PRAJ Industries Ltd.; Western Research Institute; Georgia Forestry Commission; Yeomans Wood and Timber; Truetlen County Development Authority; BioConversion Technology; Khosla Ventures; CH2MHill; Gillis Ag and Timber.

8. Ethanol mixes readily with water and causes corrosion to gasoline pipelines.

9. In addition to the inconvenience of filling up with E-85, consumers' lack of awareness of engine type contributes to underutilization of high ethanol blends.

10. See Congressional Research Service (2006).

11. See Congressional Research Service (2008).

12. Renewable Fuels Association (2007), http://www.ethanolrfa.org/resource/facts/trade.

13. Biomass Research and Development Initiative, http://www.brdisolutions.com/default.aspx

14. The program dedicated $157 million between 2002 and 2006.

7

University Research Parks

Prospective Infrastructural Policies

7.1. Introduction

The university research park (URP) organizational structure is the public/private partnership described in this chapter through which government acts as entrepreneur.[1] Government, primarily state government, allocates funds to support URPs. The allocation of these funds is direct, in terms of state resources earmarked for the creation of a park, as well as indirect in the sense that a state university allocates its operating funds for the creation and ongoing activities of the park.[2] In this chapter, we focus on the government's indirect involvement in support of such public/private partnerships. See table 7.1. Among the many objectives of the park, one important one is that the park serves as an environment conducive for industry/university research collaboration and academic entrepreneurship. Thus, the environment created by the park is a technology infrastructure that facilitates leveraging both public (i.e., the university or public-sector tenants in the park)[3] and private R&D. The innovative policy action of using public resources to establish and/or expand existing parks is The Building a Stronger America Act.

This chapter focuses on pending legislation in the U.S. Congress—The Building a Stronger America Act—that is aimed at expanding the size and scope of existing URPs and helping to create new URPs. Unlike in the previous chapters in which we generally discussed public sector initiatives from a retrospective point of view—the exceptions being IPv6 in chapter 5 and

Table 7.1.   Public/Private Partnerships: University Research Park

Government Involvement	Economic Objective	
	Leverage Public-Sector R&D	Leverage Private-Sector R&D
Indirect	university research park	university research park
Direct		
Financial Resources	...	...
Infrastructural Resources	...	...
Research Resources	...	...

biofuels in chapter 6—and accordingly offered descriptive commentary on the extent to which parties affected or targeted were inhibited by the entrepreneurial risk germane to the innovative policy, in this chapter a prospective point of view is taken because of the topical nature of the innovative policy action discussed.

A federally guaranteed loan program to expand or build URPs is the innovative policy action subject of this chapter. The resulting environment—technology infrastructure—is expected to lessen barriers to innovation (see table 1.2) by reducing technical risk (e.g., through expanded R&D activities). The entrepreneurial risk associated with the expansion and creation of new URPs is if the new park facilities will be a technological milieu to attract tenants, and if so, if the tenants will actively participate in the two-way flow of knowledge between the university and the park. See table 7.2.

Table 7.2.   Government as Entrepreneur: University Research Park

Public/Private Partnership	Technology Infrastructure	Innovative Policy Action	Entrepreneurial Risk
University research park	Environment conducive for industry/ university research collaboration and academic entrepreneurship	The Building a Stronger America Act: use of public resources to establish and/or expand existing parks	If the new or expanded park will attract tenants, and if so, whether they will actively participate in the two-way flow of knowledge between the university and the park

7.2. Evolution of Public Policy toward University Research Parks

A URP is a cluster of technology-based organizations that are located on or near a university campus in order to benefit from the university's knowledge base and ongoing research; the university not only transfers knowledge but expects to develop knowledge more effectively given the association with the tenants in the research park (Link and Scott 2007).[4] URPs have various goals, including facilitating university-based technology transfer, promoting new firm creation, encouraging the growth of existing technology-based firms, attracting firms involved in leading-edge technologies, enhancing strategic alliances, and contributing to regional economic growth and development. The end result is that URPs are designed to enhance the performance of tenant firms, to enhance the university's research activities, and to act as an anchor for regional economic growth and development.

There are more than one hundred URPs in operation in the United States with another twenty-five plus currently in the planning stage. Over time, the number of URPs in operation has increased. Dating from Stanford University Research Park, founded in 1951, the number of URPs being formed has followed three phases of growth.[5] The first phase dates from 1951 to about 1980. During this period fourteen parks were founded and are still in operation. From 1981 to about 1992 there was an explosion of new park formations; of the parks founded through 1992, forty-seven are still in operation. The third phase dates from 1993 to the present during which the number of parks founded each year is sporadic, and of those founded and still in operation there is a distinct technology focus to each (e.g., information technology, biotechnology).

On July 22, 2004, U.S. Senator Bingaman from New Mexico introduced a bill, S. 2737, The Science Park Administration Act of 2004, to facilitate the development of science parks.[6] The premise on which the bill was based is: "It is in the best interests of the Nation to encourage the formation of science parks to promote the clustering of innovation through high technology activities," where a science park means "a group of interrelated companies and institutions, including suppliers, service providers, institutions of higher education [i.e., universities], start-up incubators, and trade associations that cooperate and compete and are located in a specific area whose administration promotes real estate development, technology transfer, and partnerships between such companies and institutions...."

Building on the premise of S. 2737, U.S. Senator Pryor from Arizona introduced on May 11, 2007, a bill: S. 1373, The Building a Stronger America Act. Bill S. 1373 provides grants and loan guarantees for the development and construction of science parks to promote the clustering of innovation through high-technology activities. If passed, the Secretary of Commerce would be authorized to award grants for the development of feasibility studies and plans for the construction of new, or the expansion of existing, science [or research or technology] parks.

Both the Bingaman and Pryor bills are innovative amendments to the Stevenson-Wydler Technology Innovation Act of 1980 (see chapter 3) because, even at the time of the introduction of Senator Pryor's bill, there was little systematic information to support the contention that "[i]t is in the best interest of the Nation to encourage the formation of science parks to promote the clustering of innovation through high technology activities."

The systematic information that existed at that time to support the underlying premise of this bill was at best anecdotal. Aside from the fact that the number of URPs had increased over time, as shown in figure 7.1 (discussed below), and aside from the fact that several of the earliest founded parks had grown to international prominence—such as Stanford Research Park in California, founded in 1951, and Research Triangle Park in North Carolina, founded in 1959—there was no conclusive evidence that URPs are part of a national innovation system and there was no conclusive evidence about the net social (e.g., national, regional, or local) returns from investments in the formation and maintenance of parks.[7] Thus, this public-policy effort is certainly one that is characterized by entrepreneurial risk.[8, 9]

Many nations' sectors have to varying degrees informally encouraged the formation of industry/university linkages. France's central government, like that of Japan, the Netherlands and the United Kingdom, has actively fostered the creation of science parks (Westhead 1997; Hilpert and Ruffieux 1991; Goldstein and Luger 1990), and Germany has long promoted academic innovation centers to incubate and develop small- and medium-sized enterprises (Sternberg 1990).

7.3. Background Information on URPs

The term *research park* is more prevalent in the United States, the term *science park* is more prevalent in Europe, and the term *technology park* is more prevalent in Asia. We will use the term *research park* throughout this chapter. Because URPs are a relatively new form of public/private partnership, we carefully set forth accepted definitions not only to clarify the concept but also to emphasize the heterogeneity of parks' missions.

7.3.1. Definitions

A number of definitions of a *park* have been proffered in recent years. Beginning with the international definitions, the International Association of Science Parks (IASP 2002) offered the following:

A Science Park (or Technology Park, or Technopole or Research Park) is an organisation managed by specialised professionals, whose main aim is to increase the *wealth of its community* [emphasis added] by promoting the culture of innovation and the competitiveness of its associated businesses and knowledge-based institutions.

To enable these goals to be met, a Science Park stimulates and manages the flow of knowledge and technology amongst universities, R&D institutions, companies and markets; it facilitates the creation and growth of innovation-based companies through incubation and spin-off processes; and provides other value-added services together with high quality space and facilities.

The United Kingdom Science Park Association's (UKSPA, 2003) definition is more focused:

A science park is essentially a cluster of knowledge-based businesses, where support and advice are supplied to assist in the growth of the companies. In most instances, science parks are associated with a centre of technology such as a university or research institute. . . . A science park is a business support and technology transfer initiatives that:
- encourages and supports the start up and incubation of innovation led, high growth, knowledge based businesses.
- provides an environment where larger and international businesses can develop scientific and close interactions with a particular centre of knowledge creation for their *mutual benefit* [emphasis added].
- has formal and operational links with centres of knowledge creation such as universities, higher education institutes and research organizations.

The United Nations Educational, Scientific and Cultural Organization (UNESCO, 2004) defines a science park as

. . . an economic and technological development complex that aims to foster the development and application of high technology to industry. Research facilities, laboratories, business incubators, as well as training, business exchange and service facilities are located in the complex. It is formally linked (and usually physically close) to a centre of technological excellence, usually a university and/or research centres.

The characteristics of science parks [are to]:
- promote research and development by the *universities in partnership with industry* [emphasis added], assisting in the growth of new ventures, and promoting economic development;
- facilitate the creation and growth of innovation-based companies through incubation and venturing;
- stimulate and manage the flow of knowledge and technology amongst universities, R&D institutions, companies and markets;
- provide an environment where knowledge-based enterprises can develop close interactions with a particular centre of knowledge creation for their mutual benefit.

More specific to the United States, the Association of University Related Research Parks (AURRP, 1998) defined a research park in the following terms:

The definition of a research or science park differs almost as widely as the individual parks themselves. However, the research and science park concept generally includes three components:

- A real estate development
- An organizational program of activities for technology transfer
- A partnership between academic institutions, government and the private sector

The AURRP recently changed its name to the Association of University Research Parks (AURP 2007), and it set forth the following definition for a university research park:

A university research park is defined by AURP as a property-based venture, which has:

- Master or planned property and buildings designed primarily for private/public research and development facilities, high technology and science based companies, and support services.
- A contractual, formal or operational relationship with one or more science/research institutions of higher education.
- A role in promoting research and development through industry partnerships, in assisting in the growth of new ventures and promoting economic development.
- A role in aiding the transfer of technology and business skills between university and industry teams.
- A role in promoting technology-led economic development for the community or region.

The park may be a not-for-profit or for-profit entity owned wholly or partially by a university or a university-related entity. Alternatively, the park or incubator may be owned by a non-university entity but have a contractual or other formal relationship with a university, including joint or cooperative ventures between a privately developed research park and a university.

A priori, each of the above definitions of a park has limitations. In particular, the IASP definition only emphasizes the regional economic growth aspects associated with park activity, but in some European countries regional economic growth is the founding objective of many of their parks. The UKSPA definition appropriately emphasizes technology transfer from the university, but it is narrow in that it focuses on the growth of firms within the park. Although the recognition of "mutual benefit" by UKSPA suggests a two-way flow of knowledge, the UNESCO definition like that of the UKSPA refers only to a one-way knowledge flow from the university to the private sector. The AURP definition appropriately acknowledges that knowledge does flow in two directions between park tenants and the university. The AURP definition is appealing and formed the foundation for our working definition of a university research park. Thus, Link and Scott (2006b, 2007) posit the following definition of a URP: "A university research park is a cluster of technology-based organizations that locate on or near a university campus in order to benefit from the university's knowledge base and ongoing research. The university not only transfers knowledge but expects to develop knowledge more effectively given the association with the tenants in the research park."

In the United Kingdom, all research parks are located on or near a university. In other countries, the distance between the URP and the university varies. In the United States, for example, a number of URPs are located on or near a university as in the United Kingdom, but other UPRs can be a substantial distance from the campus due in part to the recentness of the formation of the park and thus the availability of land juxtaposed to the university (Link and Scott 2006b).

If the URP is on or directly adjacent to a university campus the university may own the park land and/or oversee, or at least advise on, aspects of the activities that take place in the park as well as on the strategic direction of the park's growth. Such oversight may include tenant criteria for leasing space in the park (Link and Link 2003).

7.3.2. Academic Literature on URPs

URPs are important for several reasons.[10] They are a mechanism for the transfer of academic research findings, a source of knowledge spillovers, and a catalyst for national and regional economic growth. This generalization about the role and impact of URPs follows indirectly from a vast literature in economics, geography, management, and public policy on the impact of basic research, which is largely performed at universities. Studies in the literature on the economics of innovation link investment in basic research to improvements in productivity growth at the firm and societal levels.[11] There is also a related literature in economic development, which focuses on the impact of research clusters on regional economic growth.[12]

The growth in URPs in the United States, as shown in figure 7.1, has stimulated an important academic debate concerning whether such property-based initiatives directly enhance over time the performance of corporations, universities, and economic regions. More practically, the growth in URPs has also led to interest among policymakers and industry leaders in identifying best practices in the formation and operation of such parks. Unfortunately, few academic studies directly address these issues. The lack of such focused research may be attributed to the somewhat embryonic nature of URPs per se (discussed below) and to the fact that most URPs are public/private partnerships, indicating that multiple stakeholders (e.g., community groups, regional and state governments) have influence over their missions and operational procedures. Thus, developing theories to characterize the precise nature of the growth models and managerial practices of parks can be somewhat complex and very difficult to test empirically. There are few managerial benchmarks to follow to ensure the growth and possible success of URPs; and, more generally, the place of URPs in a national innovation system is not yet well understood.

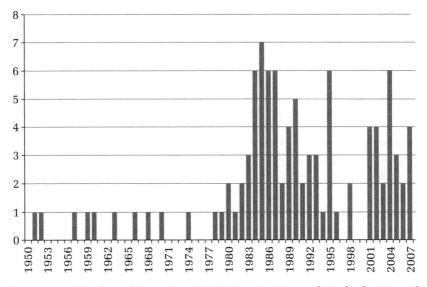

Figure 7.1. Number of Operating U.S. University Research Parks, by Year of Founding

As emphasized above, URPs are not well understood and attendant research on them is just beginning to burgeon. We speculate that this gap in understanding stems from the lack of well-defined constructs about what constitutes a URP, the variety of goals of a URP, and the general lack of clear metrics for measuring their impacts and successes.

If the URP is located on a university campus or directly adjacent to it, the university may own the park land and/or oversee, at least in part, the activities that occur in the park as well as provide advice on the strategic direction of the park's growth. Oversight may include tenant criteria for leasing space in the park (Link and Link 2003). Such criteria may specify particular technologies or state that the tenant must maintain an active research relationship with university departments and their students. When the park is located off campus, it is often the case that the park land is owned by a private venture—and sold or leased to tenants—but typically in such cases the university had contributed financial capital to the park's formation and/or intellectual capital to its operation. Therefore, there are elements of an administrative relationship between the university and these research parks.

In the United States, the form of the relationship between the university and the research park can be very explicit, as in the case when the university owns the park land and buildings and leases space to criteria-specific tenants (e.g., tenants involved in research in a particular technology area such as biotechnology); or very implicit, as in the case when the privately-owned park is juxtaposed to the university and the university owns and operates buildings on park land.

The formation of URPs is a post–World War II phenomenon.[13] See figure 7.1. Although data on park formations are very limited, examination of the number of URPs founded during the period from 1951 through 1998 for seven OECD countries[14]—the United States, the United Kingdom, Canada, France, Japan, Germany, and Italy—suggests that park formations increased sharply in the late 1970s and/or early 1980s in all countries.[15]

Link and Scott (2006b, 2007) identified several potential causes for the rise in the founding of URPs in the late 1970s and early 1980s in the United States. There were a number of U.S. policy actions in the early 1980s, initiated in response to the moderate decline in productivity growth in the early 1970s and the more pronounced decline in the late 1970s that extended into the early 1980s. These initiatives did include the Bayh-Dole Act of 1980, but also the R&E Tax Credit of 1981 and the National Cooperative Research Act of 1984.[16] As well, Link and Scott (2006b) argued that real R&D performed in U.S. industry had been decreasing since 1970 and not until 1977 did it return to its 1969 predecline level. Thus, in the late 1970s industrial firms were looking for cooperative research partnerships to expand their research portfolios, and universities were responding by providing research locations.[17]

The most complete time series of data on research park formations documented in the academic literature relates to URPs in the United States (Link and Scott 2003b, 2006b, 2007). As of the end of 2007, there are ninety-nine active URPs in the United States (these are the data that underlie figure 7.1), and at least another twenty-four are in the planning phase.[18, 19]

7.3.2a. Theories on the Formation of University Research Parks

Surprisingly, the extant literature in economics, geography, management, and public policy does not offer a fully developed theory about the formation of URPs. Case studies have documented the institutional history of a number of research parks, university affiliated or not.[20]

Scholars have not yet formally tied the emergence of URPs to cluster theory, although cluster theory has been applied to the formation of biotechnology and other science-based agglomerations of firms near universities, so the potential application is not unreasonable. Drawing on cluster theory—and location theory was, in part, a prequel to the popularization of cluster theory—one could argue that there are both demand and supply forces at work that result in the clustering of research firms near universities (Baptista 1998).[21]

On the demand side, there are sophisticated users of developed technologies within a park, and the search costs for such users are minimized by locating on a park. Of course, there are disadvantages associated with being in a park, mainly greater competition for the developed technologies. On the supply side, there is skilled and specialized labor available from the university or universities involved in the park in the form of graduate students and consulting faculty, although there is also more competition for that pool of human capital. Also, for a firm, location on a URP provides a greater opportunity for the acquisition of new knowledge—tacit knowledge in particular. As well, for the university, having juxtaposed firms provides a localized opportunity for licensing university-based innovations. The theory of agglomeration economics emphasizes knowledge spillovers and enhanced benefits and lowered costs caused by the presence of multiple organizations and the externalities they create (Swann 1998).[22]

Henderson (1986) and Krugman (1991) emphasize conceptually as well as empirically the importance of location per se with regard to knowledge spillovers. Localization has an effect on resource prices. To the extent that new technology embodies new knowledge, geographic closeness implies lower new technology prices and thus presumably greater usage. Firms achieve economies of scale more easily with newer technologies.[23]

Relatedly, Leyden, Link, and Siegel (2007) outlined a theoretical model, based on the theory of clubs, to describe the conditions under which a firm would be located in an existing URP. The authors conjecture that a URP acts like a private organization, so that membership in the research park is the result of mutual agreement between the existing park tenants including the university, the club, and a potential new member firm.

The decision to admit the new firm depends on the marginal effect of that firm on the well-being of the firms already in the park. For the representative on-park firm, the value of belonging to the park is the opportunity to engage in synergistic activities, which can be used to increase its profits in the output markets in which it participates, net of the direct cost (e.g., maintenance cost of being in the park and maintaining infrastructure) and indirect cost (e.g., congestion and competition for new knowledge) of being on the park.[24]

7.3.2b. Empirical Studies of University Research Parks

In addition to case studies documenting the institutional history of URPs in a variety of countries, as referenced above, the empirical literature on URPs broadly falls into five categories, and each is discussed below. Further, the URP empirical literature generally takes one of two forms: descriptive studies of survey data from which broad propositions are supported, or not, and econometric studies of public-domain or survey data from which specific hypotheses are tested statistically. Because the academic URP literature is burgeoning, both forms of analysis are important, and important and meaningful insights can be drawn from each.

Regarding factors affecting firm decisions to locate on a URP, the pioneering descriptive analysis of factors that attracted firms to locate on a URP was done by Westhead and Batstone (1998), based on a matched pairs sample (i.e., on-park firms and off-park firms) of 1986 U.K. data originally collected by Monck, Porter, Quintas, Storey, and Wynarczyk (1988) and later updated to 1992 and expanded by Westhead and Story (1994). The data are also summarized in Westhead (1997). Westhead and Batstone (1998) found that the major determinant of a firm's decision to locate on a URP is a desire to acquire access to research facilities and scientists at the university.

The ability to develop linkages between higher education institutions (HEIs) and firms is, according to Westhead and Bastone (1998), the key criterion by which to judge the success of the science-park phenomenon.[25] Hansson, Husted, and Vestergaard (2005) concluded from case studies of science parks in Denmark and the United Kingdom that an important role for parks is to foster the social capital needed to facilitate entrepreneurial growth and network formations within an HEI environment.

Finally, Leyden, Link, and Siegel (2007) modeled the decision of a firm to locate on a URP, or more precisely the likelihood that a firm will be invited to locate on a URP. Their empirical model shows that firms doing higher quality research are more likely to be invited to locate on a URP because of the spillover benefits to existing park tenants.[26] Certainly, more R&D-intensive firms confer benefits to existing tenants and to the university, but as well the locating firm must realize research externalities.

Regarding the formation of a URP and university performance, Link and Scott (2003b) quantified the growth in U.S. URPs over time.[27] They argued that URPs are an infrastructural innovation and universities will "adopt" this innovation over time much like product or process innovations diffuse throughout a market. In fact, when time-series data on park formations are analyzed as cumulative totals, the resulting S-shaped patterns of URP formations that result are not dissimilar to observed diffusion curves for innovations.[28, 29]

Based on responses by university provosts to a 2001 survey about the benefits associated with their universities' research parks, Link and Scott (2003b) report that the relationship of the university to the park was important. Universities with a formal relationship (e.g., an institutional arrangement such as ownership of the park land or advisory control over types of tenants) with their research park realize greater benefits from that relationship as quantified through increased publications and patenting activity, greater extramural funding success, and an enhanced ability to hire preeminent scholars and to place doctoral graduates.

The most complete study of the growth of URPs was by Link and Scott (2003b, 2006b).[30] They reported that the annual rate of employment growth in URPs is greater the closer, in miles, the park is to the university, *ceteris paribus*. This finding is expected based on cluster and location theory.[31] They also found that URPs' housing incubator facilities—and about one-half the URPs in the United States have an incubator facility—grow slower than parks without them, *ceteris paribus*. This finding reflects the fact that incubators assist the growth of small firms and then those firms leave the park for other locations.[32]

Regarding the locational advantages for a firm being on a URP, the most complete evidence about the economic effects on firm performance of being located on a URP is from the United Kingdom. Several studies were based on selected years of longitudinal data consisting of performance indicators for firms located on URPs and matched pairs of firms not located on URPs.[33] Researchers have generally found no difference between the closure rates of firms located on URPs and similar firms not located on URPs, implying that sponsored park environments did not significantly increase the probability of business survival or enhance job creation.

With respect to the importance of the university, Westhead and Storey (1994, 1997) found, from matched pairs of firms in the data for the United Kingdom for 1986 and 1992, a higher survival rate among science park firms with a university relationship than firms without such a relationship. Examining descriptively differences in R&D outputs (i.e., counts of patents, copyrights, and new products or services) and inputs (i.e., percentage of scientists and engineers in total employment, the level and intensity of R&D expenditure, and information on the thrust and nature of the research undertaken by the firm) of firms located on URPs and similar firms located off URPs, Westhead (1997) found no significant differences between the on-park and off-park firms. However, Siegel, Westhead, and Wright (2003), examining the Westhead and Story (1994) data, found that on-park firms have slightly higher research productivity than comparable off-park firms, where productivity is measured in terms of generating new products and services and patents, but not copyrights.[34]

There have also been several evaluation studies of Swedish science parks. Lindelöf and Löfsten (2003, 2004) conducted a matched pairs analysis of 134 on-park and 139 off-park Swedish firms for 1999 using descriptive techniques similar to those employed by Westhead and Storey (1994). The authors reported that there are insignificant differences between science park and non-science park firms in terms of patenting and new products. However, they found that firms located on science parks appear to have different strategic motivations than comparable off-park firms. More specifically, they seem to place a stronger emphasis on innovative ability, sales and employment growth, market orientation, and profitability.[35]

Fukugawa (2006) analyzed the 2003 value added to firms by Japanese science parks, and, unlike the United Kingdom but like the United States, in Japan not all science parks are associated with a university. He found that firms located on these parks are more likely than observationally equivalent off-park firms to develop links with universities. It appears that the range of these universities is not necessarily localized. The author also reported that on-park firms are not encouraged to develop linkages with universities more than off-park firms are. Taken together, these findings show that localized spillovers from parks are not as great as they could be.[36]

Regarding the regional economic development impact of URPs, the evidence is slim. Most URPs have financial support either directly through a governmental growth initiative or through targeted taxes. One rationale for public support of URPs is that they have the ability to leverage regional economic growth. Goldstein and Luger (1990) initiated the research in the United States on the spillover benefits from a URP to the regional economy. They argued, conceptually, that the potential economic development impacts of a URP include: location of new R&D activity, R&D firm spin-offs, location of new manufacturing activities and attendant supply chain businesses, and increased firm productivity.[37]

7.4. Conclusions

In 2002, the NSF held a workshop to discuss with academics and university administrators the economics of URPs.[38] The NSF wanted to learn about URPs in general and to begin to think about URPs as part of our national innovation system. In late 2007, the NSF convened a follow-up workshop to discuss how the academic and professional literatures have progressed and how specific U.S. parks functioned.[39] And, in early 2008, the National Academy of Sciences convened a panel of world experts to discuss global trends in URPs and how parks compared across countries.

The Building a Stronger America Act will, if passed by Congress, foster the expansion of existing parks and the construction of new parks. As parks grow in size, their scope of research will expand and the opportunity for a two-way flow of knowledge between the park (i.e., its tenants) and the university (i.e., its faculty) will increase, and we expect that potential park tenants will, over time, be less inhibited by the uncertainty associated with locating in a park and participating in the two-way flow of knowledge.

Notes

1. As discussed below, we prefer the term *research park*, but many casually use the term *science park*, or *technology park*, interchangeably.

2. Link (2008) reported, based on data from the Association of University Related Research Parks (AURRP 1998), that over 80 percent of UPRs rely in one way or another on public funds.

3. Although many private universities have research parks, those universities still have a degree of publicness in the sense that much of their internal research agenda is publicly funded.

4. Some parks are juxtaposed to a university, but the park and the university have no formal relationship. We do not include such parks in our conceptualization of a URP.

5. These three phases of growth are our ad hoc characterization of what occurred in the United States.

6. The Bill was not passed. Senator Bingaman reintroduced it on July 29, 2005 as S. 1581, but it too was not passed.

7. The elements of a national innovation system include competitive firms and a competitive environment, an effective educational system, strong university research, a legal system with property rights, and a capital market that includes venture capital (Nelson 1993; Cohen 2002).

8. The Senate Committee on Commerce, Science and Transportation held hearings in October 2007 about the Pryor bill.

9. Hand-in-hand with public-sector support is the need for public accountability, namely the development and implementation of evaluation methods and tools not only to support the assumption that URPs are in fact an important element of the national innovation system but also to quantify the net spillover benefits that result from public-sector support. The matched pairs studies discussed below are a preliminary form of evaluation. That is, it is useful to know that there is evidence that firms on a research park are more productive than firms not on a research park, *ceteris paribus*. However, when substantial public-sector resources are devoted to park formations, a more in-depth evaluation approach is warranted, namely the application of what Link and Scott (2001) call the spillover evaluation method. The spillover evaluation method applies to publicly funded, privately performed research projects, and in the case of URPs, research project is defined in terms of the research activities that occur in the park rather than simply the construction of the park. There are important projects where economic performance can be improved with public funding of privately performed research. Public funding is needed when socially valuable projects (i.e., research on a URP) would not be undertaken without it. If their expected rate of return from creating a university research park environment falls short of their required rate, called the hurdle rate, then the university or local firms would not invest in the research park environment. Nonetheless, if the benefits of the research spill over to consumers and to firms other than the ones investing in the research, the social rate of return may exceed the appropriate hurdle rate, even though the private rate of return falls short of the private hurdle rate. It would then be socially valuable to have the investments made, but since the university or local firms will not make them without public support, the public sector should support the investments. By providing public funding, thereby reducing the investment needed from the university and local firms doing the research, the expected private rate of return can be increased above the hurdle rate. In this case, the public sector's support may also suggest, or affirm, the possibility of a market for a successful project, thus reducing the investors' perceived risk as well as increasing the initial investment they are willing to make. Thus, because of the public subsidy, the university and local firms are willing to perform the research that is socially desirable because much of its output spills over to other firms in the park and sectors in the local and national economy. The question asked in the spillover evaluation method is one that facilitates an economic understanding of the potential returns to public-sector support for a portion of private-sector research, namely: What proportion of the total profit stream generated by the university's and local firms' research and innovation does the university and local firms expect to capture; and hence, what proportion is not appropriated but is instead captured by others that use knowledge generated by the URP research to produce competing

products for the social good? Link and Scott (2007) concluded that URPs should not a priori be considered a primary element of a nation's innovation system. That point of view, which evidently is held by a significant group in the U.S. Congress as well as by policymakers in other nations, needs to be substantiated through more studies. Successful two-way knowledge flow between universities and industry is a key ingredient for a national innovation system, and we do have evidence that URPs play a role in that knowledge flow. However, URPs are not a sine qua non of the knowledge flow. Perhaps, consistent with the findings of the survey of university provosts reported in Link and Scott (2003b), URPs fall under the broader category of an effective educational system. However, URPs may in the future warrant a higher status, especially as technological lifecycles continue to shorten and as basic research at universities (and to a growing extent at national laboratories [Wessner 1999, 2001]) and applied research and development {R in R&D refers to basic and applied research and we are only talking about applied research here} in industry become more intertwined.

10. This section draws directly from Link and Scott (2007).

11. See Adams (1990); Griliches (1986); Lichtenberg and Siegel (1991); Link (1981a, 1981b); Link and Siegel (2003); and Mansfield (1980).

12. See Porter (2001a, 2001b); and Swann, Prevezer, and Stout (1998).

13. Antonelli (2008, p. 212) notes: "A shift in the role and the organisation of the university within the economic system has been taking place in the last 20 years. New aspects...of the academic institution emerge as key factors. The interaction between the academic and the business system is changing, and new mechanisms have been implemented."

14. These data come from the Association of University Related Research Parks (AURRP 1998). This data set represents the most encompassing set of information about URPs that is publicly available, but, as discussed by Link and Scott (2003b, 2006b), it is not complete because the information comes from AURRP members and not all worldwide URPs are members. Nevertheless, the AURRP data are a useful starting point to discuss trends in URPs formations.

15. Siegel, Westhead, and Wright (2003) suggested that during that time period, there were two important policy initiatives in OECD countries that are alleged to have accelerated the rate of knowledge transfer from universities to firms and that may have contributed to the sharp increase in park formations. These initiatives were targeted legislation designed to stimulate cooperation in research and development (R&D) between universities and firms and to institute a major shift, favoring universities, in the intellectual property regime. Examples of the targeted stimulation of cooperative research include various European Union Framework Programmes, and the enactment of the Bayh-Dole Act of 1980 in the United States (see chapter 3) illustrates the changes favoring universities in intellectual property.

16. These latter two initiatives are public/private partnerships that are discussed in detail in Link (2006).

17. It is important to note, too, that productivity growth declined in most industrial nations during about the same periods as it did in the United States. It is thus not unreasonable to hypothesize that the international trends suggesting a pronounced increase in park formations in the late 1970s

and early 1980s are coincidentally related to the increase in R&D that occurred in the productivity growth recovery periods (Link and Siegel 2003).

18. "At least" refers to the fact that these twenty-four planned parks come from Internet information. Some universities may be planning a park, but have not yet revealed such plans.

19. The U.K. Science Park Association (UKSPA 2003) reports that there are one hundred science parks in the United Kingdom, most of which are based on or near U. K. universities. According to Lindelöf and Löftsen (2003), there were, as of 2001, twenty-three science parks in Sweden. Phan, Siegel, and Wright (2005) identified, as of 2003, over two hundred science parks in Asia, with 111 based in Japan. China has over one hundred; Hong Kong and South Korea each report two parks; and Macau, Malaysia, Singapore, Taiwan and Thailand have one each. India established thirteen parks in the late 1980s, but with the exception of Bangalore, India's Silicon Valley, all have failed.

20. Castells and Hall (1994) describe the Silicon Valley (California) and Route 128 (around Boston, Massachusetts) phenomena; Luger and Goldstein (1991), Link (1995, 2002), and Link and Scott (2003a) detail the history of Research Triangle Park (North Carolina); Gibb (1985), Grayson (1993), Guy (1996a, 1996b), and Vedovello (1997) summarize aspects of the science park phenomenon in the United Kingdom; Gibb (1985) also chronicles the science/technology park phenomenon in Germany, Italy, Netherlands, and selected Asian countries; and Chordà (1996) reports on French science parks, Phillimore (1999) on Australian science parks, Bakouros et al. (2002) and Sofouli and Vonortas (2007) on the development of science parks in Greece, and Vaidyanathan (2008) on technology parks in India.

21. See also Goldstein and Luger (1992) and Westhead and Batstone (1998).

22. And, Audretsch (1998); Audretsch and Feldman (1996, 1999); Breschi and Lissoin (2001); Jaffe (1989); Jaffe, Trajtenberg, and Henderson (1993); Wallsten (2001); and Rothaermel and Thursby (2005a, 2005b) provide empirical support for the agglomeration effect.

23. Arthur (1989) underscored the related importance of network externalities with regard to such scale economies. David (1985) also argues in general—and his argument could apply particularly well to URPs—that chance or historical events can lock a technology on a particular path of development. If that technology had a university origin, then creating a URP, from the university's perspective, and locating on the park, from a firm's perspective, gives positive feedback to continue the path dependency of the particular technology. The idea of path dependency, according to Arrow (2000), has its origins in the early writings of economists Veblen and Cournot, but it also can be traced to the Nelson and Winter (1982) concepts about evolutionary economics.

24. Leyden, Link, and Siegel (2007) modeled the decision for a firm to join a URP based on the economic theory of clubs. That is, they conceptualize membership in the park in terms of an invitation from the "club" to join the park. Based on this framework, the optimal size of a park can be determined, and the factors that can induce a change in the optimal size of a park

can be identified. Consider a URP that acts as a private organization so that membership in the research park is the result of mutual agreement between the existing park tenants including the university—the "club"—and a potential new member firm. Among the population of firms that are interested in joining the park, let each be characterized by the quality of its R&D, q. Then, the population of such firms can be characterized by the distribution of q, $f(\mathbf{q})$. The decision to admit a new firm, the jth firm into the park depends on the effect of that firm on the well-being of the firms already in the park. Assume that there is some "representative" firm already in the park so that the relevant decision rule is whether the prospective member increases the well-being of the "representative" member. For the "representative" firm, the ith firm, the value of belonging to the park is the opportunity to engage in synergistic activities that can be used to increase its well-being, defined to be profits in the output markets in which it participates. Assume that the ith firm's potential to engage in synergistic activities is linked to its ability to assimilate new knowledge, that is, to its absorptive capacity, A_i. The ith firm's absorptive capacity is a positive function of the quality of its R&D, q_i. Hence: $A=A(q_i)$. The actual level of the company's synergistic activities, S_i, which is assumed to be less than or equal to its absorptive capacity, A_i, is assumed to depend on the following factors: the number of other firms in the park and the quality of their R&D as well as the order in which potential firms are invited to join the park. The level of synergy of the ith firm is a positive, though convex, function of the number of firms, N, in the park: $S_i=S(q_i, N \mid f(\mathbf{q})) \leq A(q_i)$ such that the first and second derivatives of S with respect to N are less than 0, and in the limit as $N \rightarrow \infty$, S approaches A. The ith firm engages in synergistic activity to generate profits, Π_i, in its output markets. Assume that profits increase at a diminishing rate with the level of synergistic activity so that $\Pi_i=\Pi(S_i)$ with the first derivative with respect to S being greater than 0 and the second derivative being less than 0. It follows that $\Pi_i=\Pi(S_i)=\Pi(S(q_i, N)\mid f(\mathbf{q})))$ with the first derivative with respect to N being greater than 0 and the second derivative being less than 0. Of course, there are costs associated with belonging to a university research park. Assume that the cost to the ith firm from belonging to the park consists of a fixed component and a marginal component. The fixed component is the ith firm's proportional share of total park overhead, which includes such factors as the installation and maintenance of basic infrastructure and park administration. The marginal component, which consists of advertising and marketing, physical maintenance of the park, and the cost of joint park activities, is assumed to increase at an accelerating rate with the number of firms in the park. Thus, the ith firm's cost function (for the costs of belonging to a university research park) can be written as $C_i=c_0+c_1N^2$. The marginal cost to the ith firm of from admitting a new firm into the park is therefore $dC_i/dN=2c_iN$. Whether the ith firm is better off as a result of a new firm joining the park, and hence, whether the new firm is invited to join the park, depends on the size of the marginal profits to the ith firm in its output markets (i.e., without inclusion of the costs associated with belonging to the research park), with the new firm, compared to the marginal cost to the ith firm, with the new firm.

Thus, the decision rule is admit if and only if $\partial \Pi_i / \partial N \geq dC_i / dN$. Thus, the equilibrium number of firms in the park will be that number of firms, N^*, that solves the ith firm's objective function to maximize profit.

25. Goldstein and Luger (1992) arrived at the same conclusion from their descriptive analysis of university-based and non-university-based research parks established before 1989 in the United States.

26. Leyden, Link, and Siegel (2007) measured research quality in terms of the level of a firm's R&D expenditures, and they hold constant in their regression analysis the extent to which each firm is diversified in the output market because diversification can also afford spillover benefits to existing park tenants. Their analysis of U.S. public firms strongly suggests that the likelihood of a firm locating on a URP—that is being invited to enter and agreeing to enter—is positively related to the level of its R&D, other things, including the firm's sales, being the same.

27. Link and Scott (2003b) used a Gompertz survival-time model.

28. The Gompertz model describes the adoption of the URP innovation as a stochastic diffusion process with an increasing hazard rate. The probability of the establishment of a URP by time t, $F(t)$, is: $F(t) = 1 - S(t)$, where $S(t)$ is the probability that for a particular observation, the adoption has not occurred by time t.

29. Link and Scott (2003a) also invoked this model to explain the growth in tenants entering Research Triangle Park, North Carolina. They argue that firms adopt the location of Research Triangle Park over time and thereby adopt the URP innovation.

30. Link and Scott (2003b, 2006b) created the database and identified, within a regression framework, correlates with the growth over time in the number of employees in the park. As of 2002, there were eighty-one URPs operating in the United States with another twenty-seven in the planning stage. Their regression model begins with a growth equation: $y(t) = a\ e^{gt}\ e^{\varepsilon}$, where $y(t)$ is the URP's employment t years after being established, a is a minimum efficient start-up scale for a URP, and g is the annual rate of employment growth of the park, and ε is a random error term. Link and Scott (2006b) hypothesized that g for a park is a function of various explanatory variables (e.g., distance from the university to the URP, and the presence of an incubator) as represented by the vector $\mathbf{X}$: $g = f(\mathbf{X})$.

31. It also follows from the empirical work of Adams and Jaffe (1996), which suggests that communication costs related to collaborative R&D activity increase with distance, and Wallsten (2001), which shows geographic proximity to other successful innovating firms is associated with the firm's own success.

32. There is a vast literature on the economics and management of business incubators and business incubation, much of which has been expertly reviewed by Hackett and Dilts (2004) and McAdam et al. (2006), and in the references therein. There is a void in research specifically related to incubators on URPs.

33. See Monck, Porter, Quintas, Storey, and Wynarczyk (1988); Westhead (1995); Westhead and Cowling (1995); Westhead and Storey (1994, 1997); Westhead, Storey, and Cowling (1995).

34. Their regression analysis is based on a model of the general form: **ResearchOutput** = f (*InnovationCapacity, SciencePark*), where **Research-Output** is a vector of alternative innovation- and research-related output measures relevant to a firm (e.g., number of new products and services), *InnovationCapacity* measures the internal capabilities of the firm (e.g., internal R&D expenditures), and *SciencePark* defines dichotomously if a firm is on a science park or not. Their findings are relatively insensitive to the specification of the econometric model and control for the possibility of an endogeneity bias (i.e., a firm being on a science park is not independent of, say, its technology focus and its R&D activity). This preliminary evidence suggests that university science parks could constitute an important spill-over mechanism because they appear to enhance aspects of the research productivity of firms.

35. Lindelöf and Löfsten (2004) also found that the absolute level of interaction between the university and firms located on science parks is low, but that science park firms were more likely to have formal (e.g., contracts for research) or informal (e.g., transfer of personnel) interactions with the university than non-science park firms. Ferguson and Olofsson's (2004) analysis of Swedish science park firms, using 1995 data, found no significant differences between park and off-park firms in terms of sales or employment.

36. This conclusion complements Felsenstein's (1994, p. 93) earlier finding that there is greater interaction between on-park firms and universities in Israel, using 1992 matched-pairs firm data, than between off-park firms and universities, but their interactions have "a weak and indirect relationship with innovation."

37. Goldstein and Luger (1992) also provide some of the first descriptive evidence, based on a 1989 survey of directors of research parks in the United States that URPs have indeed contributed to regional growth. In particular, surveyed park directors state that their park has improved the quality and reputation of the host university; and the park has leveraged population growth, new business start-ups, and employment opportunities especially among minorities. Shearmur and Doloreux's (2000) analysis of Canadian science parks reached a similar conclusion.

38. This workshop was convened at the University of North Carolina at Greensboro.

39. This workshop was held at SRI International in Arlington, Virginia.

8

Small Business Innovation Research Program

An Environment to Enhance Commercialization

8.1. Introduction

The Small Business Innovation Research (SBIR) program is the public/private partnership described in this chapter through which government acts as entrepreneur. The SBIR program leverages, through the direct provision of financial resources, private-sector R&D in small firms. See table 8.1. The use of public resources to target and support private-sector R&D in small firms lessens barriers to innovation (see table 1.2; much like ATP, on which see chapter 4) and creates a funded environment conducive for commercializable research (unlike ATP) that would not otherwise have occurred.[1] It is this funded environment conducive for commercializable research, created initially through the Small Business Innovation Development Act of 1982, that is the technology infrastructure. The entrepreneurial risk associated with the activities of the SBIR is if the funded research will be successful, meaning that it will result in a commercializable product, process, or service. See table 8.2.

8.2. A Brief History of the SBIR Program

The SBIR program helped to fulfill the government's mission to enhance private-sector R&D and to complement the results of federal research.[2] A prototype of the SBIR program began at the National Science Foundation (NSF) in 1977 (Tibbetts 1999). At that time, the goal of the program was

Table 8.1. Public/Private Partnerships: Small Business Innovation Research Program

Government Involvement	Economic Objective	
	Leverage Public-Sector R&D	Leverage Private-Sector R&D
Indirect	. . .	. . .
Direct		
Financial Resources	. . .	Small Business Innovation Research program
Infrastructural Resources	. . .	. . .
Research Resources	. . .	. . .

Table 8.2. Government as Entrepreneur: Small Business Innovation Research Program

Public/Private Partnership	Technology Infrastructure	Innovative Policy Action	Entrepreneurial Risk
Small Business Innovation Research program	Funded environment conducive for commercializable research	Small Business Innovation Development Act of 1982: use of public resources to target and support research in small firms	If the funded research will result in a commercializable product, process, or service

to encourage small businesses (hereafter firms)—increasingly recognized to be a source of innovation and employment in the U.S. economy—to participate in NSF-sponsored research, especially research with commercial potential. Because of the early success of the program at NSF, Congress passed the Small Business Innovation Development Act of 1982 (hereafter, the 1982 Act).

The 1982 Act required all government departments and agencies with external research programs of greater than $100 million to establish their own SBIR program and to set aside funds equal to 0.20 percent of the external research budget.[3] In 1983, this amount totaled $45 million.

The 1982 Act stated that the objectives of the program are:

(1) to stimulate technological innovation
(2) to use small business to meet Federal research and development needs
(3) to foster and encourage participation by minority and disadvantaged persons in technological innovation, and
(4) to increase private-sector commercialization of innovations derived from Federal research and development.

As part of the 1982 Act, SBIR program awards were structured as defined by three phases (National Research Council 2004; Wessner 2004, 2007).[4] Phase I awards are small, generally less than $100,000 for the six month award period. The purpose of Phase I awards is to assist businesses as they assess the feasibility of an idea's scientific and commercial potential in response to the funding agency's objectives.[5] Phase II awards typically range up to $750,000 over two years.[6] These awards are for the firm to develop further its proposed research, ideally leading to a commercializable product, process, or service.[7] The Phase II awards of public funds for development are sometimes augmented by outside private funding (Wessner 2000). Further work on the projects launched through the SBIR program occurs in what is called Phase III, which does not involve SBIR funds.[8] At this stage businesses needing additional financing—to ensure that the product, process, or service can move into the marketplace—are expected to obtain it from sources other than the SBIR program.

In 1992, the SBIR program was reauthorized until 2000 through the Small Business Research and Development Enactment Act. Under the 1982 Act, the set aside had increased to 1.25 percent; the 1992 reauthorization raised that amount over time to 2.50 percent and reemphasized the commercialization intent of SBIR-funded technologies (see point (4) of the 1982 Act above).[9] The 1992 reauthorization broadened objective (3) above to also focus on women: "to provide for enhanced outreach efforts to increase the participation of . . . small businesses that are 51 percent owned and controlled by women." The Small Business Reauthorization Act of 2000 extended the SBIR program until 2008 and kept the 2.50 percent set aside.[10]

Eleven agencies currently participate in the SBIR program: the Environmental Protection Agency (EPA), the National Aeronautics and Space Administration (NASA), the National Science Foundation (NSF), and the Departments of Agriculture (USDA), Commerce (DoC), Defense (DoD), Education (ED), Energy (DoE), Health and Human Services (HHS, particularly the National Institutes of Health [NIH]), Transportation (DoT), and, most recently, Homeland Security (DHS). In 2006, DoD maintained the largest program, awarding about 51 percent of total dollars and funding about 57 percent of total awards in that year. Five agencies—DoD, HHS, NASA, DoE, and NSF—account for nearly 97 percent of the program's expenditures, with HHS (which includes NIH) being the second largest program, accounting for 30 percent of awards and 19 percent of total dollars in 2005. See table 8.3.

Table 8.3. Small Business Innovation Research Awards and Dollars, FY2005

Agency	Phase I Awards	Phase I Dollars	Phase II Awards	Phase II Dollars	Total Awards	Total Dollars
DoD	2344	$213,482,152	998	$729,285,508	3342	$942,767,660
HHS	732	$149,584,038	369	$412,504,975	1101	$562,089,013
DoE	259	$25,757,637	101	$77,852,565	360	$103,610,202
NASA	290	$20,183,648	139	$83,014,853	429	$103,198,501
NSF	152	$15,054,750	132	$64,101,179	284	$79,155,929
USDA	91	$7,195,211	40	$11,738,536	131	$18,933,747
DHS	62	$6,158,240	13	$10,241,202	75	$16,399,442
ED	22	$1,646,603	14	$6,749,980	36	$8,396,583
DoC	34	$2,373,433	19	$5,469,846	53	$7,843,279
EPA	38	$2,652,216	14	$3,540,251	52	$6,192,467
DoT	7	$679,154	3	$1,765,468	10	$2,444,622
Total	4031	$444,767,082	1842	$1,406,264,363	5873	$1,851,031,445

Note: Department of Defense (DoD), Health and Human Services (HHS), Department of Energy (DoE), National Aeronautics and Space Administration (NASA), National Science Foundation (NSF), U.S. Department of Agriculture (USDA), Department of Homeland Security (DHS), Department of Education (ED), Department of Commerce (DoC), Environmental Protection Agency (EPA), Department of Transportation (DoT).

Source: U.S. Small Business Administration (2006).

8.3. Case Studies of SBIR Projects

The following seven case studies were conducted in 1999.[11] Although all were funded by the Department of Defense SBIR program, they nevertheless illustrate the scale and scope of the innovative activities funded under Phase II SBIR awards. As with SBIR awards, the funding agency, DoD in these examples, is the likely consumer of the resulting product or process technology.

8.3.1. Analysis and Prediction of Antenna Interactions

Matis, Inc., an Atlanta-based firm founded in 1990, received a DoD Phase II award for a project entitled, "A Novel Computational System for Real-Time Analysis and Prediction of Antenna-to-Aircraft and Antenna-to-Antenna Interactions." To summarize, there was at that time a major problem with antenna communication systems. If antennas have no obstructions, then signals are transmitted and received clearly. However, such an environment rarely exists. On aircraft and ships, there often are obstructions of one form or another. These obstructions could be communications hardware or parts of the vehicle on which the antenna system is mounted. It is therefore critical to the quality of the communication system that the antennas be in an optimal position to minimize interference. Matis, Inc. proposed to develop software to simulate the antenna's environment and to measure the communication quality of alternative antenna placements. Given simulated information on alternative placements, it is the responsibility of engineers to trade off communication efficiency with engineering feasibility.[12]

8.3.2. Imaging Automatic Gain Control

OPTS, Inc., a Huntsville, Alabama, firm founded in 1994, received a DoD Phase II award for a project entitled, "Imaging Automatic Gain Control for Target Acquisition, Automatic Target Recognition, and Tracking." According to the firm, it is important for a missile to know what it is going to hit as opposed to where it is going to hit. For example, a missile might see two vehicles, a tank and a truck, at a predetermined location. To be most effective, the missile should be able to distinguish between vehicles and thus hit the most militarily important one. To be able to do this, the missile guidance system must be able to translate infrared images to a pattern recognition program; however, there is tremendous noise in infrared imaging. Existing technology relies on what is called signal gain, meaning that the sighted image is enlarged in all dimensions. OPTS, Inc. developed hardware to install on missiles that will enhance images selectively, or apply gain selectively, so as to improve recognition. This will take place in real time on a missile.[13]

8.3.3. Virtual Reality Scene Generation

CG2, Inc., a Huntsville, Alabama firm founded in 1995, received a DoD Phase II award for a project entitled, "Virtual Reality Scene Generation by Means of Open Standards." To test a missile, it has to be developed, tested under controlled conditions, and then fired. The model must be fired a significant number of times to verify its capabilities. The cost for each firing is between $10 million and $15 million. CG2 investigated a lower-cost process for verifying the capabilities of a missile under development. The software that was developed is designed to run a hardware-in-loop process. After a missile is launched once, all of the information from that launch is stored in a simulation computer. The simulation computer is then connected to the circuitry of a new missile, and to an image scene generator. Then the image scene generator is connected to the missile, completing the loop. The loop first repeats for the new missile the flight of the tested missile. Then, there is what is called a validated simulation. Once the simulation is validated, the missile can be tested in various environments that are created by the image scene generator. For example, the image scene generator can tell the missile that it is seeing various things (e.g., a mountain), and it will measure how the missile reacts. The missile's reaction is stored in the simulation computer. This technology has the potential to save the DoD billions of dollars per year in unneeded missile firings.[14]

8.3.4. Resilient Video Communication

Summitec Corporation, an Oak Ridge, Tennessee, firm founded in 1987, received a DoD Phase II award for a project entitled, "Very-Low-Bit-Rate-Error-Resilient Video Communications." At the time of the award, the lack of available bandwidth was the technical constraint on video imaging, especially wireless video imaging. With limited bandwidth, transmission of pictures is difficult and slow, and video is nearly impossible. Summitec Corporation is developing a compression-like software that will select only the important pieces of information to transmit over a narrow bandwidth so that video images will be clear. The primary use of the software is in surveillance. Video information can be transmitted to planes to assist them in locational bombing.[15]

8.3.5. Intelligence Data Fusion

Bevilacqua Research Corporation, a Huntsville, Alabama, firm founded in 1992, received a DoD Phase II award for a project entitled, "A Dialectic Approach to Intelligence Data Fusion for Threat Identification." The project produced a software architecture that will make computers think more like people think. DoD had a strong desire to be able to do intelligent programming at the time the project began in the late 1990s. DoD had attempted intelligent programming in the past through what was called role-based expert systems. That technology worked fine in a FORTRAN world of "if this, then that." But, the needs of DoD were more complex, and thus an alternative technology was needed. The software developed took systematic concepts and translated them into numbers so that the computer could process them. For example, when people think of a concept, they do so in terms of a vector of characteristics of the concept. However, if two concepts are combined, the then vector of characteristics of the combined concepts will not necessarily be a linear combination of the individual concept vectors. Bevilacqua Research Corporation called this architecture a cognitive-reasoning engine.[16]

8.3.6. Non-Chromate Coatings for Naval Engine Components

MicroCoating Technologies, an Atlanta, Georgia firm founded in 1993, received a DoD Phase II award for a project entitled, "Non-Chromate Combustion Chemical Vapor Deposition (CCVD) Coating for Naval Engine Components." Hexavalent chrome is widely used in the navy as well as in industry. However, it is a known carcinogen, and thus its use creates a toxic waste problem. The U. S. Environmental Protection Agency (EPA) had long known of the problems associated with hexavalent chrome, but had not at the time of this award mandated that it cease to be used because, at that time, no replacement was available. Congress had given DoD an internal directive to find a replacement material; MicroCoating Technologies undertook the task of finding such a material. The firm's approach was based on a thin-film oxide that could be applied to metal during a CCVD process. During such a process, the thin film is deposited onto the metal substrate using a flame, resulting in a replacement molecular coating that performs like hexavalent chrome but has more environmentally friendly properties.[17]

8.3.7. Microelectromechanical Accelerometer

Optical E.T.C., Inc., a Huntsville, Alabama firm founded in 1990, received a DoD Phase II award for a project entitled, "High-G Microelectromechanical Accelerometer." The Air Force used, at the time of the award, light gas guns for testing the air dynamics of various devices. These guns are 300 to 500 feet long. Artillery shells or small missiles are shot through these guns and pictures are taken of events such as ionization, tumbling, and other aerodynamic properties. When these pictures are taken, the acceleration of the object must be known. Acceleration needs to be measured up to 120,000 Gs.[18] A sensor was needed that could be mounted on the object to measure acceleration in such an environment. The firm built such a sensor on silicon chips using infrared devices that can withstand the acceleration. The technology underlying the project is known as microelectromechanical systems.[19]

Table 8.4.   Descriptive Statistics on the National Research Council Survey of Phase II Small Business Innovation Research Awards

Agency	Phase II Sample Size	Respondents	Response Rate
DoD	3055	920	42%
NIH	1680	496	44%
NASA	779	181	34%
NSF	457	162	48%
DoE	439	157	47%
Total	6408	1916	42%

Note: NIH is within HHS; see Table 8.3.

8.4. National Research Council Evaluation of the Small Business Innovation Research Program

The Small Business Reauthorization Act of 2000 mandated that, among other things, the National Research Council (NRC) within the National Academies conduct "an evaluation of the economic benefits achieved by the SBIR program" and make recommendations for "improvements to the SBIR program."[20] In response, the NRC constructed a survey-based database on SBIR-awarded projects for five agencies: DoD, NIH (within HHS), NASA, DoE, and NSF.

The five-agency database has information on 1,916 Phase II projects funded between 1992 and 2001, as described in table 8.4.[21, 22] This quantitative information in the NRC database is based on extensive and balanced surveys. The purpose of the survey, among other things, was to quantify if the funded project would have been undertaken without the SBIR award, and if there were spillover benefits to society from SBIR-supported projects.[23] Answers to these survey questions provide some indication of the extent to which the entrepreneurial risk associated with the policy action of using direct funding to target and support research in small firms has been overcome. More specific information on the success of the SBIR program in overcoming entrepreneurial risk is in the following section of this chapter.

Table 8.5 reports descriptive statistics related to whether the funded project would have been undertaken without the SBIR award. To the extent that these expressed opinions represent what the firm's actual behavior would have been, in the absence of the award, the majority of firms responding to the NRC survey "probably" or "definitely" would not have undertaken their Phase II research project in the absence of SBIR support. The range of negative responses was 67 percent for NSF projects to 82 percent for DoE projects.

As discussed in chapter 1 (see table 1.2), there are at least eight factors creating barriers to innovation. These include: high technical risk associated with the underlying R&D, high capital costs to undertake the underlying R&D, long time to complete the R&D and commercialize the resulting technology,

Table 8.5.   Descriptive Statistics to the Survey Question: *In the absence of this SBIR award, would your firm have undertaken this project?*

Agency	Response Categories to the Survey Question				
	Definitely Yes	Probably Yes	Uncertain	Probably Not	Definitely Not
DoD	3%	10%	17%	33%	37%
NIH	5%	8%	14%	28%	46%
NASA	3%	15%	14%	36%	32%
NSF	4%	10%	19%	43%	24%
DoE	1%	4%	13%	44%	38%

underlying R&D spills over to multiple markets and is not appropriable, market success of the technology depends on technologies in different industries, property rights cannot be assigned to the underlying R&D, resulting technology must be compatible and interoperable with other technologies, and high risk of opportunistic behavior when sharing information about the technology. Based on the survey responses, and based on the NRC case studies (not summarized herein), SBIR funding appears to lower the capital costs associated with R&D. Others (e.g., Link and Scott 2001, 2005a) have found that inadequate capital costs to undertake the underlying R&D is more prevalent in smaller firms than in larger firms because larger firms can more easily benefit from economies of financial scope.[24] From the survey data, as reported in table 8.5, more than 50 percent of the respondents stated that they would "probably not" or "definitely not" have proceeded with their research absent the SBIR award.[25] This finding is similar to the comments in the examples in the previous section of this chapter (and these examples of previously funded SBIR projects did not come from the NRC evaluation study).

Regarding the spillover benefits to society from the funded SBIR Phase II awards, the responses in table 8.6 and table 8.7 illustrate that if the firms had undertaken the research project in the absence of SBIR funding, the projects would definitely not have been broader in scope and generally would have been narrower in scope, and they would have taken longer to complete by, on average, slightly more than twelve months. Unfortunately, information is not available on the ability of a firm to appropriate the spillover benefits—the underlying research knowledge—embodied in commercialized products or processes.

8.5. The Commercial Success of SBIR Projects

The entrepreneurial risk associated with the SBIR program is if the publicly funded research will result in a commercializable product, process, or service. Based on information from the NRC survey contained in table 8.8, it appears

Table 8.6. Descriptive Statistics to the Survey Question: *If you had undertaken this project in the absence of this SBIR award, this project would have been...?*

| | Response Categories to the Survey Question | | |
Agency	Broader in Scope	Similar in Scope	Narrower in Scope
DoD	7%	44%	50%
NIH	5%	44%	51%
NASA	10%	48%	43%
NSF	11%	5%	84%
DoE	0%	17%	83%

Table 8.7. Descriptive Statistics to the Survey Question: *In the absence of this SBIR award, the start of this project would have been delayed by about ___ months.*

Agency	Response
DoD	11 months
NIH	8 months
NASA	19 months
NSF	13 months
DoE	11 months

Table 8.8. Descriptive Statistics on the Percentage of Firms that Had Actual Sales of Products, Processes, or Services from Small Business Innovation Research Phase II Projects

Agency	Percent Commercialization
DoD	61%
NIH	58%
NASA	59%
NSF	63%
DoE	70%

that the SBIR program has overcome innovation barriers and has been successful in terms of this dimension.[26, 27] While we eschew a cross-agency comparison of the percentage of projects that had actual sales, it is clear that the probability of success is greater than the flip of a fair coin. Unfortunately, the SBIR-mandated evaluation did not include any matched pairs, so there is no way to tell if comparable (i.e., in terms of size, experience, and area of technology) small firms would have had similar success. That fact aside, it is a fair statement that on average, funded SBIR projects have been successful.

Regarding commercialization, Link and Scott (2009) proposed an entrepreneurial strategy for government to consider. Their analysis of DoD SBIR projects shows a positive correlation between the probability of commercialization and the presence of outside investment funds for the technology being researched. Link and Scott conjectured that a prediction market could be used to provide useful information to DoD to make the commercialization performance of the SBIR program more effective.

8.6 Conclusions

Much like the programmatic outcomes of ATP, the SBIR program has funded a significant amount of research in small firms that would otherwise not have been undertaken. And, in response to counterfactual questions, these small firms generally agreed that if they had undertaken the research on their own it would have taken longer to complete and would have been narrower in scope.

More important to the theme of this book, the small firms that received funding from SBIR are commercializing outputs from their research, and presumably, commercializing more and at a faster rate than if they did not receive SBIR support. Thus, we conclude (based on indirect evidence) that firms participating in the SBIR program have not been inhibited by entrepreneurial risk.

Notes

1. ATP was concerned with accelerating the development of generic technology.

2. This section draws on Link and Scott (2000); Audretsch, Link, and Scott (2002); and Wessner (2000, 2007, 2008). For a taxonomy of public/private partnerships, see Link (1999, 2006).

3. Since SBIR is a set-aside program, it redirects existing R&D funds for competitive awards to small businesses rather than appropriating new monies for R&D. The 1982 Act allowed for this percentage to increase over time.

4. As stated in the 1982 Act, to be eligible for an SBIR award, the small business must be: independently owned and operated; other than the dominant firms in the field in which they are proposing to carry out SBIR projects; organized and operated for profit; the employer of five hundred or

fewer employees, including employees of subsidiaries and affiliates; the primary source of employment for the project's principal investigator at the time of award and during the period when the research is conducted; and at least 51 percent owned by U.S. citizens or lawfully admitted permanent resident aliens. Our database does not cover projects funded under the related Small Business Technology Transfer (STTR) program, which has similar aims but different eligibility requirements.

5. "The objective of Phase I is to determine the scientific or technical feasibility and commercial merit of the proposed research or R&D efforts and the quality of performance of the small business concern, prior to providing further Federal support in Phase II." See http://grants.nih.gov/grants/funding/SBIRContract/PHS2008-1.pdf, page 1.

6. It is not uncommon, however, for NIH Phase II awards to exceed the $750,000 threshold. While NIH offers no research assessment–based justification, the NRC, as part of its evaluation of SBIR programs (discussed below) has recommended that NIH formalize criteria for larger awards (Wessner 2008).

7. "The objective of Phase II is to continue the research or R&D efforts initiated in Phase I. Funding shall be based on the results of Phase I and the scientific and technical merit and commercial potential of the Phase II proposal." See http://grants.nih.gov/grants/funding/SBIRContract/PHS2008-1.pdf, page 1.

8. "The objective of Phase III, where appropriate, is for the small business concern to pursue with non-SBIR funds the commercialization objectives resulting from the outcomes of the research or R&D funded in Phases I and II." See http://grants.nih.gov/grants/funding/SBIRContract/PHS2008-1.pdf, page 1.

9. The percentage increased to 1.5 in 1993 and 1994, 2.0 in 1995, and 2.5 in 1997.

10. At the time of writing this book, the SBIR/STTR Authorization Act was introduced in the House of Representatives as H. R. 5819. It would, *inter alia*, extend the SBIR program until 2010, increase agency set asides from 2.50 percent to 3.00 percent, and increase Phase I and Phase II funding limits to $300,000 and $2.2 million, respectively. If passed, we augur that additional legislation to support small firms will follow.

11. These studies draw on Link (2000) and were, by intent, focused on awards to firms located in southern states.

12. The technology to develop this software comes from previous research projects. Absent SBIR funding, Matis, Inc. would have taken on this project on a limited scale. Although the capital and labor costs to undertake this research are extraordinarily high, Matis, Inc. had previous investment relationships with firms and could acquire partial research funding from them.

13. Absent the SBIR award, the firm would not have undertaken this research. The reason is that the capital costs are very high and there are few investment sources. Also, there is a limited commercial market for this technology; hence, finding a commercial investor would have been, at best, extremely difficult.

14. Because of the high capital costs for this research and the lack of available funding sources, CG2, Inc. would not have undertaken this research in the absence of the SBIR award. Outside investors would not have

been interested because the commercial market is very small, and the technology can be imitated quickly.

15. Outside investors were not interested in this project because the commercial returns to the technology were not expected to occur quickly, and because the complementary technology (i.e., bandwidth) could change rapidly.

16. The company would not have undertaken this research absent SBIR funding for two reasons. One, it did not have access to sufficient funding and the commercial application of the technology would not have been readily understood by investors. Two, the architecture could be quickly imitated once commercialized. It made sense for the government to be the third-party investor, and thus to undertake the entrepreneurial risk, in this project.

17. This research project would not have occurred absent SBIR funding. In fact, the firm itself would not be operating absent the award. Venture capital was not available to support the technology, although industry would eventually need it, but not until the EPA mandated a replacement. The firm holds the flame deposition patent.

18. Human beings black out at 8 to 10 Gs.

19. The technical risk associated with this project was large because the sensors needed to be very small (i.e., 0.33in.^3).

20. Much of this section draws on Link and Wessner (2007).

21. In addition, the NRC conducted more than one hundred case studies.

22. The surveys were administered in 2005, thus assuming that all 2001-funded Phase II projects would be completed, and the firm would have had time to commercialize any resulting products or processes or services.

23. The survey asked many other questions related to project characteristics and commercialization efforts, but these two areas of questions are most in line with the implementation of the spillover evaluation method.

24. This is not to say that those advocating new products and new technologies in large firms do not encounter similar challenges in obtaining the necessary financial support.

25. Link and Wessner (2007) calculated that the probability that a project would "probably not" or "definitely not" have been undertaken in the absence of SBIR support decreases the larger the firm conducting the research. Based on their probit analysis, they concluded that the calculated probability of not undertaking the projects decreases by 2 percent for each 100 additional employees; the range of employees is 1 to 460 with a mean of 31.1. The estimated marginal effect of employment size is minimal.

26. The percentages in table 8.8 are based on all survey responses. No controls for survey response bias have been made.

27. See Link and Ruhm's (forthcoming) analysis of commercialization from NIH awards, and see Link and Scott's (2009) analysis of commercialization from DoD awards.

9

Conclusions

Our theme is that government acts as entrepreneur in the provision of technology infrastructure when its involvement is both innovative and characterized by entrepreneurial risk.[1] Thinking of government as entrepreneur is, we have argued, a unique lens through which to view particular government policy actions.

As summarized in table 9.1, we have, as means of illustrating our premise, summarized six innovative policy actions: the National Cooperative Research Act of 1984, the Omnibus Trade and Competitiveness Act of 1988, the Organic Act of 1901, the Biomass Research and Development Act of 2000 as amended by the Food, Conservation, and Energy Act of 2008, the Building a Stronger America Act (pending), and the Small Business Innovation Development Act of 1982.

Each of these six policy actions resulted in a public/private partnership that had the economic objective of leveraging either public-sector R&D or private-sector R&D, or both. See table 9.2.

Figure 9.1 summarizes the public/private partnerships (see table 9.2) that resulted from the innovative policy actions (see table 9.1) within the context of our nonlinear model of innovation (see figure 2.1). The public/private partnerships are shown in brackets. Our objective in using the nonlinear model of innovation for this illustration is to underscore the potential positive impact of government, when it acts as entrepreneur, on the economy and on society.

RJVs were discussed in chapter 3. Trends in U.S. RJVs were illustrated in an effort to underscore the entrepreneurial risk (i.e., if the benefits from

Table 9.1. Examples of Government as Entrepreneur: Summary of the Book

Public/Private Partnership	Technology Infrastructure	Innovative Policy Action	Entrepreneurial Risk
RJV structure	Legal environment conducive for cooperative research	National Cooperative Research Act of 1984: use of antitrust laws to stimulate private-sector R&D	If the benefits to firms from participating in an RJV outweigh the costs
Advanced Technology Program	Cost-sharing environment conducive for cooperative research	Omnibus Trade and Competitiveness Act of 1988: use of public resources to leverage private-sector R&D, that would otherwise not have been undertaken, through cooperative research	If the jointly funded research will be successful and if so, whether it will accelerate the development of generic technology
National Institute of Standards and Technology	Voluntary industrial standards	Organic Act of 1901: use of public resources to promulgate voluntary standards to reduce the technical and market risk of private-sector R&D	If the promulgated voluntary standard will be accepted by industry, and if accepted in a timely manner, whether it will enhance competitiveness
Biomass Research and Development Initiative	Cost-sharing environment conducive for developing domestic biofuels that are cost competitive with gasoline	Biomass Research and Development Act of 2000 as amended by the Food, Conservation, and Energy Act of 2008: use of public resources to accelerate the development of biofuels	If the publicly supported research will be successful in generating advanced biofuels to meet the renewable fuel standard

Table 9.1. (*continued*)

Public/Private Partnership	Technology Infrastructure	Innovative Policy Action	Entrepreneurial Risk
University research park	Environment conducive for industry/university research collaboration and academic entrepreneurship	The Building a Stronger America Act: use of public resources to establish and/or expand existing parks	If the new or expanded park will attract tenants, and if so, whether they will actively participate in the two-way flow of knowledge between the university and the park
Small Business Innovation Research program	Funded environment conducive for commercializable research	Small Business Innovation Development Act of 1982: use of public resources to target and support research in small firms	If the funded research will result in a commercializable product, process, or service

Table 9.2.   Public/Private Partnership Mechanisms and Structures: Summary of the Book

Government Involvement	Economic Objective	
	Leverage Public-Sector R&D	Leverage Private-Sector R&D
Indirect	university research park	research joint venture structure university research park
Direct		
Financial Resources	Biomass Research and Development Initiative	Advanced Technology Program Biomass Research and Development Initiative Small Business Innovation Research program
Infrastructural Resources	National Institute of Standards and Technology	National Institute of Standards and Technology
Research Resources	National Institute of Standards and Technology	National Institute of Standards and Technology

participating in a research partnership outweigh the costs) that surrounds the NCRA policy action even today. The jury is still out as to whether the benefits to all firms from participating in an RJV outweigh the costs. *Federal Register* filings suggest that the entrepreneurial risk associated with the passage of the NCRA remains; but, in contrast, the NSF-sponsored survey data, albeit not in the public domain, suggest that the firms affected by the NCRA were not inhibited by partnership participation—if not for all firms then certainly some.

The two RJV case studies discussed in chapter 4 clearly indicate that the R&D activity of firms recipient of ATP's public resources to leverage their R&D were not swayed by the entrepreneurial risk inherent in RJVs. Most of the participants in the PWB RJV and all of the participants in the flat panel display RJV agreed that in the absence of ATP funding, industry would not have undertaken the research. And, in response to counterfactual questions, all agreed that if industry had undertaken the research it would have taken longer to conduct and would have been more expensive. Thus, ATP's funding of RJVs did accelerate the development of the two generic technologies.

In chapter 5 we illustrated, through examples, that the research activities at NIST did in fact reduce the technical and market risk of private-sector R&D related to optical fiber and alternative refrigerant technology in a timely manner, and that action did enhance competitiveness. In these two examples, the entrepreneurial risk associated with the promulgation of standards did

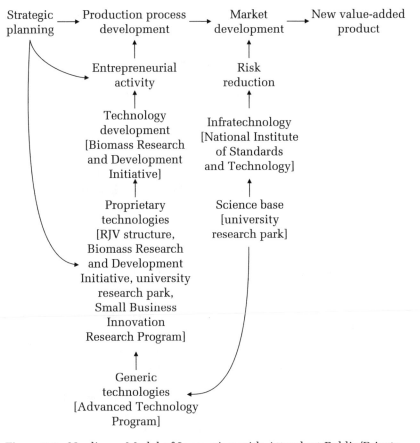

Figure 9.1. Nonlinear Model of Innovation with Attendant Public/Private Partnerships: A Manufacturing Firm

not inhibit industry accepting the standards in a timely manner. The adoption of the standards enhanced competitiveness. The due diligence of NIST did not similarly result in the same economic benefits with respect to ISDN or IPv6 technology. With respect to ISDN, NIST's actions did not remove all market risk; with respect to IPv6, the jury is still out. Nevertheless, NIST, that is government, did act entrepreneurially; it was just the case that the entrepreneurial risk associated with its actions inhibited firm acceptance.

As discussed in chapter 6, the U.S. renewable fuel standard is a target mandating the incorporation of specific renewable fuels into the transportation fuel supply over time. The renewable fuel standard set by the EISA of 2007 is unique in that it sets targets for the incorporation of specific types of advanced biofuels and requires the incorporation of renewable fuels that are not yet commercially available. In order to help meet the RFS, the government provides R&D support through the BRDI, designed to accelerate the development and commercialization of biofuels.

The Building a Stronger America Act will, if passed by Congress, foster the expansion of existing parks and the construction of new parks, as discussed in chapter 7. As parks grow in size, their scope of research will expand and the opportunity for a two-way flow of knowledge between the park (i.e., its tenants) and the university (i.e., its faculty) will increase and, we expect, that potential park tenants will, over time, be less inhibited by the uncertainty associated with locating in a park and participating in the two-way flow of knowledge.

Much like the programmatic outcomes of ATP, the SBIR program has funded a significant amount of research in small firms that would otherwise not have been undertaken. As shown through the data described in chapter 8 in response to counterfactual questions, these small firms generally agreed that if they had undertaken the research on their own it would have taken longer to complete and would have been narrower in scope. More important to the theme of this book, the small firms that received funding from SBIR are commercializing outputs from their research, and presumably, commercializing more and at a faster rate than if they did not receive SBIR support. Thus, we conclude (based on indirect evidence) that firms participating in the SBIR program have not been inhibited by entrepreneurial risk.

While the examples and data presented and discussed in this book were selectively chosen, based primarily on our previous research experiences and current research interests, they do illustrate the entrepreneurial dimensions of government's provision of technology infrastructure. While these examples and data are specific to the United States' policy experience, the concept of government as entrepreneur is, we believe, universal and is an applicable lens through which to characterize a subset of governmental policy actions.

All too often, policy initiatives that do involve entrepreneurial risk are criticized a priori because they lack precedent and/or predictable outputs as well as outcomes. When precedent and/or predictable outputs are not available, the status quo is to retreat to tried and true policy instruments. Our challenge to policymakers is to leapfrog the status quo and thereby to embrace innovative policy actions through their entrepreneurial behavior.[2]

Hopefully, this book will serve as a vehicle for policymakers and scholars to think about entrepreneurship, or more specifically the entrepreneurial actors in an economy, in a new way. Through examples we have discussed realistic situations—albeit specific to the United States and to U.S. innovation policy—that demonstrate our theme. As such, viewing government as entrepreneur broadens the scope of thinking about tools and frameworks available for providing technology infrastructure. If innovation policy to provide technology infrastructure is to be used effectively as a national competitive strategy, imitating what has been done in the past or what other nations are doing may well be a second-best approach. Perception of new infrastructure opportunities may require actions that are characterized by what we have called entrepreneurial risk.

With such policy actions comes accountability for how resources have been or are expected to be used, and an aspect of such accountability is systematic evaluation of the outputs and outcomes from the new infrastructure.[3] While there are a number of alternative approaches to evaluation accepted in U.S. policy circles (Link and Scott 1998, 2005a),[4] all rely on metrics that relate actual and/or expected benefits to actual and/or expected costs.[5]

Three elements are critical, from an evaluation perspective, when government acts as entrepreneur. The first element is a full identification of all benefits. This is a more formidable task than when traditional innovative policies are evaluated because of the myriad spillover benefits that could be associated with entrepreneurial risk (and by definition of uncertainty these spillover benefits will not be known a priori).

The second element is a consideration of a time period over which one can be certain that all spillover benefits have been identified both in concept and in value. A difficulty with any evaluation exercise, be it retrospective or prospective, is the time period of analysis. Often analysts rely on expert opinion to bound the evaluation study, but by the nature of the entrepreneurial risk associated with an entrepreneurial governmental policy action that is innovative, there may be no basis for expert opinion.

The third element is an appropriate discount rate to relate a stream of benefits to a stream of costs. In our opinion the discount rate should equal the rate at which those who are not excluded from the technology infrastructure would be willing to be taxed to have access to the technology infrastructure (i.e., the rate to borrow to purchase the public or quasi-public infratechnology were it marketable in a less than perfectly competitive market), plus an entrepreneurial risk factor that approximates the ability of the government to successfully supply the socially desirable amount of the technology infrastructure. But, because of the conceptual and operational difficulty in quantifying such a rate, an across-the-board benchmark rate is frequently used.[6]

These and related evaluation issues will be on the table for future academic and policy discussions because they are important, but they should not stifle government acting entrepreneurially.

Notes

1. By intent, this final chapter is a brief summary of the book as well as a call for more scholarly discussion on this topic.

2. Former U.S. Secretary of Energy Spencer Abraham stated in an address to Department of Energy senior staff on October 24, 2001: "...I believe we need to leapfrog the *status quo* and prepare for a future that under any scenario requires a revolution in how we produce, deliver, and use energy." While Secretary Abraham was charging his department to embrace leapfrog technologies, we are charging policymakers to embrace leapfrog policy actions.

3. In the United States, the concept of fiscal accountability is rooted in the fundamental principles of representation of the people and by the people.

However, as a more modern concept, accountability can be traced to the Budget and Accounting Act of 1921, and that Act began the modern tradition of fiscal accountability in U.S. public institutions. Building on the general concept of accountability established in the more recent legislation, including the Government Performance and Results Act (GPRA) of 1993, focus changed to performance accountability in order to improve the confidence of the American people in the capability of the federal government, initiate program performance reform, and improve federal program effectiveness and public accountability. More recent legislation has again focused on fiscal accountability.

4. Griliches (1958) and Mansfield, et al. (1977) pioneered the so-called traditional evaluation method. It involves the application of fundamental economic insight to the development of estimates of private and social rates of return to investments in R&D. Streams of investment outlays through time—the costs—generate streams of economic surplus through time—the benefits. Once identified and measured, these streams of costs and benefits are used to calculate rates of return, benefit-to-cost ratios, or other related metrics.

A different question should be considered when publicly funded, publicly performed investments are evaluated. Holding constant the very stream of economic surplus that the Griliches/Mansfield model seeks to measure, and making no attempt to measure that stream, the counterfactual evaluation method asks the question: What would the private sector have had to invest to achieve those benefits in the absence of the public sector's investments? The answer to this question gives the benefits of the public's investments—namely, the costs avoided by the private sector. With those benefits—obtained in practice through extensive interviews with administrators, federal research scientists, and those in the private sector who would have to duplicate the research in the absence of public performance—counterfactual rates of return and benefit-to-cost ratios can be calculated to answer the fundamental evaluation question: Are the public investments a more efficient way of generating the technology than private sector investments would have been? The answer to this question is more in line with the public accountability issues implicit in GPRA, and certainly is more in line with the thinking of those public-sector stakeholders who may doubt the appropriateness of government's having a role in the innovation process in the first place.

There are important projects where economic performance can be improved with public funding of privately performed research. The question asked in the spillover evaluation method is one that facilitates an economic understanding of whether the public sector should be underwriting the private-sector firms' research, namely: What is the net social rate of return from the program (including spillovers) compared to the net private rate of return? Or: What proportion of the total profit stream generated by the private firm's R&D and innovation does the private firm expect to capture; and hence, what proportion is not appropriated but is instead captured by other firms that imitate the innovation or use knowledge generated by the R&D to produce competing products for the social good? The part of the stream of expected profits captured by the innovator is its private return, while the entire stream is the lower bound on the social rate of return. In essence, this method weighs the private return, estimated through extensive interviews with firms receiving public support regarding their expectations of future patterns of events and future abilities to appropriate R&D-based knowledge, against private investments. The social rate of return weights the social returns against the social investments. The application of the spillover model to the evaluation of publicly funded, privately performed research is appropriate because the output of the research is only partially appropriable by the private firm with the rest spilling over to society. The extent of the spillover of such knowledge with public-good characteristics determines whether or not the public sector should fund the research.

5. For an evaluation of a public/private partnership, two time series of data are needed. One time series is on the costs associated with the partnership, public costs and private costs. The other time series is on the benefits to those whose innovative activity is being leveraged, measured in constant dollars. Several metrics are common in evaluations, especially when the traditional or counterfactual evaluation method is used.

The internal rate of return (IRR) is the value of the discount rate, i, that equates the net present value (NPV) of the stream of net benefits (benefits less costs associated with a research project to zero. The time series runs from the beginning of the research project, $t=0$, to a terminal point, $t=n$.

Mathematically,

$$NPV = [(B_0 - C_0)/(1+i)^0] + \ldots + [(B_n - C_n)/(1+i)^n] = 0$$

where, $(B_t - C_t)$ represents the net benefits associated with the project in year t, and n represents the number of time periods—years in the case studies below—being considered in the evaluation. For unique solutions for i, the IRR can be compared to a value, r, that represents the opportunity cost of funds invested by the technology-based public institution. Thus, if the opportunity cost of funds is less than the internal rate of return, the project was worthwhile from an ex post social perspective.

The ratio of benefits-to-costs (B/C) is the ratio of the present value of all measured benefits to the present value of all measured costs. Both benefits and costs are referenced to the initial time period, $t=0$, when the project began as:

$$B/C = \left[\sum\nolimits_{t=0 \text{ to } t=n} B_t/(1+r)^t\right] \Big/ \left[\sum\nolimits_{t=0 \text{ to } t=n} C_t/(1+r)^t\right]$$

A benefit-to-cost ratio of 1 is said to indicate a project that breaks even. Any project with $B/C > 1$ is a relatively successful project as defined in terms of benefits exceeding costs. Fundamental to implementing the ratio of benefits-to-costs is a value for the discount rate, r.

The information developed to determine the benefit-to-cost ratio can be used to determine net present value (NPV) as:

$$NPV_{\text{initial year}} = B - C$$

where, as in the calculation of B/C, B refers to the present value of all measured benefits and C refers to the present value of all measured costs and where present value refers to the initial year or time period in which the project began, $t=0$ in terms of the B/C formula. Note that NPV allows, in principle, one means of ranking several projects *ex post*, providing investment sizes are similar.

6. In the United States, a 7 percent real discount rate is used, following Office of Management and Budget (1992) guidelines.

References

Abramovitz, M. (1981). "Welfare Quandaries and Productivity Concerns." *American Economic Review* 71: 1–17.

Adams, J. D. (1990). "Fundamental Stocks of Knowledge and Productivity Growth." *Journal of Political Economy* 98: 673–702.

Adams, J. D., and Jaffe, A. B. (1996). "Bounding the Effects of R&D: An Investigation Using Matched Establishment-Firm Data." *Rand Journal of Economics* 27: 700–21.

Alic, J. A. (1990). "Cooperation in R&D." *Technovation* 10: 319–31.

America COMPETES Act, Public Law 110–69, passed on August 9, 2007.

American Jobs Creation Act of 2004, Public Law 108–357, passed on October 22, 2004.

American Technology Preeminence Act of 1991, Public Law 102–245, passed on February 14, 1992.

Anthony, R. N., and Day, J. S. (1952). *Management Controls in Industrial Research Organizations.* Boston: Harvard University Press.

Antonelli, C. (2008). *Localised Technological Change.* London: Routledge.

Arrow, K. J. (1962). "Economic Welfare and the Allocation of Resources for Invention." In *The Rate and Direction of Inventive Activity.* Princeton: Princeton University Press.

———. (2000). "Increasing Returns: Historiographic Issues and Path Dependence." *European Journal of the History of Economic Thought* 7: 171–80.

Arthur, W. (1989). "Competing Technologies, Increasing Returns, and Lock-in by Historical Small Events." *Economic Journal* 99: 116–31.

Association of University Related Research Parks (AURRP) (1998). "World-wide Research & Science Park Directory 1998." BPI Communications report.

Association of University Research Parks (AURP) (2007). http://www.aurp.net/about/whatis.cfm.

Audretsch, D. B. (1998). "Agglomeration and the Location of Innovative Activity." *Oxford Review of Economic Policy* 14: 18–29.

Audretsch, D. B., and Feldman, M. P. (1996). "R&D Spillovers and the Geography of Innovation and Production." *American Economic Review* 86: 630–40.

———. (1999). "Innovation in Cities: Science-based Diversity, Specialization, and Localized Competition." *European Economic Review* 43: 409–29.

Audretsch, D. B., Link, A. N., and Scott, J. T. (2002). 'Public/Private Technology Partnerships: Evaluating SBIR-Supported Research', *Research Policy*, 31: 145–58.

Bakouros, Y. L., Mardas, D. C., and Varsakelis, N. C. (2002). "Science Parks, a High Tech Fantasy? An Analysis of the Science Parks of Greece." *Technovation* 22: 123–28.

Baldwin, W., and Link, A. N. (1998). "Universities as Research Joint Venture Partners: Does Size of Venture Matter?" *International Journal of Technology Management* 15: 895–913.

Baptista, R. (1998). "Clusters, Innovation, and Growth: A Survey of the Literature." In *The Dynamics of Industrial Clustering,* edited by G. M. P. Swann, M. Prevezer, and D. Stout. Oxford: Oxford University Press.

Bator, F. M. (1958). "The Anatomy of Market Failure." *Quarterly Journal of Economics* 72: 351–79.

Baumol, W. J. (1990). "Entrepreneurship: Productive, Unproductive, and Destructive." *Journal of Business Venturing.* 11: 3–22.

Baumol, W. J., Litan, R. E., and Schramm, C. J. (2007). "Sustaining Entrepreneurial Capitalism." *Capitalism and Society* 2: 1–36.

Belderbos, R., Carree, M., and Lokshin, B. (2004). "Cooperative R&D and Firm Performance." *Research Policy* 33: 1477–92.

Bernal, J. D. (1939). *The Social Function of Science.* London: Routledge & Sons.

Berndt, E. R. (1980). "Energy Price Increases and the Productivity Slowdown in the United States." In *The Decline in Productivity Growth.* Boston: Federal Reserve Bank of Boston.

———. (1984). "Comment on Jorgenson." In *International Comparisons of Productivity and Causes of the Slowdown,* edited by J. W. Kendrick. Cambridge, Mass.: Ballinger Publisher.

Bichowsky, F. R. (1942). *Industrial Research.* New York: Chemical Publishing.

Biomass Research and Development Act of 2000, Public Law 106–224, passed on February 14, 2000.

Bozeman, B., and Link, A. N. (1983). *Investments in Technology: Corporate Strategies and Public Policy Alternatives.* New York: Praeger.

Bozeman, B., Link, A. N., and Zardkoohi, A. (1986). "An Economic Analysis of R&D Joint Ventures." *Managerial and Decision Economics* 7: 263–66.

Braswell, A. (1989). "Testimony Before the Subcommittee on Oversight and Investigations of the Committee on Energy and Commerce." U.S. House of Representatives.

Breschi, S., and Lissoin, F. (2001). "Knowledge Spillovers and Local Innovation Systems: A Critical Survey." *Industrial and Corporate Change* 10: 975–1005.

Brod, A. C., and Link, A. N. (2001). "Trends in Cooperative Research Activity: Has the National Cooperative Research Act Been Successful?" In *Innovation Policy in the Knowledge-Based Economy*, edited by M. Feldman and A. Link. Norwell, Mass.: Kluwer Academic Publishers.

Brozen, Y. (1951). "Research, Technology and Productivity." In *Industrial Productivity*, edited by L. R. Tripp. Champaign, Ill.: Industrial Relations Research Association.

Budget and Accounting Act of 1921, Public Law 67–13, passed on June 10, 1921.

Bush, V. (1945). *Science—the Endless Frontier*. Washington, D.C.: U.S. Government Printing Office.

Caloghirou, Y., Ioannides, S., and Vonortas, N. S. (2003). "Research Joint Ventures." *Journal of Economic Surveys* 17: 541–70.

Cantillon, R. (1931). *Essai sur la nature du commerce en general,* edited by H. Higgs. London: Macmillan.

Castells, M., and Hall, P. (1994). *Technopoles of the World*. London: Oxford University Press.

Chaffee, C. D. (1988). *The Rewiring of America: The Fiber Optic Revolution*. Orlando, Fla.: Academic Press.

Chordà, I. M. (1996). "Towards the Maturity State: An Insight into the Performance of French Technopoles." *Technovation* 16: 143–52.

Clark, P. K. (1981). "Inflation and Productivity Growth." Paper presented at the Third Annual Conference on Current Issues in Productivity, Rutgers University.

———. (1982). "Inflation and Productivity Decline." *American Economic Review* 72: 149–54.

Clayton Act of 1914, 15 U.S Code, Title 15, passed on October 15, 1914.

Coburn, C. (1995). *Partnerships: A Compendium of State and Federal Technology Programs*. Columbus, Ohio: Battelle Press.

Cogan, D. G. (1988). *Stones in a Glass House: CFCs and Ozone Depletion*. Washington, D.C.: Investor Responsibility Research Center, Inc.

Cohen, W. (2002). "Thoughts and Questions on Science Parks." Paper presented at the National Science Foundation Workshop on Science Parks Indicators, University of North Carolina at Greensboro.

Combs, K. L., and Link, A. N. (2003). "Innovation Policy in Search of an Economic Foundation: The Case of Research Partnerships in the United States." *Technology Analysis & Strategic Management* 15: 177–87.

Congressional Research Service (2006). "Biofuels Incentives: A Summary of Federal Programs." Washington, D.C.: Library of Congress.

———. (2008). "Biofuels Provisions in the 2007 Energy Bill and the 2008 Farm Bill: A Side-by-Side Comparison." Washington, D.C.: Library of Congress.

Council on Competitiveness (1991). *Gaining New Ground: Technology Priorities for America's Future.* Washington, D.C.: Council on Competitiveness.

———. (1994). *Critical Technologies Update 1994.* Washington, D.C.: Council on Competitiveness.

———. (1996). *Endless Frontiers, Limited Resources: U.S. R&D Policy for Competitiveness.* Washington, D.C.: Council on Competitiveness.

Cyber Security Research and Development Act of 2002, Public Law 107–305, passed on November 2, 2003.

David, P. A. (1985). "Clio and the Economics of QWERTY." *American Economic Review* 75: 332–37.

———. (1987). "Some New Standards for the Economics of Standardization in the Information Age." In *Economic Policy and Technological Performance,* edited by P. Dasgupta and P. Stoneman. Cambridge: Cambridge University Press.

Dearborn, D. C., Kneznek, R. W., and Anthony, R. N. (1953). "Spending for Industrial Research, 1951–52." Cambridge, Mass.: Harvard University Graduate School of Business report.

Economic Recovery Tax Act of 1981, Public Law 97–34, passed on August 13, 1981.

Energy Independence and Security Act of 2007 (EISA), Public Law 110–140, passed on December 19, 2007.

Energy Policy Act of 2005, Public Law 109–58, passed on September 8, 2005.

Energy Tax Act of 1978, Public Law 9–618, passed on November 9, 1978.

Farm Security and Rural Investment Act of 2002, Public Law 107–171, passed on May 13, 2002.

Felsenstein, D. (1994). "University-Related Science Parks—'Seedbeds' or 'Enclaves' of Innovation?" *Technovation* 14: 93–110.

Ferguson, R., and Olofsson, C. (2004). "Science Parks and the Development of NTBFs: Location, Survival and Growth." *Journal of Technology Transfer* 29: 5–17.

Flamm, K. S. (1994). "Flat-Panel Displays: Catalyzing a U.S. Industry." *Issues in Science and Technology* 11: 27–32.

Flatt, M. (1992). *Printed Circuit Board Basics.* 2nd ed. San Francisco: Miller Freeman Books.

Fligstein, N. D. (1991). "The Structural Transformation of American Industry: An Institutional Account of the Causes of Diversification in the Largest Firms." In *The New Institutionalism,* edited by W. Powell and P. DiMaggio. Chicago: University of Chicago Press.

Food, Conservation, and Energy Act of 2008, Public Law 110–234, passed on May 22, 2008.

Fukugawa, N. (2006). "Science Parks in Japan and Their Value-Added Contributions to New Technology-Based Firms." *International Journal of Industrial Organization* 24: 381–400.

Furnas, C. D. (1948). *Research in Industry: Its Organization and Management.* Princeton, N.J.: van Nostrand.

Gallaher, M. P, Link, A. N., and Petrusa, J. E. (2006). *Innovation in the U.S. Service Sector.* London: Routledge.

Gallaher, M. P., Link, A. N., and Rowe, B. R. (2008). *Cyber Security: Economic Strategies and Public Policy Alternatives*. Cheltenham, U.K.: Edward Elgar Publishers.

Gallaher, M. P., and Rowe, B. R. (2005). *IPv6 Quantitative Economic Impact Assessment*. Gaithersburg, Md.: National Institute of Standards and Technology.

———. (2006). "The Costs and Benefits of Transferring Technology Infrastructure Underlying Complex Standards: The Case of IPv6." *Journal of Technology Transfer* 31: 519–44.

Gibb, M. J. (1985). *Science Parks and Innovation Centres: Their Economic and Social Impact*. Amsterdam: Elsevier.

Godin, B. (2006). "The Linear Model of Innovation: The Historical Construction of an Analytical Framework." *Science, Technology, & Human Values* 31: 639–67.

Goldstein, H. A., and Luger, M. I. (1990). "Science/Technology Parks and Regional Development Theory." *Economic Development Quarterly* 4: 64–78.

———. (1992). "University-Based Research Parks as a Rural Development Strategy." *Policy Studies Journal* 20: 249–63.

Government Performance and Results Act of 1993, Public Law 103–62, passed on August 3, 1993.

Grayson, L. (1993). *Science Parks: An Experiment in High Technology Transfer*. London: The British Library Board.

Griliches, Z. (1958). "Research Costs and Social Returns: Hybrid Corn and Related Innovations." *Journal of Political Economy* 66: 419–31.

———. (1986). "Productivity Growth, R&D, and Basic Research at the Firm Level in the 1970s." *American Economic Review* 76: 141–54.

Guy, I. (1996a). "A Look at Aston Science Park." *Technovation* 16: 217–18.

———. (1996b). "New Ventures on an Ancient Campus." *Technovation* 16: 269–70.

Hackett, S. M., and Dilts, D. M. (2004). "A Systematic Review of Business Incubation Research." *Journal of Technology Transfer* 29: 55–82.

Hagedoorn, J., Link, A. N., and Vonortas, N. S. (2000). "Research Partnerships." *Research Policy* 29: 567–86.

Hall, B. H., Link, A. N., and Scott, J. T. (2000). "Universities as Research Partners." NBER Working Paper No. 7643.

———. (2001). "Barriers Inhibiting Industry from Partnering with Universities: Evidence from the Advanced Technology Program." *Journal of Technology Transfer* 26: 87–98.

———. (2003). "Universities as Research Partners." *Review of Economics and Statistics* 85: 485–91.

Hansson, F., Husted, K., and Vestergaard, J. (2005). "Second Generation Science Parks: From Structural Holes Jockeys to Social Capital Catalysts of the Knowledge Society." *Technovation* 25: 1039–49.

Hayes, R. H., and Abernathy, W. J. (1980). "Managing Our Way to Economic Decline." *Harvard Business Review* 58: 67–77.

Hébert, R. F., and Link, A. N. (1988). *The Entrepreneur: Mainstream Views and Radical Critiques*. New York: Praeger.

———. (2006a). "The Entrepreneur as Innovator." *Journal of Technology Transfer* 31: 589–97.

————. (2006b). "Historical Perspectives on the Entrepreneur." *Foundation and Trends in Entrepreneurship* 2: 261–408.

Henderson, J. V. (1986). "The Efficiency of Resource Usage and City Size." *Journal of Urban Economics* 19: 47–70.

Hertzfeld, H. R., Link, A. N., and Vonortas, N. S. (2006). "Intellectual Property Protection Mechanisms in Research Partnerships." *Research Policy* 35: 825–38.

High Performance and Communication Act of 1991, Public Law 102–194, passed on December 9, 1991.

Hilpert, U., and Ruffieux, B. (1991). "Innovation, Politics, and Regional Development: Technology Parks and Regional Participation in High-Technology in France and West Germany." In *Regional Innovation and Decentralization: High Technology Industry and Government Policy,* edited by U. Hilpert. London: Routledge.

Hirsch, B. T., and Link, A. N. (1987). "Labor Union Effects on Innovative Activity." *Journal of Labor Research* 8: 323–32.

Holcombe, R. G. (2002). "Political Entrepreneurship and the Democratic Allocation of Economic Resources." *The Review of Austrian Economics* 15: 143–59.

Huston, G. (2003). "Waiting for IP version 6." http://www.potaroo.net/papers/isoc/2003–01/Waiting.html.

Huxley, J. S. (1934). *Scientific Research and Social Needs.* London: Watts and Company.

Institute for Interconnecting and Packaging Electronic Circuits (IPC). (1992). *Analysis of the Market: Rigid Printed Wiring Boards and Related Materials for the Year 1991.* Lincolnwood, Ill.

————. (1995a). *Analysis of the Market: Rigid Printed Wiring Boards and Related Materials for the Year 1994.* Lincolnwood, Ill.

————. (1995b). Minutes from the May 21–23, 1995, meeting in Washington, D.C.

International Association of Science Parks (ISAP). (2002). http://www.iasp.ws.

International Trade Commission (ITC). (1988). *U.S. Global Competitiveness: Optical Fibers, Technology, and Equipment.* Washington, D.C.: U.S. Government Printing Office.

Jaffe, A. B. (1989). "Real Effects of Academic Research." *American Economic Review* 79: 957–70.

Jaffe, A. B, Trajtenberg, M., and Henderson, R. (1993). "Geographic Localization of Knowledge Spillovers as Evidenced by Patent Citations." *Quarterly Journal of Economics* 108: 577–98.

Knight, F. H. (1921). *Risk, Uncertainty and Profit.* New York: Houghton Mifflin.

Krishna, K., and Thursby, M. (1996). "Wither Flat Panel Displays?" NBER working paper 5415.

Krugman, P. (1991). *Geography and Trade.* Cambridge, Mass.: MIT Press.

Levine, J. B., and Byrne, J. A. (1986). "Corporate Odd Couples." *Business Week,* July 21: 100.

Leyden, D. P., and Link, A. N. (1993). "Tax Policies Affecting R&D: An International Comparison." *Technovation* 13: 17–25.

————. (1999). "Federal Laboratories as Research Partners." *International Journal of Industrial Organization* 17: 572–92.

Leyden, D. P., Link, A. N., and Siegel, D. S. (2007). "A Theoretical and Empirical Analysis of the Decision to Locate on a University Research Park." *IEEE Transactions on Engineering Management.*

Lichtenberg, F. R., and Siegel, D. (1991). "The Impact of R&D Investment on Productivity—New Evidence Using Linked R&D-LRD Data." *Economic Inquiry* 29: 203–28.

Lindelöf, P., and Löfsten, H. (2003). "Science Park Location and New Technology-Based Firms in Sweden: Implications for Strategy and Performance." *Small Business Economics* 20: 245–58.

———. (2004). "Proximity as a Resource Base for Competitive Advantage: University-Industry Links for Technology Transfer." *Journal of Technology Transfer* 29: 311–26.

Link, A. N. (1978). "Rates of Induced Technology from Investments in Research and Development." *Southern Economic Journal* 45: 370–79.

———. (1981a). "Basic Research and Productivity Increase in Manufacturing: Some Additional Evidence." *American Economic Review* 71: 1111–12.

———. (1981b). *Research and Development Activity in U.S. Manufacturing.* New York: Praeger.

———. (1982). "Productivity Growth, Environmental Regulations and the Composition of R&D." *Bell Journal of Economics* 13: 548–54.

———. (1983). "Market Structure and Voluntary Product Standards." *Applied Economics* 15: 393–401.

———. (1987). *Technological Change and Productivity Growth.* London: Harwood Academic Publishers.

———. (1991). *Economic Impacts of NIST-Supported Standards for the U.S. Optical Fiber Industry: 1981–Present.* Gaithersburg, Md.: National Institute of Standards and Technology.

———. (1995). *A Generosity of Spirit: The Early History of the Research Triangle Park.* Research Triangle Park: University of North Carolina Press for the Research Triangle Park Foundation.

———. (1996a). *Evaluating Public Sector Research and Development.* New York: Praeger Publishers.

———. (1996b). "On the Classification of Industrial R&D." *Research Policy* 25: 397–401.

———. (1997). *ATP Early Stage Impacts of the Printed Wiring Board Joint Venture,* Gaithersburg, Md.: Advanced Technology Program report.

———. (1999). "Public/Private Partnerships in the United States." *Industry and Innovation* 6: 191–217.

———. (2000). "An Assessment of the Small Business Innovation Research Fast Track Program in Southeastern States." In *The Small Business Innovation Research Program: An Assessment of the Department of Defense Fast Track Initiative,* edited by C. W. Wessner. Washington, D.C.: National Research Council.

———. (2002). *From Seed to Harvest: The History of the Growth of the Research Triangle Park.* Research Triangle Park: University of North Carolina Press for the Research Triangle Park Foundation.

———. (2006). *Public/Private Partnerships: Innovation Strategies and Policy Alternatives.* New York: Springer.

———. (2008). "The Evaluation Challenge." Paper presented at the National Academy of Sciences Workshop on Understanding Research and Technology Parks, Washington, D.C.

Link, A. N., and Link, K. R. (2003). "On the Growth of U.S. Science Parks." *Journal of Technology Transfer* 28: 81–85.

Link, A. N., and Rees, J. (1990). "Firm Size, University-Based Research, and the Returns to R&D." *Small Business Economics* 2: 25–31.

Link, A. N., and Ruhm, C. J. (forthcoming). "Bringing Science to Market: Commercializing from NIH SBIR Awards." *Economics of Innovation and New Technology.*

Link, A. N., and Scott, J. T. (1998). *Public Accountability: Evaluating Technology-Based Institutions.* Norwell, Mass.: Kluwer Academic Publishers.

———. (2000). "Estimating the Social Returns to SBIR-Sponsored Projects." In *The Small Business Innovation Research Program: An Assessment of the Department of Defense Fast Track Initiative,* edited by C. W. Wessner. Washington, D.C.: National Academy Press.

———. (2001). "Public/Private Partnerships: Stimulating Competition in a Dynamic Market." *International Journal of Industrial Organization* 19: 763–94.

———. (2003a). "The Growth of Research Triangle Park." *Small Business Economics* 20: 167–75.

———. (2003b). "U.S. Science Parks: The Diffusion of an Innovation and Its Effects on the Academic Mission of Universities." *International Journal of Industrial Organization* 21: 1323–56.

———. (2005a). *Evaluating Public Research Institutions: The U.S. Advanced Technology Program's Intramural Research Initiative.* London: Routledge.

———. (2005b). "Opening the Ivory Tower's Door: An Analysis of the Determinants of the Formation of U.S. University Spin-Off Companies." *Research Policy* 34: 1106–12.

———. (2005c). "Universities as Research Partners in U.S. Research Joint Ventures." *Research Policy* 34: 385–93.

———. (2006a). "An Economic Evaluation of the Baldrige National Quality Program." *Economics of Innovation and New Technology* 15: 83–100.

———. (2006b). "U.S. University Research Parks." *Journal of Productivity Analysis* 25: 43–55.

———. (2007). "The Economics of University Research Parks." *Oxford Review of Economic Policy* 23: 661–74.

———. (2009). "Private Investor Participation and Commercialization Rates for Government-Sponsored Research and Development: Would a Prediction Market Improve the Performance of the SBIR Program." *Economica* 76: 264–81.

Link, A. N., and Siegel, D. S. (2003). *Technological Change and Economic Performance.* London: Routledge.

———. (2007). *Innovation, Entrepreneurship, and Technological Change.* Oxford: Oxford University Press.

Link, A. N., and Tassey, G. (1993). "The Technology Infrastructure of Firms: Investments in Infratechnology." *IEEE Transactions on Engineering Management* 40: 312–15.

Link, A. N., and Wessner, C. W. (2007). "Public Accountability: Evaluating the U.S. Small Business Innovation Research Program." Mimeograph.

Luger, M. I., and Goldstein, H. A. (1991). *Technology in the Garden*. Chapel Hill: University of North Carolina Press.

Machlup, F. (1980). *Knowledge and Knowledge Production*. Princeton, N.J.: Princeton University Press.

Maddison, A. (1984). "Comparative Analysis of the Productivity Situation in the Advanced Capitalist Countries." In *International Comparisons of Productivity and Causes of the Slowdown,* edited by J. W. Kendrick. Cambridge, Mass.: Ballinger Publishers.

Magaziner, I., and Patinkin, M. (1989). *The Silent War*. New York: Random House.

Mansfield, E. (1980). "Basic Research and the Productivity Increase in Manufacturing." *American Economic Review* 70: 863–73.

Mansfield, E., Rapoport, J., Romeo, A., Wagner, S., and Beardsley, G. (1977). "Social and Private Rates of Return from Industrial Innovations." *Quarterly Journal of Economics* 91: 221–40.

Markoff, J. (2005). "Early Look at Research Project to Re-Engineer the Internet." *New York Times,* August 29.

Martin, S., and Scott, J. T. (2000). "The Nature of Innovation Market Failure and the Design of Public Support for Private Innovation." *Research Policy* 29: 437–47.

Marx, M. L., and Link, A. N. (1995). *NIST Support of the Integrated Services Digital Network (ISDN)*. Gaithersburg, Md.: National Institute of Standards and Technology.

McAdam, M., Galbraith, B., McAdam, R., and Humphreys, P. (2006). "Business Processes and Networks in University Incubators: A Review and Research Agendas." *Technology Analysis & Strategic Management* 18: 451–72.

McLoughlin, G. J., and Nunno, R. M. (1995). "Flat Panel Display Technology: What Is the Federal Role?" Congressional Research Service Report.

Mees, C. E. K. (1920). *The Organization of Industrial Scientific Research*. New York: McGraw-Hill.

Mees, C. E. K., and Leermakers, J. A. (1950). *The Organization of Industrial Scientific Research*. New York: McGraw Hill.

Menger, C. (1950). *Principles of Economics,* translated by J. Dingwall and B. F. Hoselitz. Glencoe, Ill.: Free Press; first published, 1871.

Mill, J. S. (1965). *Principles of Political Economy,* edited by W. J. Askley. New York: Augustus M. Kelley; first published, 1848.

Monck, C. S. P., Porter, R. B., Quintas, P., Storey, D. J., and Wynarczyk, P. (1988). *Science Parks and the Growth of High Technology Firms*. London, Croom Helm.

Morgan, R. P. (1998). "University Research Contributions to Industry: The Faculty View." In *Trends in Industrial Innovation: Industry Perspectives & Policy Implications,* edited by P. Blain and R. Frosch. Research Triangle Park: Sigma Xi, The Scientific Research Society.

Myers, S., and Marquis, D. G. (1969). *Successful Industrial Innovations: A Study of Factors Underlying Innovation in Selected Firms*. Washington, D.C.: National Science Foundation.

National Cooperative Research Act of 1984, Public Law 98–462, passed on October 11, 1984.

National Cooperative Research and Production Act of 1993, Public Law 103–42, passed on June 10, 1993.

National Research Council (2004), *SBIR: Program Diversity and Assessment Challenges*, Washington, DC: National Academy Press.

National Science Foundation (NSF) (1956). "Science and Engineering in American Industry: Final Report on a 1953–1954 Survey." Washington, D.C.: National Science Foundation.

Nelson, R. R. (1993). *National Innovation Systems: A Comparative Analysis*. New York: Oxford University Press.

Nelson, R. R., and Winter, S. G. (1982). *An Evolutionary Theory of Economic Change*. Cambridge, Mass.: Harvard University Press.

Nightingale, P. (1998). "A Cognitive Model of Innovation." *Research Policy* 27: 689–709.

Nordhaus, W. D. (1980). "Policy Responses to the Productivity Slowdown." In *The Decline in Productivity Growth*. Boston: Federal Reserve Bank of Boston.

Norsworthy, J. R., Harper, M. J., and Kunze, K. (1979). "The Slowdown in Productivity Growth: An Analysis of Some Contributing Factors." *Brookings Papers on Economic Activity* 3: 387–421.

Office of Management and Budget (1992). *Circular No. A-94: Guidelines and Discount Rates for Benefit-Cost Analysis of Federal Programs*. Washington, D.C.: Government Printing Office.

Office of Technology Policy (1996). *Effective Partnering: A Report to Congress on Federal Technology Partnerships*. Washington, D.C.: U.S. Department of Commerce.

Omnibus Budget Reconciliation Act of 1990, Public Law 101–508, passed on November 5, 1990.

Omnibus Trade and Competitiveness Act of 1988, Public Law 100–148, passed on August 23, 1988.

Organization for Economic Co-operation and Development (OECD) (2005). *Frascati Manual: Proposed Standard Practice for Surveys on Research and Experimental Development*, Paris: OECD.

Phan, P., Siegel, D. S., and Wright, M. (2005). "Science Parks and Incubators: Observations, Synthesis and Future Research." *Journal of Business Venturing* 20: 165–82.

Phillimore, J. (1999). "Beyond the Linear View of Innovation in Science Park Evaluation: An Analysis of Western Australian Technology Park." *Technovation* 19: 673–80.

Porter, M. E. (2001a). "Clusters and Competitiveness: Findings from the Cluster Mapping Project." Presentation at the Corporate Strategies for the Digital Economy conference.

Porter, M. (2001b). *Clusters of Innovation: Regional Foundations of U.S. Competitiveness*. Washington, D.C.: Council on Competitiveness.

Quesnay, F. (1888). *Oeuvres economiques et philosophiques*. Frankfurt: M. J. Baer.

Rasche, R. M., and Tatom, J. A. (1977a). "The Effects of the New Energy Regime on Economic Capacity, Production, and Prices." *Federal Reserve Bank of St. Louis Review* 59: 2–10.

Rasche, R. M., and Tatom, J. A. (1977b). "Energy Resources and Potential GNP." *Federal Reserve Bank of St. Louis Review* 59: 12–21.

Renewable Fuels Association (2007). http://www.ethanolrfa.org/resource/facts/trade/.

Reuter, J. J., and Zollo, M. (2005). "Termination Outcomes of Research Alliances." *Research Policy* 34: 101–15.

Ronayne, J. (1988). *The Integrated Services Digital Network: From Concept to Application.* London: Pitman Publishing.

Rosenberg, N., and Nelson, R. R. (1994). "American Universities and Technical Advance in Industry." *Research Policy* 23: 323–48.

Rothaermel, F. T., and Thursby, M. C. (2005a). "Incubator Firm Failure or Graduation? The Role of University Linkages." *Research Policy* 34: 1076–90.

———. (2005b). "University-Incubator Firm Knowledge Flows: Assessing Their Impact on Incubator Firm Performance." *Research Policy* 34: 302–20.

Say, J. B. (1840). *Cours complet d'economie politique pratique.* 2nd ed. Paris: Guillaumin.

Schultz, T. W. (1980). "Investment in Entrepreneurial Ability." *Scandinavian Journal of Economics* 82: 437–48.

Schumpeter, J. A. (1928). "The Instability of Capitalism." *Economic Journal* 38: 361–86.

———. *The Theory of Economic Development*, translated by R. Opie from the 2nd German edition [1926]. Cambridge: Harvard University Press.

———. (1939). *Business Cycles.* New York: McGraw-Hill.

———. (1950). *Capitalism, Socialism and Democracy.* 3rd ed. New York: Harper & Row.

———. (1954). *History of Economic Analysis*, edited by E. B. Schumpeter. New York: Oxford University Press.

Shearmur, R., and Doloreux, D. (2000). "Science Parks: Actors or Reactors? Canadian Science Parks in their Urban Context." *Environment and Planning* 32: 1065–82.

Shedlick, M. T., Link, A. N., and Scott, J. T. (1998). *Economic Assessment of the NIST Alternative Refrigerants Research Program.* Gaithersburg, Md.: National Institute of Standards and Technology.

Siegel, D. S., Thursby, J. G., Thursby, M. C., and Ziedonis, A. A. (2001). "Organizational Issues in University-Industry Technology Transfer: An Overview of the Symposium Issue." *Journal of Technology Transfer* 26: 5–11.

Siegel, D. S., Westhead, P., and Wright, M. (2003). "Assessing the Impact of Science Parks on Research Productivity: Exploratory Firm-Level Evidence from the United Kingdom." *International Journal of Industrial Organization* 21: 1357–69.

Small Business Innovation Development Act of 1982, Public Law 97–219, passed on July 22, 1982.

Small Business Reauthorization Act of 2000, Public Law 106–554, passed on December 26, 2000.

Small Business Research and Development Enactment Act, Public Law 102–564, passed on October 28, 1992.

Smith, A. (1976a). *An Inquiry into the Nature and Causes of the Wealth of Nations*, edited by R. A. Campbell and A. S. Skinner. Oxford: Oxford University Press; first published, 1776.

———. (1976b). *The Theory of Moral Sentiments*, edited by D. D. Raphael and A. L. Macfie. Oxford: Oxford University Press; first published, 1759.

Sofouli, E., and Vonortas, N. S. (2007). "S&T Parks and Business Incubators in Middle-Sized Countries: The Case of Greece." *Journal of Technology Transfer* 32: 525–44.

Spengler, J. J. (1959). "Adam Smith's Theory of Economic Growth, Part II." *Southern Economic Journal* 26: 1–12.

Standards Development Organization Advancement Act of 2004, Public Law 108–237, passed on June 22, 2004.

Stenbet, J. (2003). "Internet Protocol Version 6 (IPv6)." U.S. Department of Defense memorandum of intent, June 9.

Sternberg, R. (1990). "The Impact of Innovation Centres on Small Technology-based Firms: The Example of the Federal Republic of Germany." *Small Business Economics* 2: 105–18.

Stevens, R. (1941). *A Report on Industrial Research as a National Resource.* Washington, D.C.: U.S. Government Printing Office.

Stevenson-Wydler Technology Innovation Act of 1980, Public Law 96–480, passed on October 21, 1980.

Swann, G. M. P. (1998). "Towards a Model of Clustering in High-Technology Industries." In *The Dynamics of Industrial Clustering,* edited by G. M. P. Swann, M. Prevezer, and D. Stout. Oxford: Oxford University Press.

Swann, G. M. P., Prevezer, M., and Stout, D. (1998). *The Dynamics of Industrial Clustering.* Oxford: Oxford University Press.

Tassey, G. (1992). *Technology Infrastructure and Competitive Position.* Norwell, Mass.: Kluwer Academic Publishers.

———. (1997). *The Economics of R&D Policy.* Westport, Conn.: Quorum Publishers.

———. (2000). "Standardization in Technology-Based Markets." *Research Policy* 20: 587–602.

———. (2005). "Underinvestment in Public Good Technologies." *Journal of Technology Transfer* 30: 89–113.

———. (2007). *The Technology Imperative.* Chettenham, U.K.: Edward Elgar.

Tibbetts, R. (1999). 'The Small Business Innovation Research Program and NSF SBIR Commercialization Results', mimeograph report, Washington, DC: National Science Foundation.

Tuttle, C. A. (1927). "The Entrepreneur Function in Economic Literature." *Journal of Political Economy* 35: 501–21.

United Kingdom Science Park Association's (UKSPA) (2003). http://www.ukspa.org.uk/default.asp?t=1&channel_id=2374&editorial_id=13661.

United Nations Educational, Scientific and Cultural Organization (UNESCO) (2004). http://www.unesco.org/science/psd/thm_innov/unispar/sc_parks/overview.shtml.

U.S. Congress (1983). 'Research and Development Joint Venture Act of 1983,' House of Representatives Report 98–571, Washington, D.C.: U.S. Congress.

U.S. Department of Commerce (1990). 'Emerging Technologies: A Survey of Technical and Economic Opportunities,' Washington, D.C.: Technology Administration.

———. (2004). "Request for Comments on Deployment of Internet Protocol Version 6." *Federal Register*, January 21.

U.S. Department of Energy (1995). "Renewable Energy Annual 1995." Washington, D.C.: U. S. Department of Energy, Energy Information Administration.

U.S. Department of Justice (1980). *Antitrust Guide Concerning Research Joint Ventures.* Washington, D.C.: U. S. Department of Justice.

U.S. Small Business Administration (2006). http://tech-net.sba.gov/.

Utterback, J. M. (1974). "Innovation in Industry and the Diffusion of Technology." *Science* 183: 620–26.

Vaidyanathan, G. (2008). "Technology Parks in a Developing Country: The Case of India." *Journal of Technology Transfer* 33: 285–99.

Vedovello, C. (1997). "Science Parks and University-Industry Interaction: Geographical Proximity between the Agents as a Driving Force." *Technovation* 17: 491–502.

Walker, A. (1866). *The Science of Wealth.* Boston: Little, Brown.

Wallsten, S. (2001). "An Empirical Test of Geographic Knowledge Spillovers Using Geographic Information Systems and Firm-Level Data." *Regional Science and Urban Economics* 31: 571–99.

Walras, L. (1954). *Elements of Pure Economics,* translated by W. Jaffe. Homewood, Ill.: Richard D. Irwin, Inc.; first published, 1874.

Wessner, C. W. (1999). *A Review of the Sandia Science and Technology Park Initiative.* Washington, D.C.: National Academy Press.

———. (2000). *The Small Business Innovation Research Program: An Assessment of the Department of Defense Fast Track Initiative.* Washington, D.C.: National Academy Press.

———. (2001). *A Review of the New Initiatives at the NASA Ames Research Center: Summary of a Workshop.* Washington, D.C., National Academy Press.

———. (2003). *Government-Industry Partnerships for the Development of New Technologies.* Washington, D.C.: National Academy Press.

———. (2004). *SBIR Program Diversity and Assessment Challenges.* Washington, D.C.: National Academy Press.

———. (2007). *SBIR and the Phase III Challenge of Commercialization: Report of a Symposium.* Washington, D.C.: National Academy Press.

———. (2008). *An Assessment of the SBIR Program.* Washington, D.C.: National Academy Press.

Westhead, P. (1995). "New Owner-Managed Businesses in Rural and Urban Areas in Great Britian: A Matched Pairs Comparison." *Regional Studies* 29: 367–80.

———. (1997). "R&D 'Inputs' and 'Outputs' of Technology-Based firms Located On and Off Science Parks." *R&D Management* 27: 45–61.

Westhead, P., and Batstone, S. (1998). "Independent Technology-Based Firms: The Perceived Benefits of a Science Park Location." *Urban Studies* 35: 2197–219.

Westhead, P., and Cowling, M. (1995). "Employment Change in Independent Owner-Managed High-Technology Firms in Great Britain." *Small Business Economics* 7: 111–40.

Westhead, P., and Storey, D. (1994). *An Assessment of Firms Located On and Off Science Parks in the United Kingdom*. London: HMSO.

———. (1997). "Financial Constraints on the Growth of High-Technology Small Firms in the U.K." *Applied Financial Economics* 7: 197–201.

Westhead, P., Storey, D. J., and Cowling, M. (1995). "An Exploratory Analysis of the Factors Associated with the Survival of Independent High-Technology Firms in Great Britain." In *Small Firms: Partnerships for Growth*, edited by F. Chittenden, M. Robertson, and I. Marshall. London: Paul Chapman.

Index